VOICES OF AMERICA

La Plata

Tri-cultural Traditions in the Upper San Juan Basin

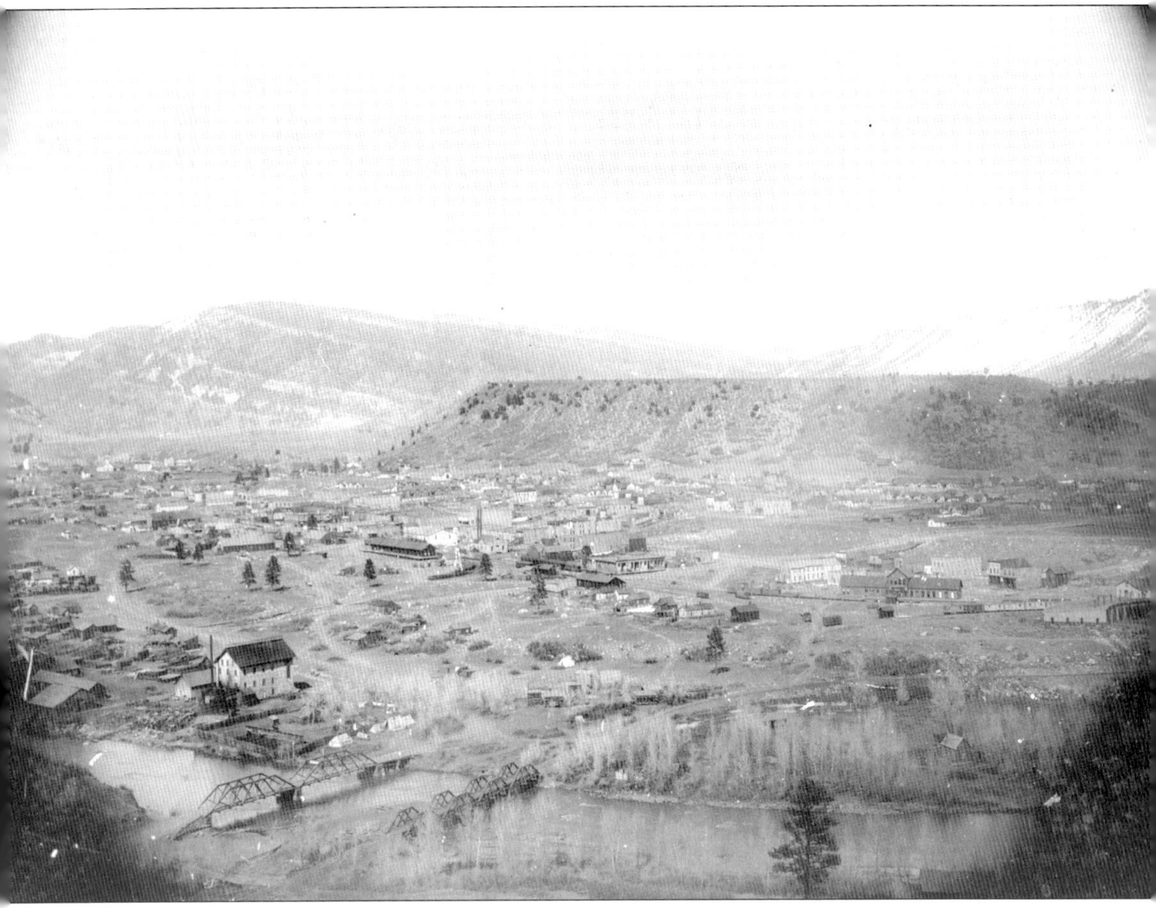

The town of Durango, Colorado, was founded in 1880 as a railroad town, headquarters for the Silverton branch of the Denver and Rio Grande Railroad. Note the depot on the right in this turn-of-the century photo. Soon after its founding, Durango became the county seat of La Plata County. (Courtesy La Plata County Historical Society)

(cover photo) *It is believed that this turn-of-the-century photo of downtown Durango may have been taken from the balcony of the Rochester Hotel. (Courtesy Duane A. Smith)*

VOICES OF AMERICA

La Plata

Tri-cultural Traditions in the Upper San Juan Basin

Written by
Frederic B. Wildfang

TEMPUS

ISBN 0-7385-2050-0

Published by Arcadia Publishing,
an imprint of Tempus Publishing, Inc.
3047 N. Lincoln Ave., Suite 410
Chicago, IL 60657

Printed in Great Britain.

Library of Congress Catalog Card Number: 2001098144

For all general information contact Arcadia Publishing at:
Telephone 843-853-2070
Fax 843-853-0044
E-Mail sales@arcadiapublishing.com

For customer service and orders:
Toll-Free 1-888-313-2665

Visit us on the internet at http://www.arcadiapublishing.com

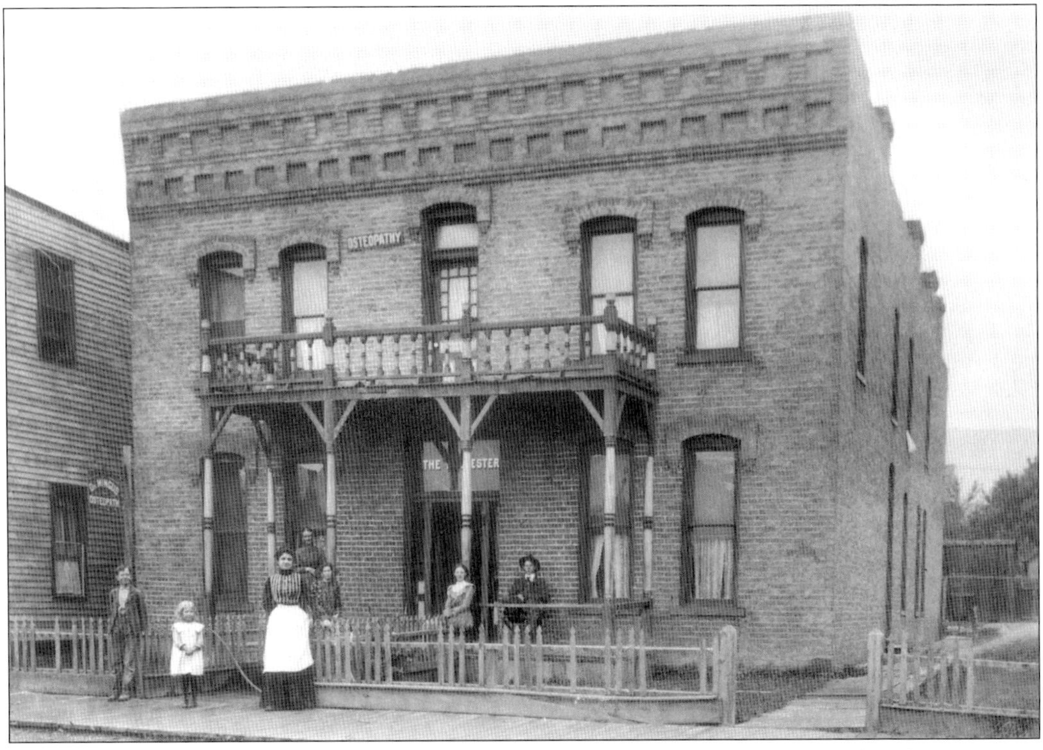

Built in 1892 and restored in 1994, the Rochester Hotel has accommodated visitors to Durango, Colorado, the county seat of La Plata County, for well over 100 years. (Courtesy La Plata County Historical Society)

CONTENTS

ACKNOWLEDGMENTS

It was a couple of years after I had moved to Durango, Colorado. I was sitting in my favorite corner spot at the bar in the Diamond Belle Saloon, part of the historic Strater Hotel, the same bar Louis L'Amour used to frequent for his inspiration. I was sitting there in the afternoon, as I am wont to do, working on one of my several unpublished novels or un-produced screenplays, when the bartendress, Jamie Adams, came up to me and said, "You're a writer, aren't you?"

And that was the beginning of this book.

Every Friday night, as Jamie informed me, the Diamond Belle fills up with a variety of old-timers—cowboys and Indians, ranchers and miners, outlaws and inlaws, bull-riders and bull-throwers—all of them coming here since the turn of the century to spill drinks and spill stories incidental to this corner of Colorado. And as Jamie pointed out, these old-timers are fast disappearing—all the old farms and ranches are breaking up (the kids don't give a damn)—and going with them, all the old stories.

So it fell upon us to collect these old stories—preserve them (because once they're gone, they're gone)—in an effort to capture a truly unique aspect of the Old West in a book I have subtitled "Tri-Cultural Traditions in the Upper San Juan Basin."

***

Despite what you may have heard about the Meeker Massacre, "Mexican Flats," and the Ku Klux Klan, the fact is that Utes, Anglos, and Hispanics have co-existed peacefully together in the upper San Juan Basin for well over a hundred years. As witnessed in this collection of oral histories, these peoples have truly epitomized the spirit of "*naná-ma*"—as the Utes say—"together," a word meant to stand for a spirit of cooperation among all the peoples in this land. It is to these peoples—the turn-of-the-century Ute, Anglo, and Hispanic families still surviving here—that I dedicate this book.

As much as I respect the academic urge to structure a publication such as this to reflect a preconceived purpose, what Jamie Adams and I hoped to accomplish in this case is simply to preserve the "old stories" in the historical context of the turn-of-the-century families we interviewed. Any methods employed were intended only to serve that purpose.

Usually, when we embarked upon an interview, we first would attempt to document the family history—names, dates, etc.—and then we would try to draw out the stories. Whenever an opportunity presented itself, we would also ask specific questions dealing with cross-cultural concerns.

By hindsight, of course, it is possible to draw all kinds of conclusions—such as the interesting thesis Dr. Joel Jones proposes in the introduction to this manuscript—focusing on interviews of "personalities who undermine in the most dramatic ways the currently popular myth of the nuclear family." "Dysfunctional families," Dr. Jones concludes, "were as much the norm 50 years ago as they are now." However, this is just one of the many possible "themes, commonalities, confluences of events and personalities that establish the character of a place and an era." Perhaps the full significance of this collection of oral histories can be left to future scholars.

Frederic B. Wildfang

INTRODUCTION

From Wallace Stegner and Willa Cather to Wendell Berry and Terry Tempest Williams, American novelists and naturalists have given us the narrative structures and psychic landscapes by which we have established the vocabulary articulating "sense of place." So often the fictional characters created by regional writers are simply re-creations or re-embodiments of individuals close to the "felt life" of the region in question.

When historians began to develop the skill of oral history, they proffered to us a new avenue for approaching and exploring "sense of place," a new way to capture the tempo and taste of a place in time. In this collection of conversational and pictorial reminiscences, Fred Wildfang has given us a rich and engaging, poignant and reflective profile of this corner in Colorado history. By giving a focus to his words, thoughts, and pictures of these varied historical personages, he allows us an insider's view of the Four Corners region.

Anyone who wants to capture the true spirit of the American West must always confront, of course, the Hollywood image of this world. Wildfang presents a range of characters, from one who seems to be a Hollywood manifestation of the cowboy, to several frontier personalities who undermine in the most dramatic ways some of the currently popular myths that cultural analysts and politicians perpetrate. One of the thoughts I had while reading the narratives gathered by Wildfang was how effective these stories and recollections are in redressing some

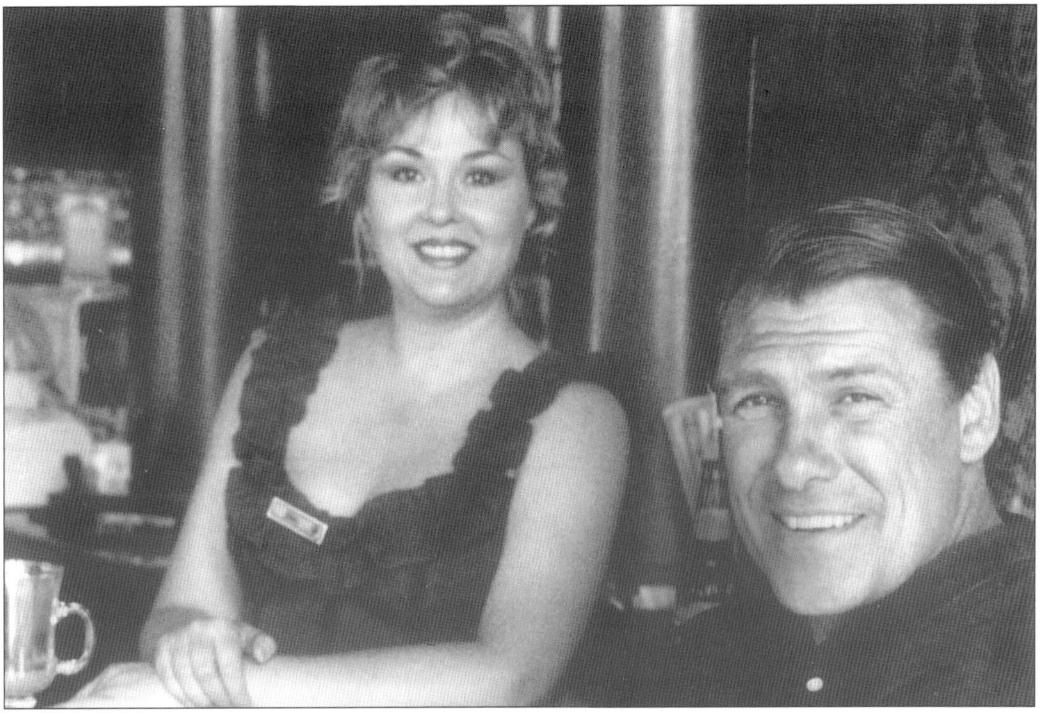

Jamie Adams and Fred Wildfang confer at the Diamond Belle Saloon in Durango, Colorado. (Courtesy Mike Rosso)

of these myths—the myth of the nuclear family, for example, which politicians so vehemently and mistakenly have wanted to associate with the core of American culture.

In fact, what one sees in these personal portraits are young women who ran away at fifteen or sixteen to get married, men who traded wives (with one throwing a cow in for good measure to balance the trade), and women who married as many as seven times.

Though there obviously was much affection and familial connection in the families discussed herein, there was also no such thing as the purely functional family. Dysfunctional families were as much the norm fifty years ago as they are now. The beauty of this text, however, rests in the fact that Wildfang does not try to draw these editorial extrapolations. Rather, to his credit, he simply lets the reader come to these recognitions through the text, both narrative and pictorial.

In short then, we have in front of us an extraordinary collection of materials pertaining to quite ordinary (but in their own light, quite exceptional) individuals.

We can never know the previous period exactly as it was, even if we are the individuals who have lived through it. Reflections, reminiscence, remembrance—all of these are creative and re-creative acts. However, there obviously are themes, commonalities, confluences of events, and personalities that establish the character of a place and an era. Wildfang lets us enter such a scenario.

Dr. Joel Jones, President Emeritus
Fort Lewis College
Durango, Colorado

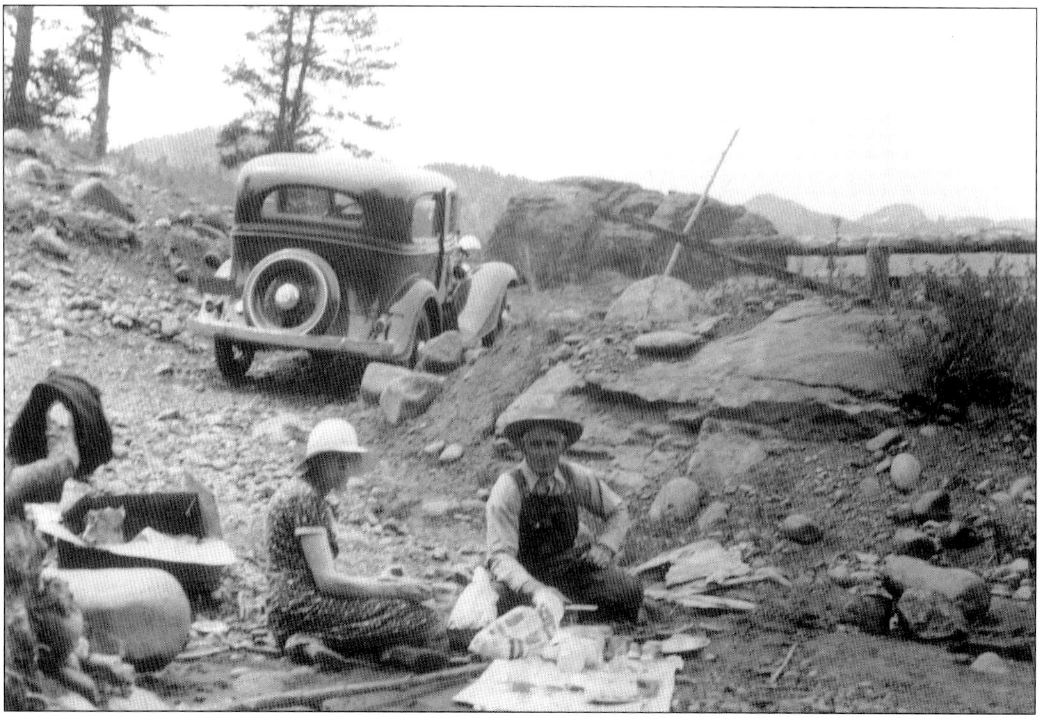

Chapter 1

HORSEMAN FROM HERRERA

ANTONIO "TONY" GILBERT HERRERA

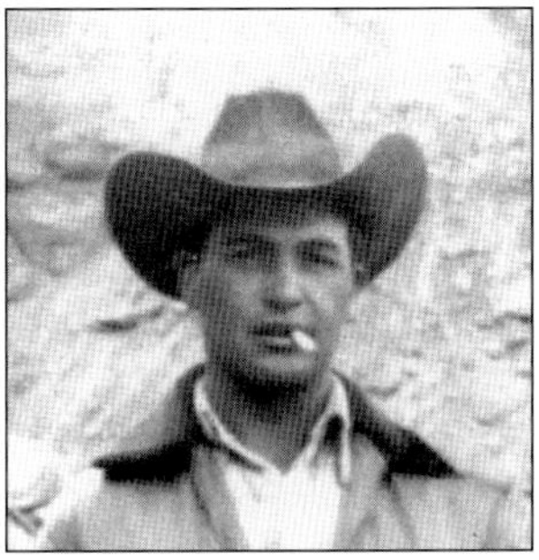

Antonio "Tony" Gilbert Herrera comes from a long line of horsemen. His family was raising horses in Herrera, Spain, when Tony's great grandfather first came to this country in the early 1800s. And Tony's grandfather, Tomas Herrera, raised horses on a ranch near Espanola, New Mexico. Then in the late 1890s, Tomas married Natividad Martinez and homesteaded 160 acres near Marvel, Colorado, in order to raise horses and start a family there.

Tony Herrera was born in the original ranch house on July 12, 1930, but grew up in the adobe house his father built along the banks of Long Hollow Creek. Tony's father, Marcelino Herrera, and his mother, Teofila Sanchez Herrera, raised seven children in this house: six boys and one girl. When he was a boy, Tony walked five miles from this house to the old schoolhouse in Marvel, through hip-high snow, his feet wrapped in burlap feed bags, carrying a lard can full of lunches for his brothers. Or at least that's how Tony likes to tell it.

***

Tony himself rode horses all his life, first trying his hand at riding bareback broncos in rodeos when he was only 16. He also rode saddle broncs, Tony tells us, whenever he thought he had a chance to win.

"Now if I'd see guys like Tibbs [Casey Tibbs, World Champion Rodeo Cowboy], you know, or Bill Linderman [famous rodeo bronc rider] or them old good cowboys, you knew you didn't have a chance. There wasn't no sense in entering, 'cause them guys, they were tough, you know, they were tough."

Tony participated in rodeos all over the country, but he was also a "wrangler" in the movies.

You can tell Tony likes to talk about the movies. Leaning back at the dining room table in front of the window, dressed in a black Justin cowboy hat and starched, striped shirt, Tony begins to tell us all about his "wrangling" jobs.

He first worked in *Westward the Women* in 1947, he tells us, and then later in *Across the Wide Missouri*, *The Naked Spur*, *Cimarron*, *The Cowboys*, and *Around the World in Eighty Days*, among others. Tony talks a lot with his hands, taking hold of the reins while talking about wrangling in *Cimarron*. "We had teams there, some four-ups, some just regular teams. We had 1,100 wagons on that."

"Three months on location," says Tony, "$75 a day on wardrobe, plus wrangler's wages."

Tony has even done a little stunt work in the movies, though he says it's just riding. "Horse falls," he says, "yeah, but you just bail out, you just step out."

"Have you ever been hurt while working on any of the movies, Tony?"

A tentative smile crosses Tony's face.

That curious vertical scar above his right eye, Tony's wife Virginia tells us, was picked up while riding an ostrich in *Around the World in Eighty Days*. Tony was bucked off the ostrich during a benefit at the fairgrounds after the filming. "Nothing there but muscles and feathers," laughs Tony, wrestling his hands counter-clockwise in front of him.

***

It was while riding in the rodeo that Tony's wife Virginia first spotted him. Tony was 21 years old and Virginia was just 16. "A friend of his introduced us," says Virginia, "and I thought he was about the funniest thing I ever saw. He had the real tight jeans tucked into his boots, you know, a satin shirt, and this *great* big cowboy hat. I couldn't believe it!"

Tony and Virginia were married after a summer romance in 1951. They raised 4 children on their 480-acre ranch, 40 acres of which are part of the old original Herrera homestead.

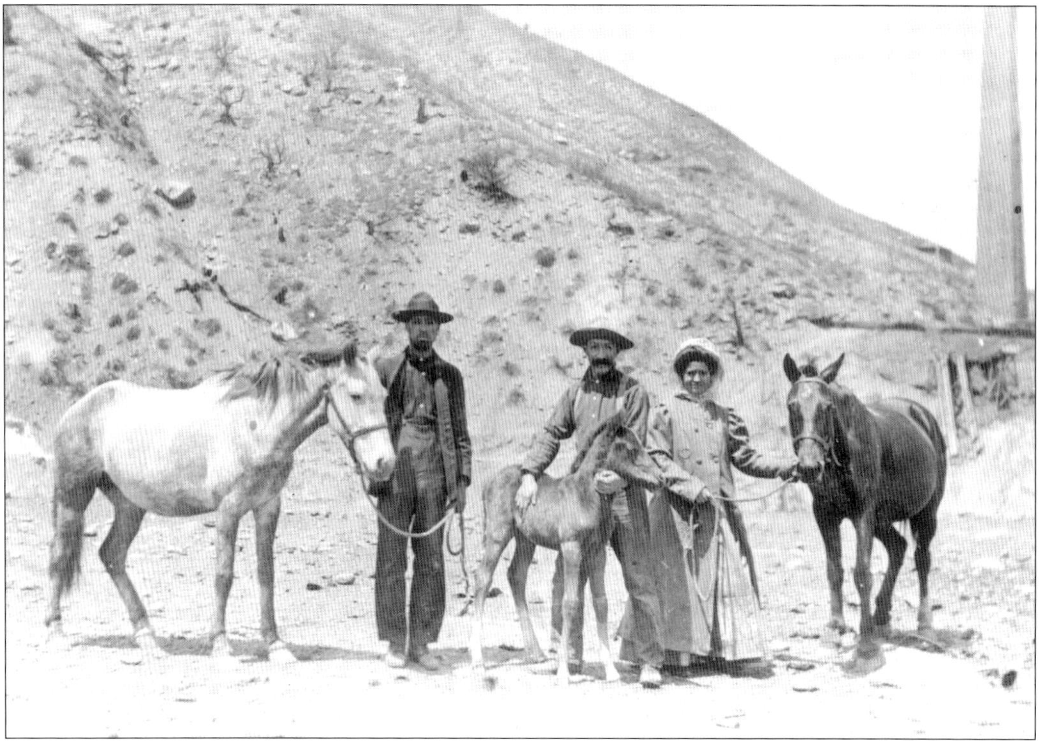

Tony Herrera's grandfather, Tomas Herrera (center), came to La Plata County from Rio Ariba County, New Mexico, sometime in the late 1890s. Tony's great grandfather emigrated to New Mexico from Herrera, Spain. In the background can be seen a smokestack from the old San Juan Smelter in Durango, relocated there from Silverton in 1882.

In this photo, Tony's grandmother, Natividad Martinez (left), is seated in front of her son, Tony's father, Marcelino Herrera (right). Tony's grandparents, Tomas and Natividad, homesteaded 160 acres of land near the town of Marvel, Colorado in La Plata County and started a family there.

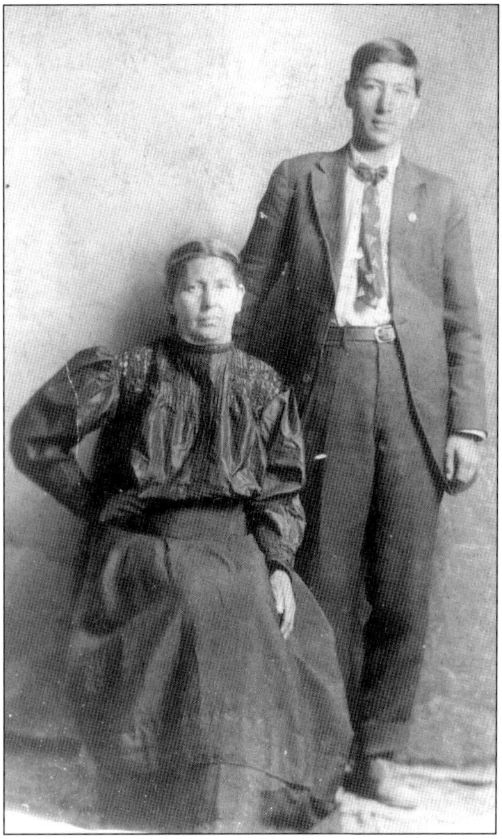

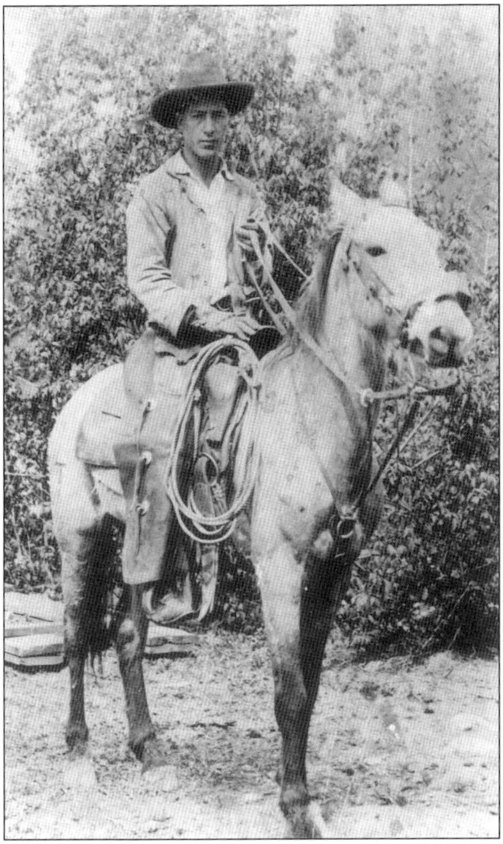

Here we see a young Marcelino Herrera interrupting his work on the ranch to pose for a picture. Although the Herreras were running sheep on the original homestead, Marcelino became best known for his horses, sometimes showing off one of his golden palominos during the annual Spanish Trails Fiesta in Durango, Colorado.

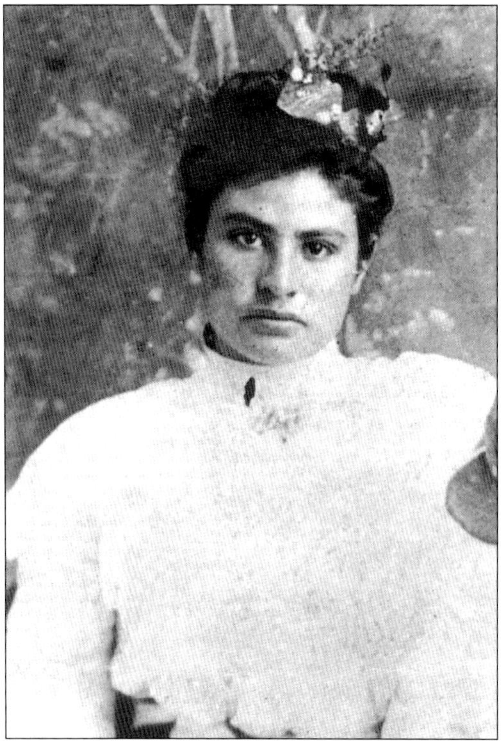

Tony's grandmother on his mother's side, Doloritas Valencia Sanchez (pictured here), also came from Spain. Her daughter, Teofila "Dorothy" Sanchez, married Tony's father, Marcelino Herrera.

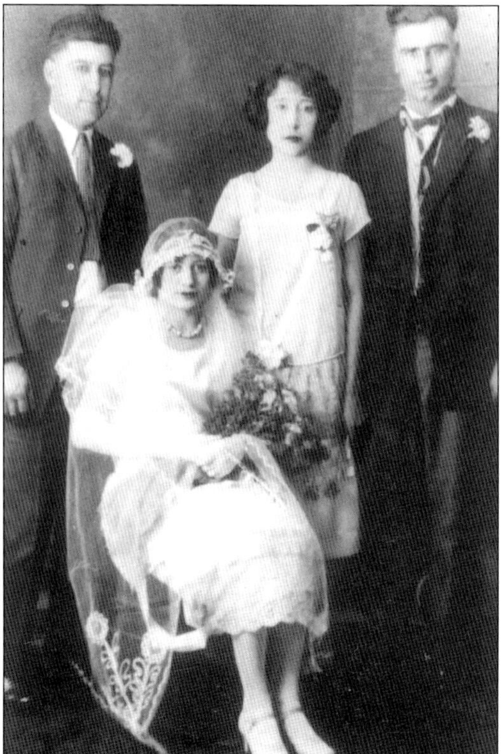

Marcelino Herrera and Teofila "Dorothy" Sanchez Herrera (seated) pose for their wedding picture. Marcelino and Dorothy raised seven children in an adobe house Marcelino built on the banks of Long Hollow Creek on the old homestead.

Tony's mother, Dorothy, poses with five of her seven children, from bottom to top in order: Levi, Marshall, Tony, Tom, and (in his mother's arms) the youngest brother, Pete. Tony's brothers were all skilled horsemen. Pete became a jockey, winning the first $1 million purse ever at Ruidoso Downs in New Mexico.

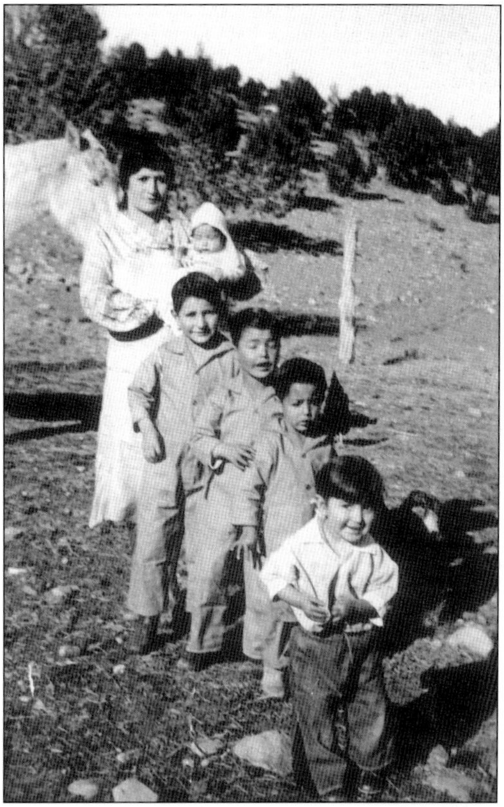

Tony (center) sits mounted on his favorite paint in this photo, out for a ride with his younger brothers Pete, Marshall, and Levi (on the left), and his older brother Tom (on the right).

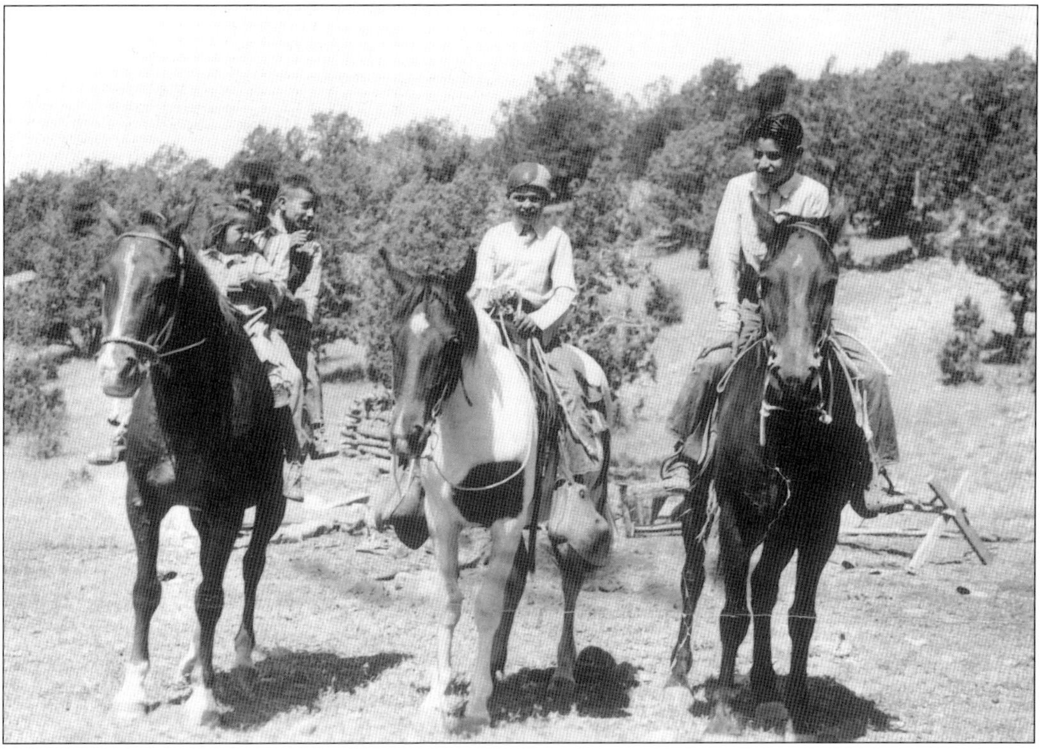

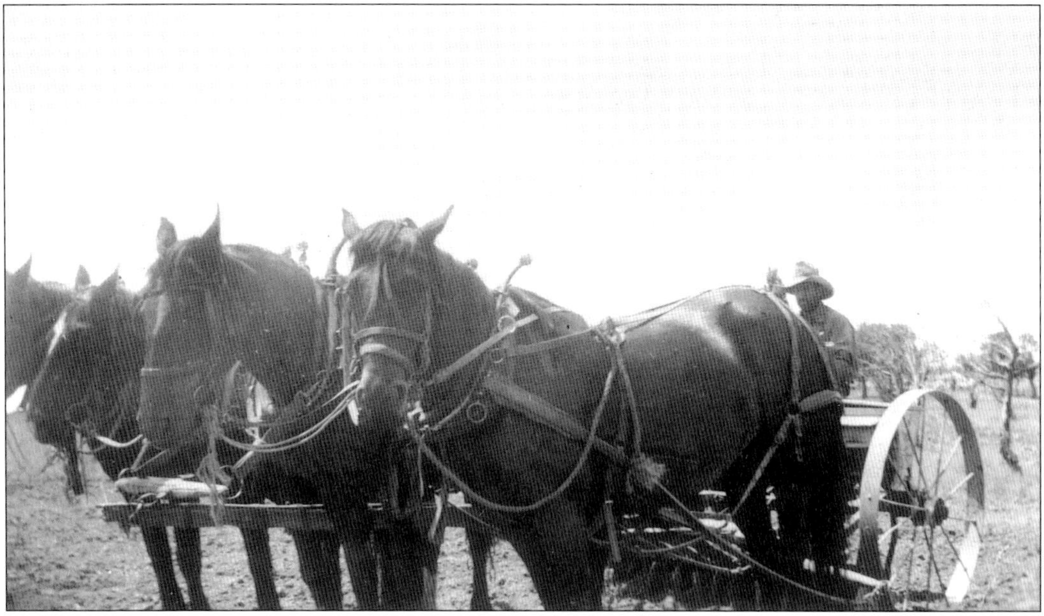

Tony's father, Marcelino, drives a hay rig on the old place. Tony's father and mother, Marcelino and Dorothy, continued to live on the old homestead until they died. After Marcelino died in 1966, Dorothy lived there by herself until she died in 1985.

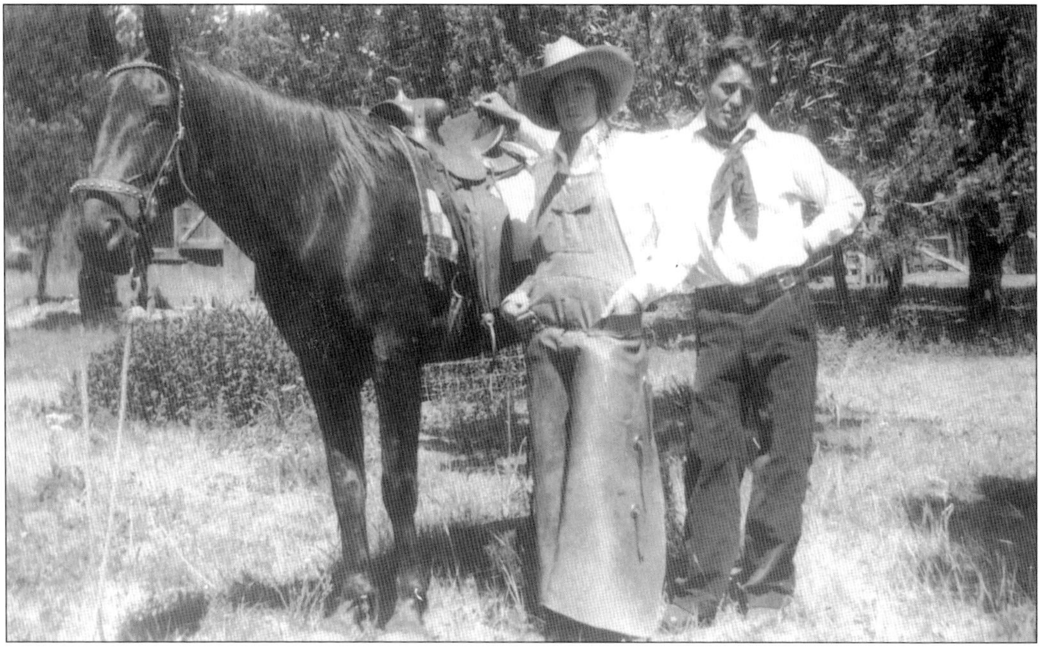

Tony's aunt and uncle, Martha and David Sanchez, pose on the old ranch where Tony grew up. The old adobe house Tony's dad Marcelino built in 1928 and most of the 160-acre tract Tony's grandfather Tomas homesteaded in the 1890s still remain intact.

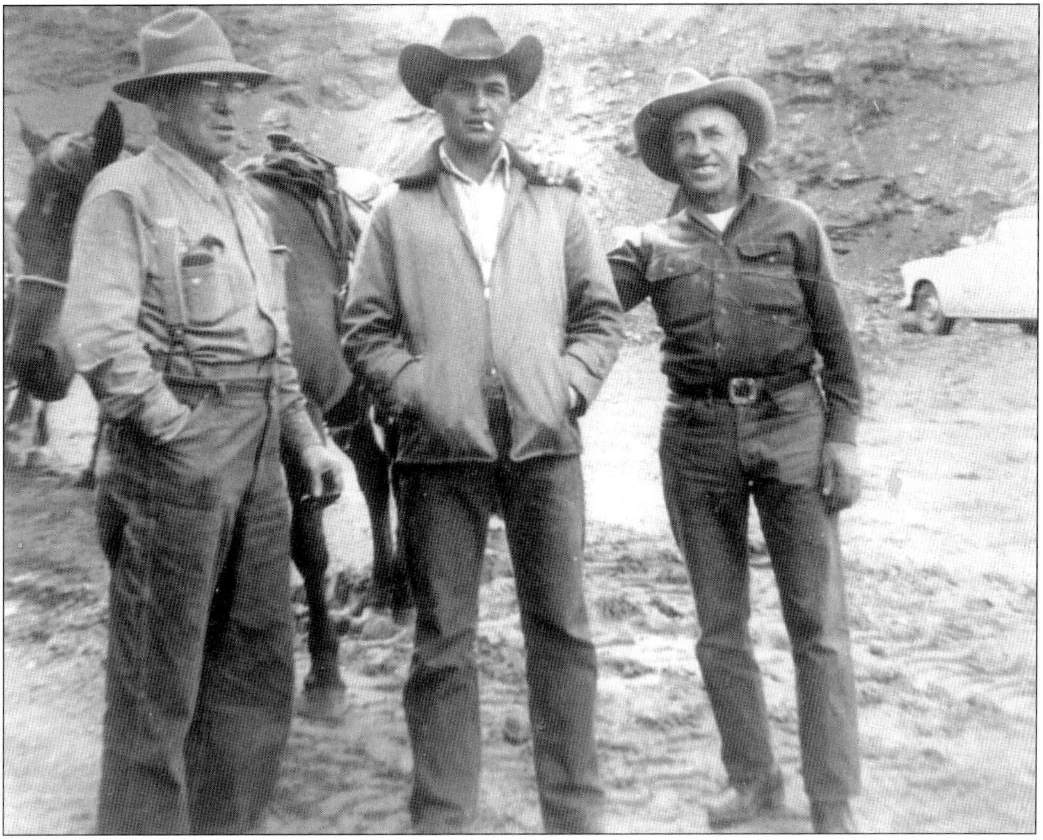

Tony (center), posing here with his buddies on location, became a "wrangler" on Westward the Women *in 1947, when he was still just a teenager. "They paid you $35 dollars a day for you and your horse back then," says Tony.*

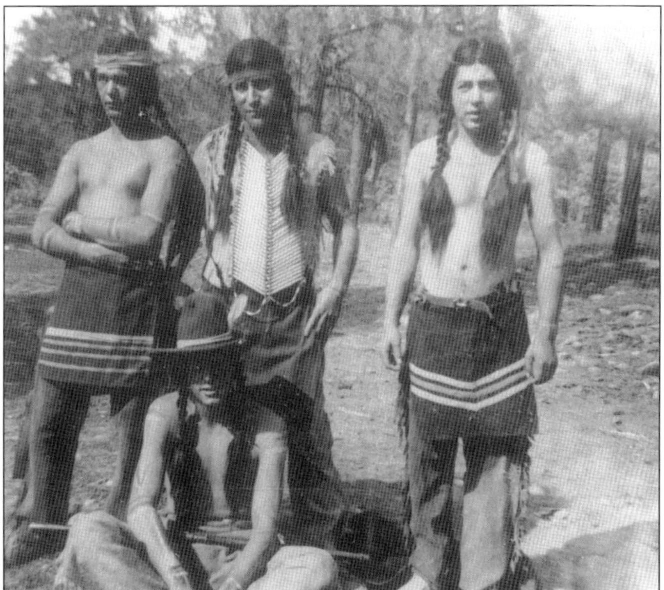

Tony (rear, left) and his brothers, Tom and Marshall (rear, center and right), in Indian garb were sometimes cast in the movies as extras. "They paid me $15 dollars a day to put that get-up on," says Tony.

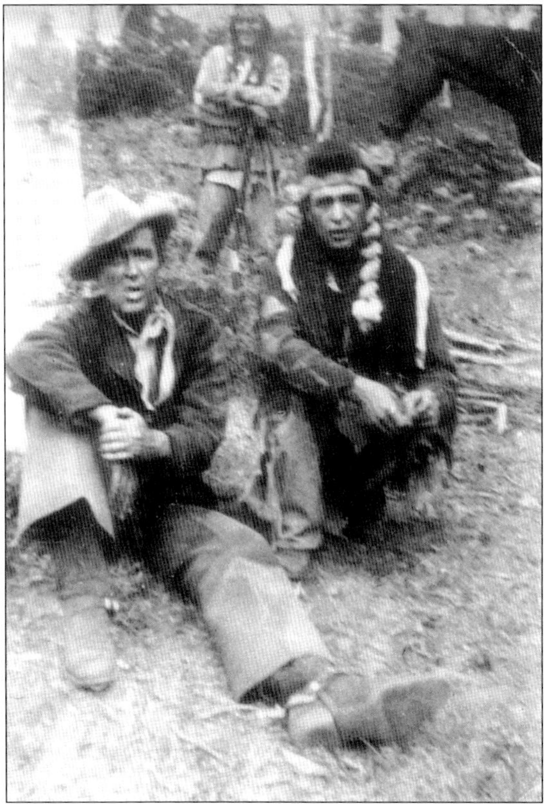

Jimmy Stewart (left) and Tony (right) take a break on location during the filming of The Naked Spur.

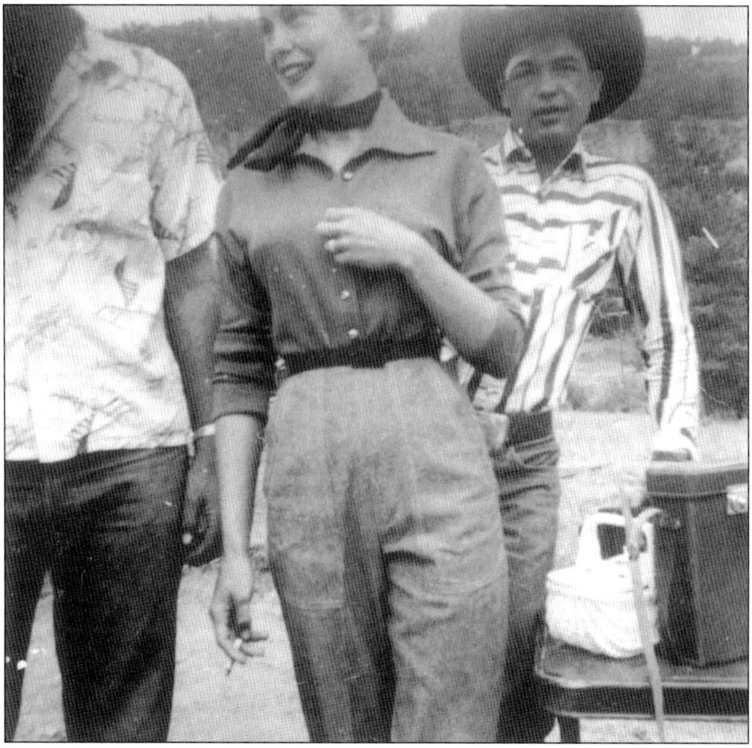

Here, Janet Leigh (center) and Tony (right) are caught together on location.

Chapter 2

Runaway Bride

Virginia Jeanette Huntsman Herrera

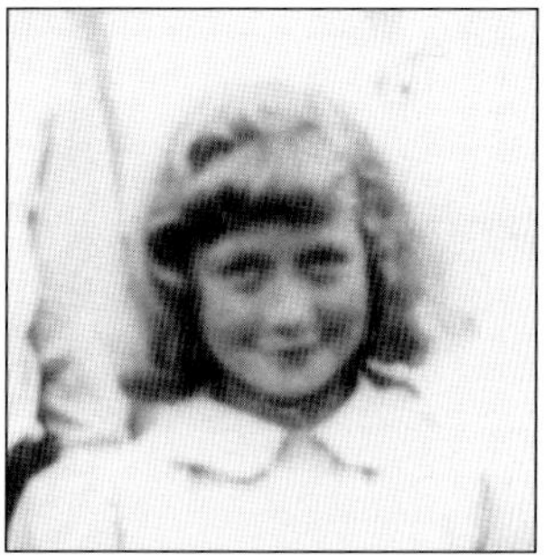

Virginia Jeanette Huntsman Herrera, Tony's wife, has a long history in southwestern Colorado herself. Virginia's mother comes from the Juby and Bartholomew clans, both local pioneer families. According to Virginia, Dan and Minerva Bartholomew came west from Minnesota in 1877, in a covered wagon drawn by a team of oxen.

"First, they went to Lake City and stayed there for a while before they came here to Bayfield. And he was the first Baptist minister here in the Pine River Valley. And of that marriage, there were eight children. Zebbie Bartholomew, my grandmother, was one of those children."

Then the lines get complicated:

"Ok, now, my mother, Lucella May Juby, was married first to a man by the name of Arthur West. And of that marriage, there were two children. Then he died and she married my dad, Richard Lloyd Huntsman.

See, my mother was a widow at that time and had two children, and my dad was also a widower at that time and my dad also had two children, though one had died before he married my mother. So they had three children between them when they were married. Then they had three more. At one time there were nine children in the family."

Virginia's father, Richard, came to La Plata County from Missouri with his mother, Janet Garrison Huntsman, in 1886.

Richard had a lot of jobs in his lifetime: logger, carpenter, rancher, game warden in the Vallecito area, deputy sheriff for the county, and at one time, consultant for the Southern Utes in Ignacio. "He taught the Indians how to build fences and raise crops," says Virginia. "He worked with them on the King Irrigation Ditch. He would go to the Indian agency and would live during the week in a little cabin down there, and then he would come back home on the weekend." He also worked for the Porter Fuel Company at the coal mine in Wildcat Canyon. "In fact, Mr. Porter left him money in his will," says Virginia, "$500."

In addition to raising the children, Virginia's mother, Lucella, used to play the piano and the guitar.

"Mama used to play for country dances at Oxford. And Mama had to fix me up to go to those dances. I had real long hair and it was naturally curly and it was naturally matted most of the time. So when she got me to wash my hair and she rolled it up on rags to make the long curls. She wasn't very easy."

In 1945, Virginia's father sold the ranch at Oxford and went to Durango and built a home in what was then known as Animas City. So Virginia went to high school in Durango and that's when she met Tony.

Virginia was working at Woolworth's the summer after her junior year in high school when Tony asked her to go to a rodeo with him in Tucumcari, New Mexico. After the rodeo, on September 13, 1951, Virginia and Tony ran off to Gallup, New Mexico and got married. Of course, this was bound to cause some problems. "My biggest problem was with my older brother Elmer and his wife," explains Virginia. "There was not a move that I made that they didn't know about and they ran home and told mama. Now, dad, he never did say nothing to me. But they would run home and tell mama. And one time she did tell me that if I continued to see Tony she would send me away to a girl's school. So when I came back, I had to face the music." But Virginia's mother didn't do anything. She just said, "How's about coming out to the house for supper?"

And everything was just fine.

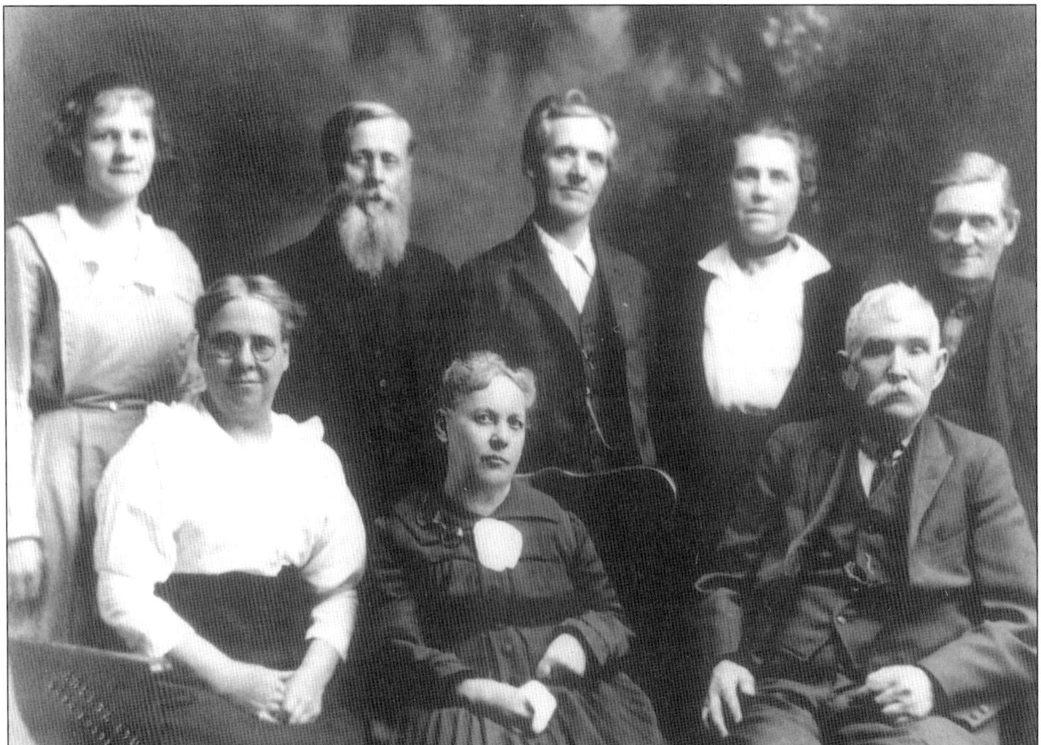

Virginia's grandmother on her mother's side, Zebbie Bartholomew Juby (front row, left), poses here with family. Virginia's great grandparents, Dan and Minerva Bartholomew, came to La Plata County from Minnesota in 1877.

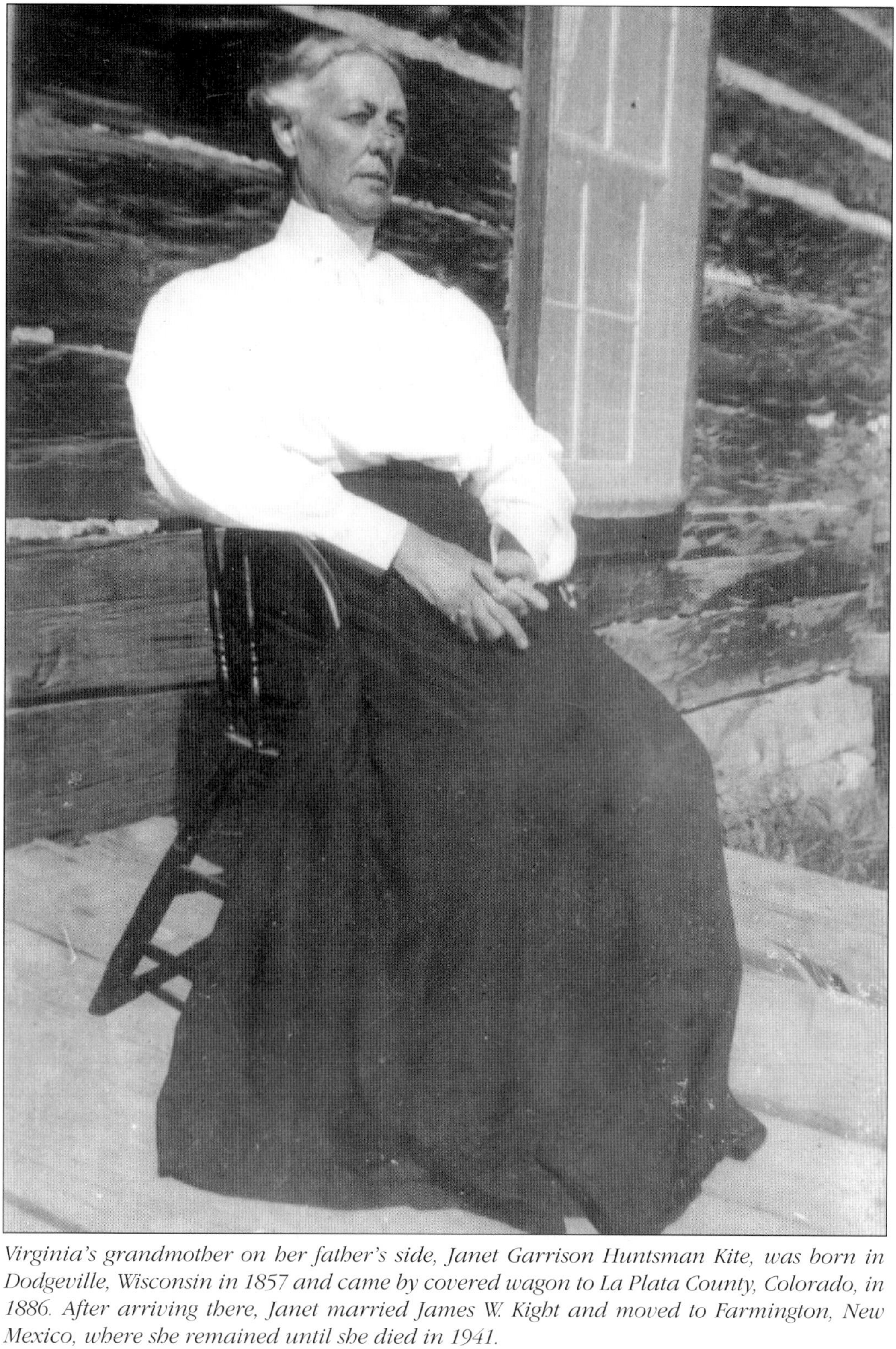

Virginia's grandmother on her father's side, Janet Garrison Huntsman Kite, was born in Dodgeville, Wisconsin in 1857 and came by covered wagon to La Plata County, Colorado, in 1886. After arriving there, Janet married James W. Kight and moved to Farmington, New Mexico, where she remained until she died in 1941.

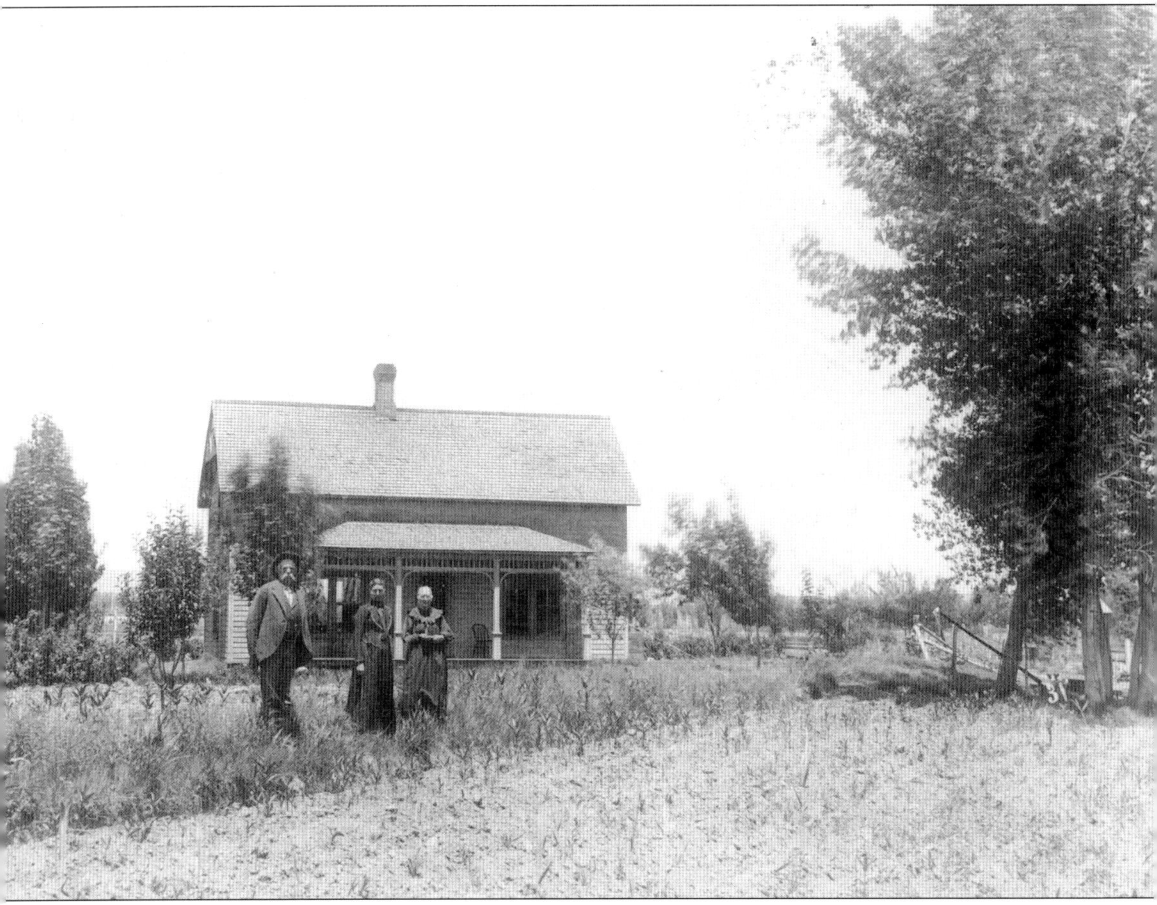

Janet Kite (right) stands in front of the Bartholomew house in Bayfield, Colorado.

Pictured left is a close-up of Virginia's father, Richard Lloyd Huntsman, from a postcard dated April 15, 1920. "Dear Mother," reads the postcard, "from Sawpit, Colorado."

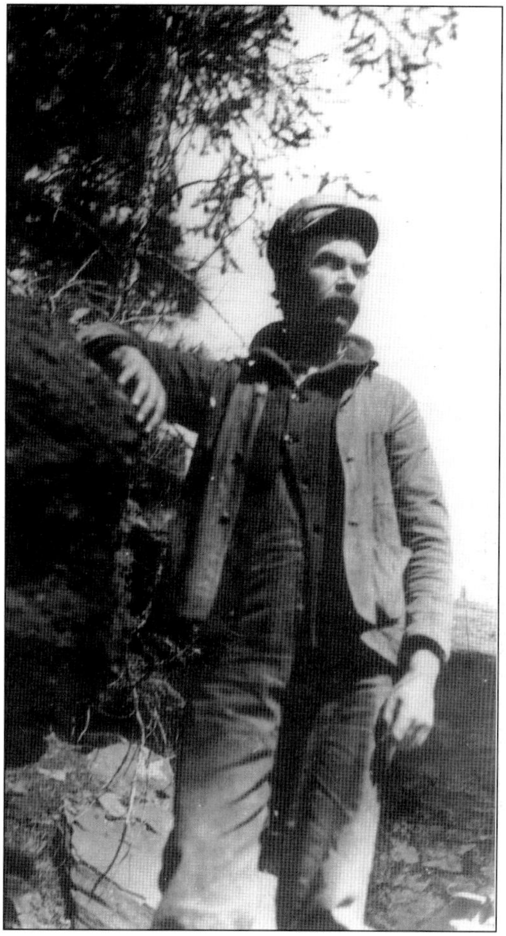

Below, Richard (center) hauls logs. He was born in Springfield, Missouri in 1880 and came to La Plata County with his mother in 1886. Richard was married one time before he married Virginia's mother and had two children from that marriage.

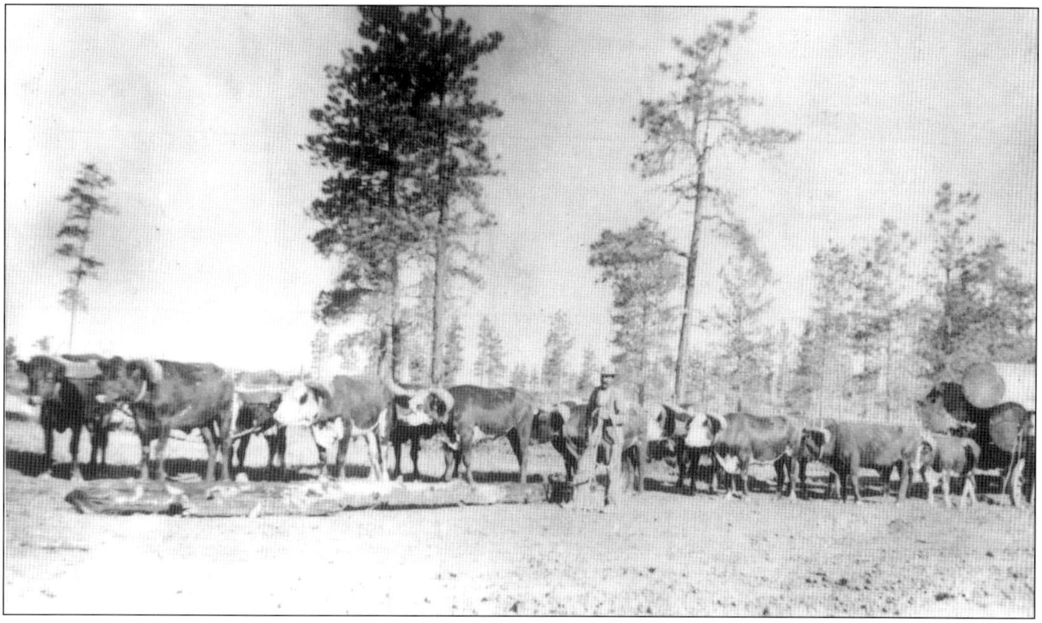

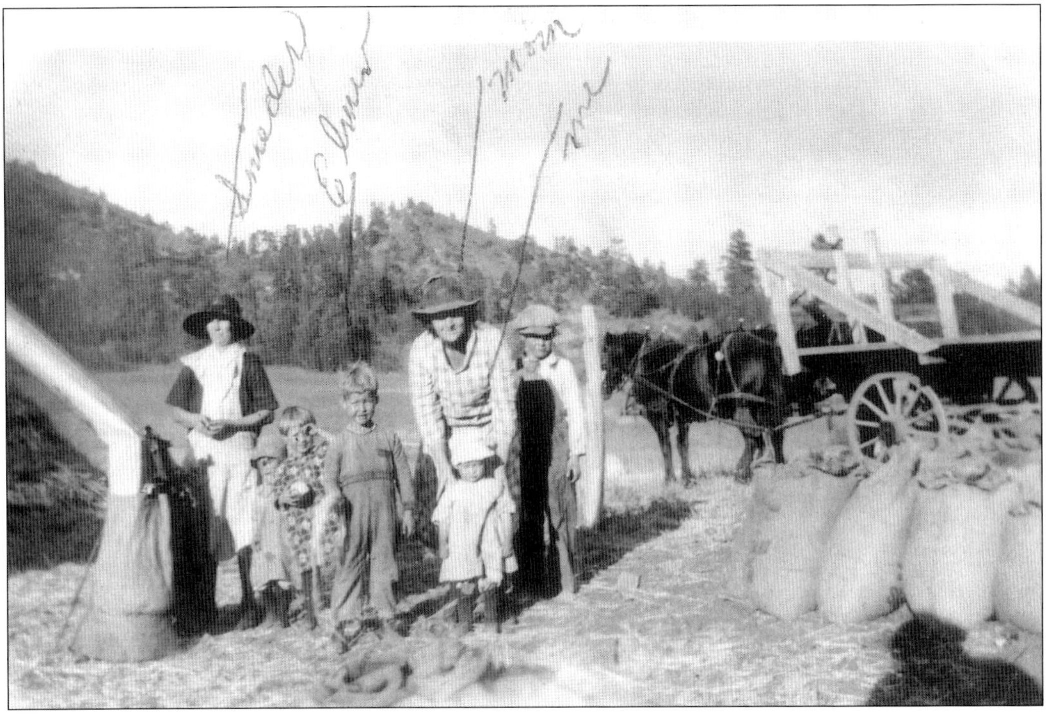

Virginia's mother, Lucella (fifth from left), and kids pose for picture during a threshing operation on the family ranch. All the kids helped sack the grain.

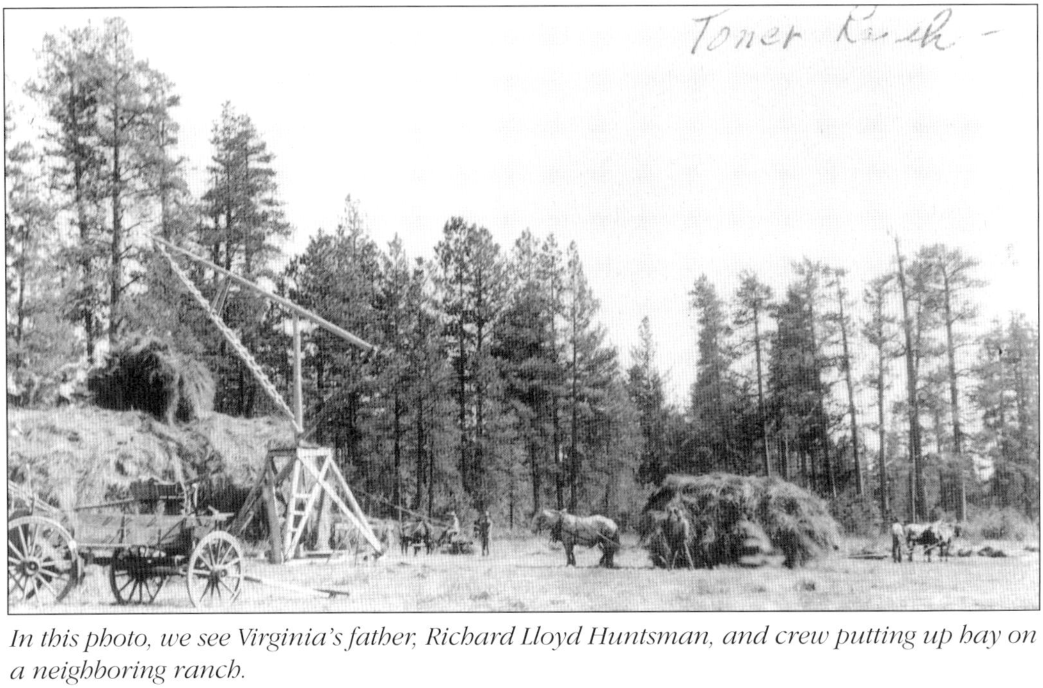

In this photo, we see Virginia's father, Richard Lloyd Huntsman, and crew putting up hay on a neighboring ranch.

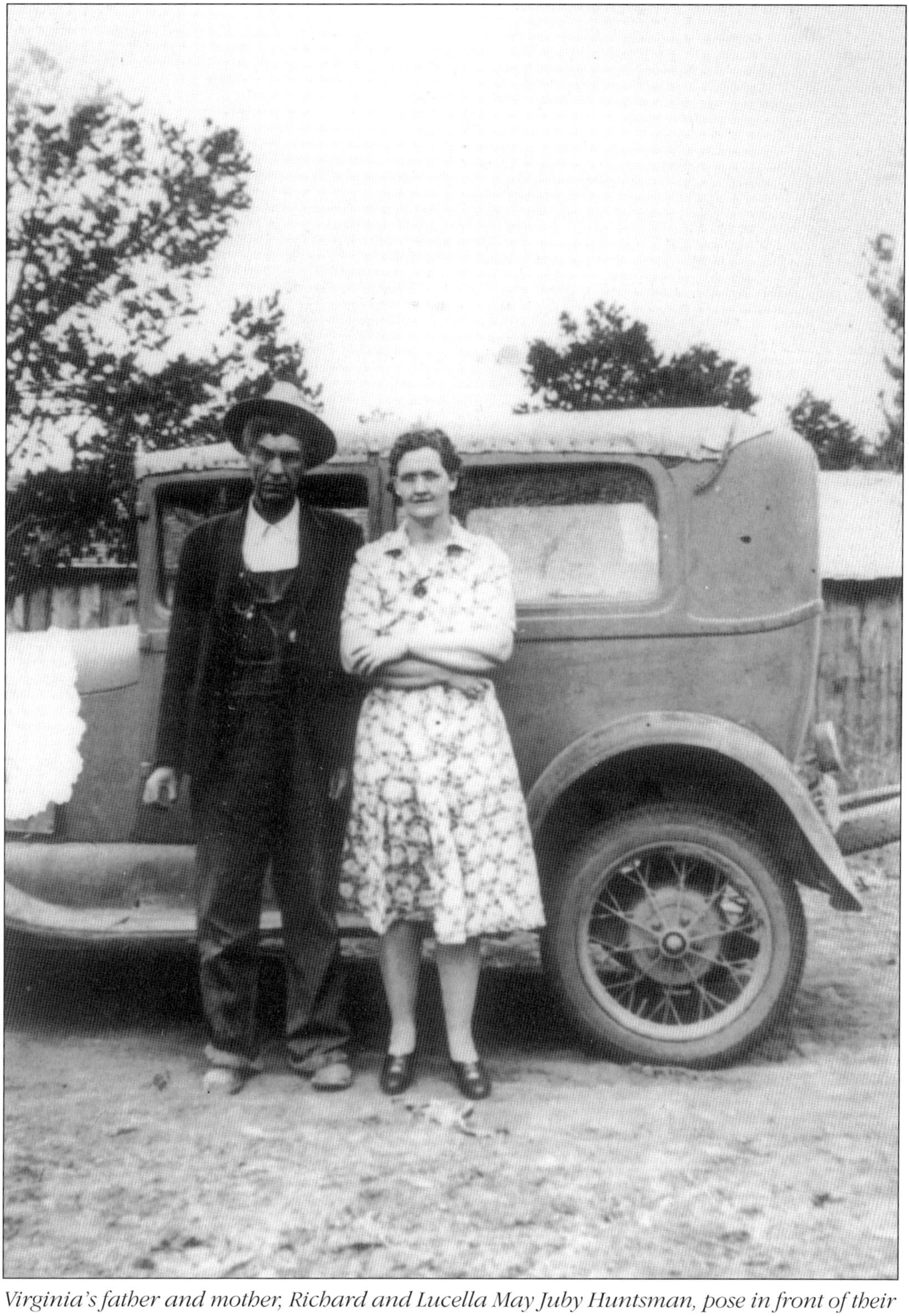

Virginia's father and mother, Richard and Lucella May Juby Huntsman, pose in front of their car, c. 1945. Virginia's parents were married in 1923 and raised six children on their ranch near Oxford, Colorado.

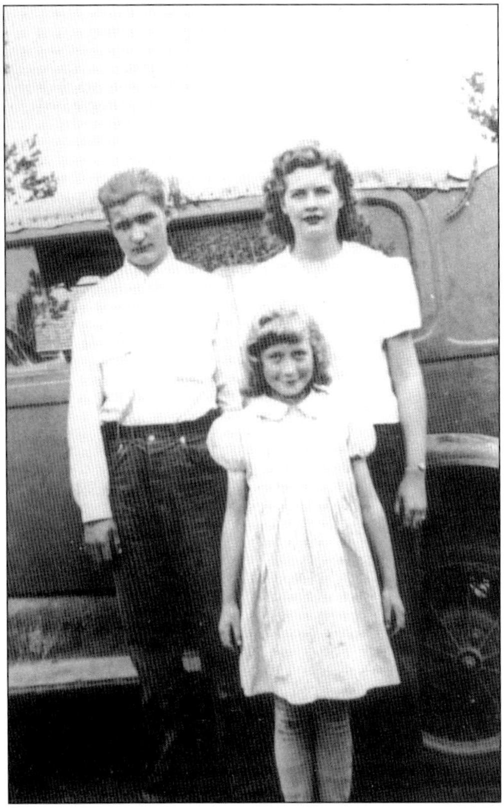

Virginia's brother Bill (rear, left) and sister Mary (rear, right) and Virginia (front) pose in front of their car at about the time the family moved from Oxford to Durango, Colorado.

Virginia's mother, Lucella (on horse, middle), with family and various cousins, heads for Emerald Lake to go fishing.

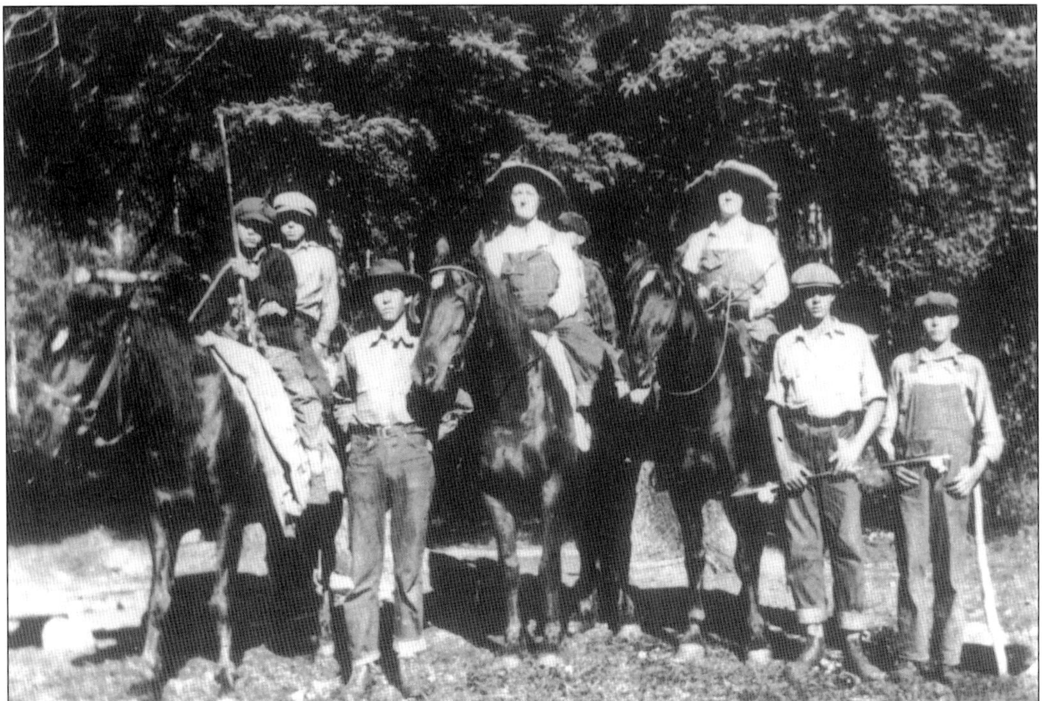

Chapter 3

Picking Up the Pieces

Jim, Joe, and Virginia Martinez

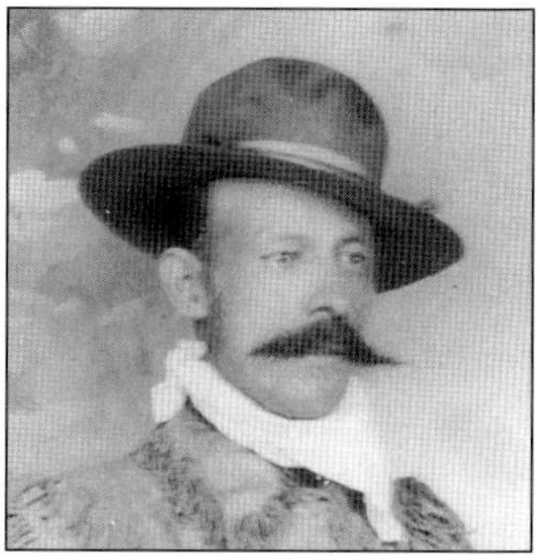

We meet Jim, Joe, and Virginia Martinez all gathered in Jim's backyard, fenced off from the road by a high picket fence decorated with all kinds of relics from the old place: a skid hook for skidding logs, old wagon wheels, tractor tires, kerosene lanterns. "All this stuff I got at the ranch," says Jim, the youngest son, showing us around.

***

We all go inside the house to continue the tour.

"Here's all the arrowheads my dad and I found at the ranch," says Jim. "We got all kinds of stuff around here—that old flat iron, those old logging tongs, an old well-weight. . . . You know what this is, doncha? A corn husker."

Over the fireplace, Jim has paneled the wall with old barn-wood from the ranch.

"These are some old pictures of my grandparents," says Jim. "That's Raymundo Trujillo, my grandfather, and my grandmother, Adelina. And here's a picture of our mom, Mary, and my dad, George Trujillo."

"And here's a picture of our mom and *my* dad, Trinidad Martinez," interrupts Virginia, "with my brother Joe and I."

"You see, Mom was married twice," Jim explains. "She was also a Martinez before she was married, different family. Then she married Trinidad Martinez. And then she married my dad, George Trujillo."

"Talking about my dad," says Jim, "he made the best moonshine in the county. I got the old copper kettle here. I keep wood in it for my fireplace. It's got the copper coils and everything. And I've got a picture of the old Pontiac he used to haul it in. You ask the people around here," emphasizes Jim, "and they say it was the best moonshine in the Four Corner area!"

The kids' mom, Maria "Mary" Delfinia Martinez, was also part German. Mary's mother, Emilia, was the daughter of Walter and Christina VonBuddenbrock. Walter VonBuddenbrock came from Germany to the Pine River area before the turn of the century.

Virginia knew her grandma Emilia very well. "After Grandpa Delfido died, she moved in with us at the ranch," says Virginia. "Grandma Emilia was a lot of fun."

"She'd teach me how to do some sewing —a little embroidery— and making tortillas. And we had them big gardens," continues Virginia, "and my grandma dried fruit. And my grandma canned. And the meat, we'd either dry it or we'd fry the meat and put it in lard and it never did spoil."

"We used to speak German when my grandmother was alive," says Jim. "She spoke it fluently."

And Joe used to speak German with his great grandpa Walter, he tells us. Joe used to go hunting with his great grandpa, and Walter used to talk to him in several languages—German, Spanish, and English.

***

"The old homestead down there, the old ranch, after Grandpa and Grandma died and when Mom and Daddy died, they gave that to my younger sister and brother," says Joe, "since I already had some of it."

"Our parents worked hard. They hand-tilled the land with a one-bottom plow with horses. And they picked up the rock, piles of rock. They worked hard to make that place something."

"Maybe one of these days we'll have a big house down there, ourselves," says Jim. "Mom and Dad were always going to build a cabin down there and go down and spend the summers there, but they were always working and they never did make it.

"The old building, it's pretty dilapidated, but there's three main beams that are still good. And when I build the house I can use them."

"It's frame and adobe. They made their own brick," says Joe.

"They got places down there where there's natural springs," he adds. "It's just a beautiful place."

"Huge panoramic views," says Jim, "the La Platas, the Needles. It's fantastic down there."

"You know, Junie Arney from around Red Basin?" muses Joe. "He's an old timer. And he said to me, 'You ever going to be a cowboy like your daddy used to be?' And that's what I want to do," says Joe. "I want to get that place going again."

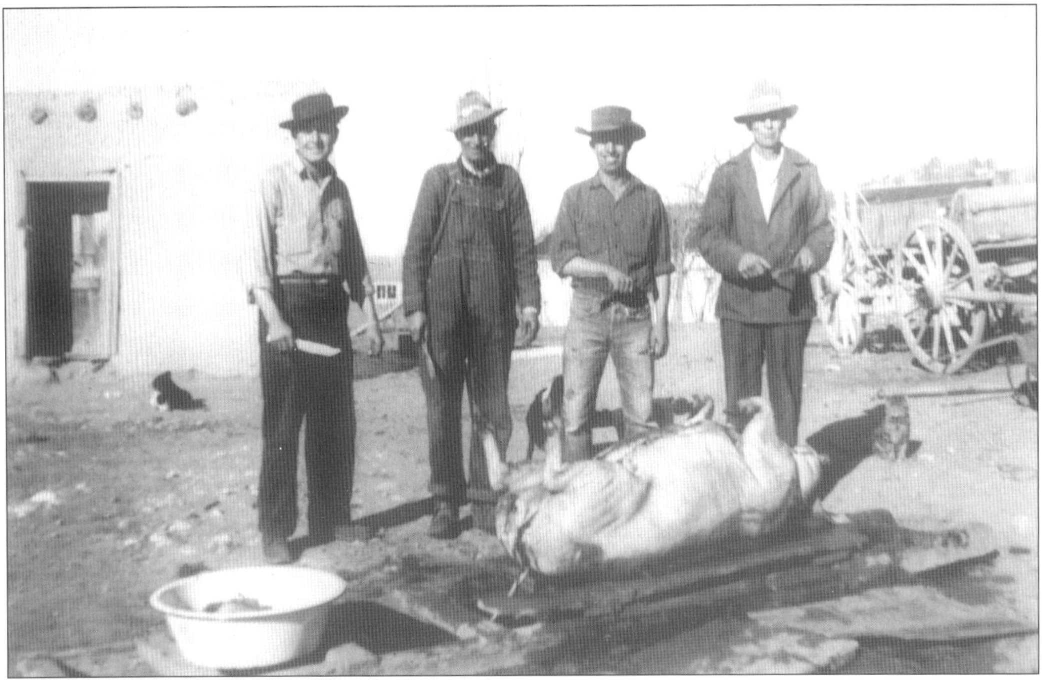

Jim Martinez' grandfather, Raymundo Trujillo (second from left), prepares to help skin a pig at a pig roast at the family ranch in Chimayo, New Mexico.

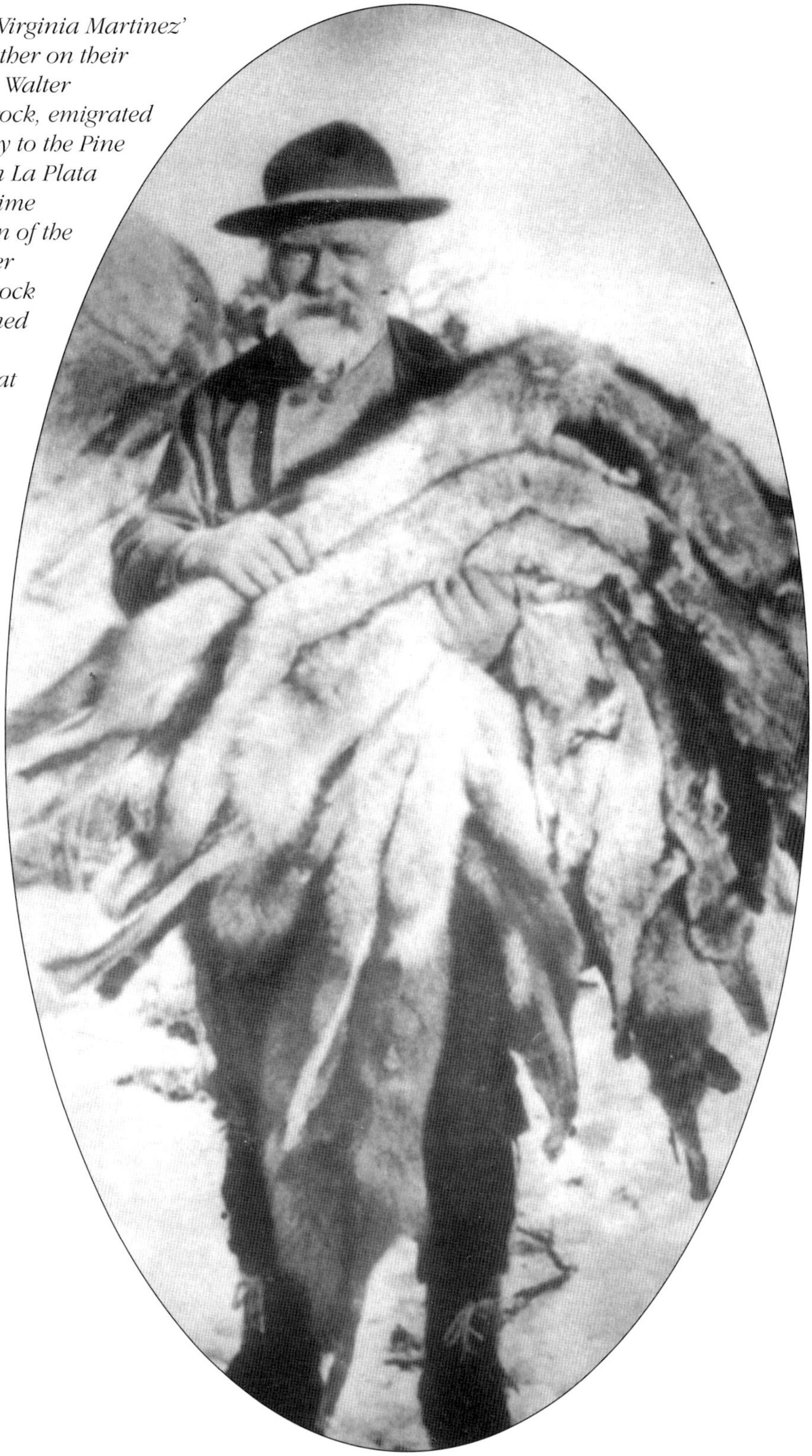

Jim, Joe, and Virginia Martinez' great grandfather on their mother's side, Walter VonBuddenbrock, emigrated from Germany to the Pine River Valley in La Plata County sometime before the turn of the century. Walter VonBuddenbrock was a renowned hunter and taught his great grandson Joe how to hunt. In this photo, Walter proudly exhibits an armful of wolf pelts.

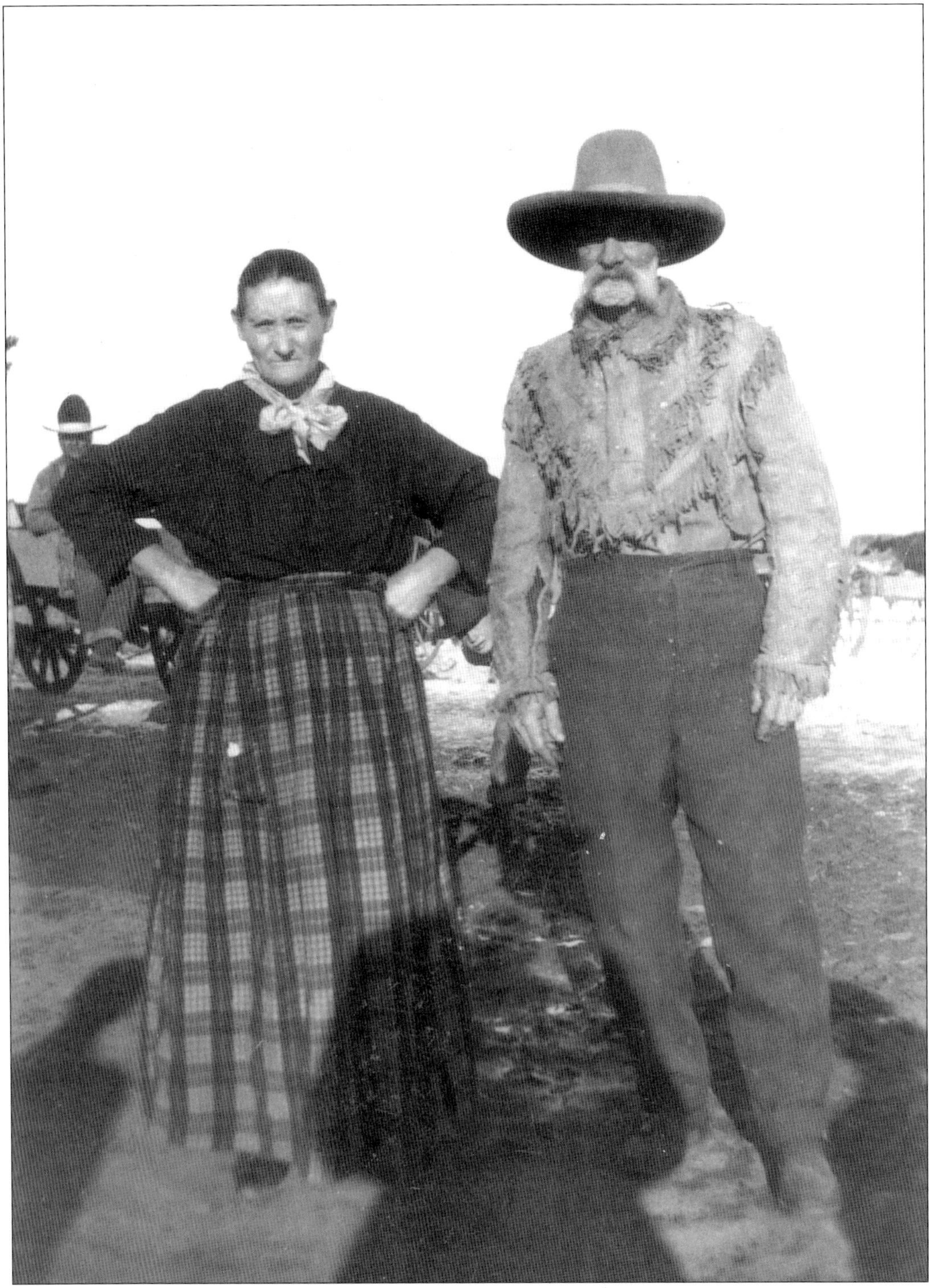

Pictured here are Joe and Virginia Martinez' grandparents on their father's side, Urselita and Luis Martinez. Joe and Virginia's father, Trinidad Martinez, was the first husband of Jim, Joe, and Virginia's mother, Maria "Mary" Delfinia Martinez, their mother's maiden name also being Martinez.

Frank Martinez, pictured on the right, was the brother of Joe and Virginia's grandfather, Luis Martinez.

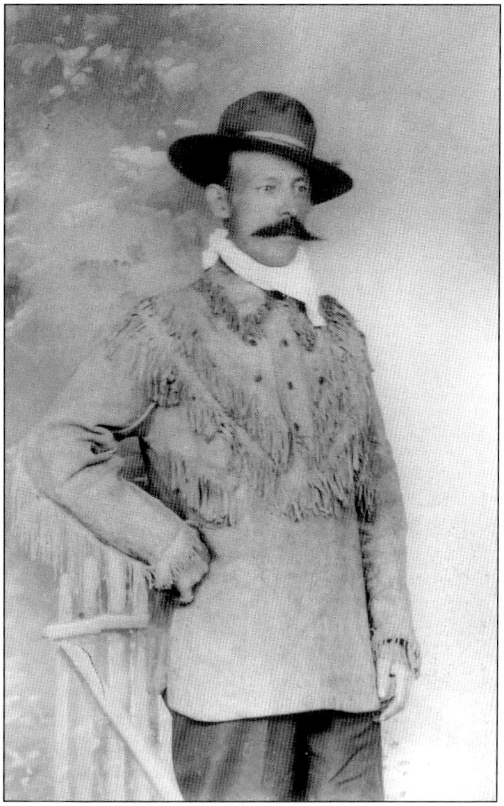

Joe and Virginia's father, Trinidad Martinez, was another renowned hunter and trapper. "He used to trap mountain lions and bobcats, bring them back alive, and keep them as pets," says Joe.

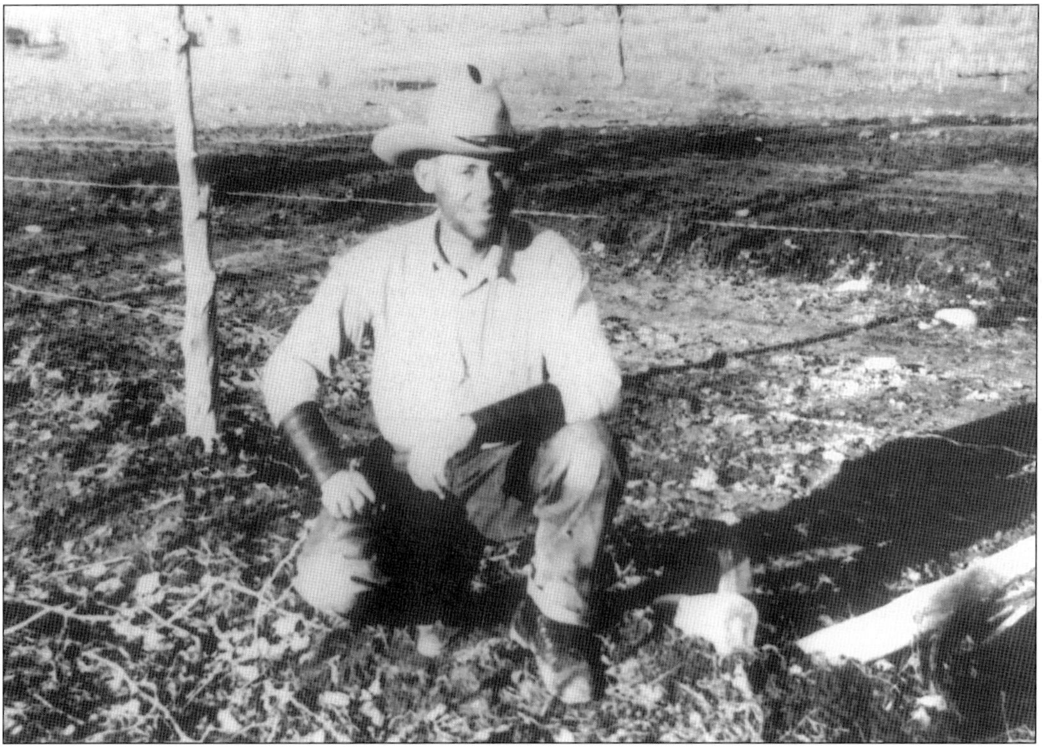

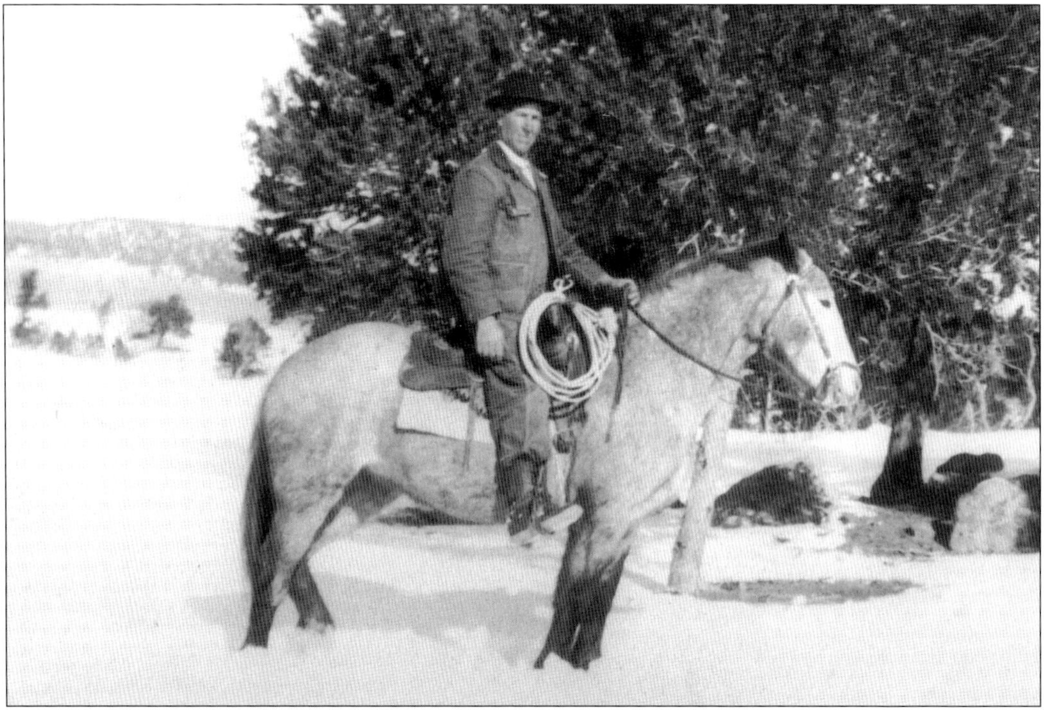

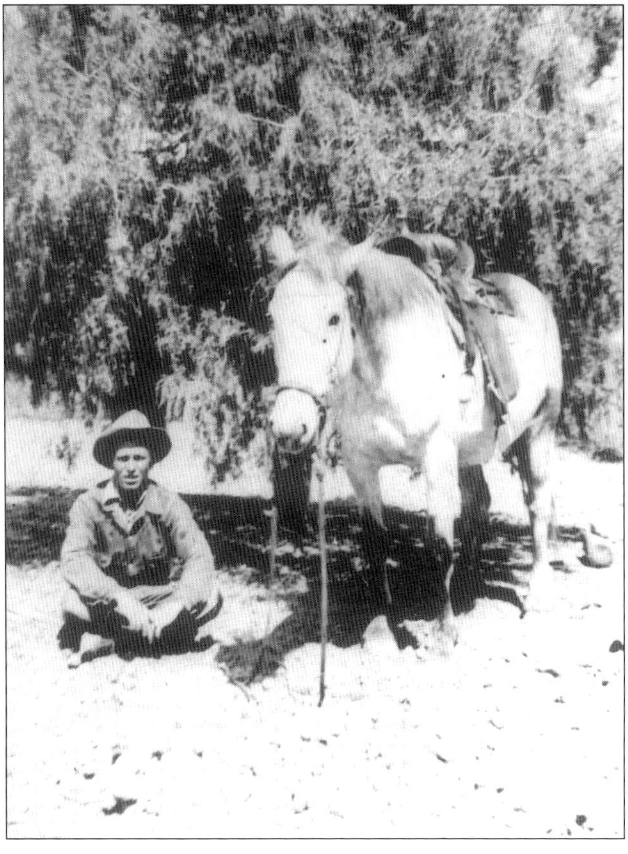

Pictured above is Jim Martinez' grandfather on his father's side, Raymundo Trujillo. Jim's father, George Trujillo, was the second husband of Jim, Joe, and Virginia's mother, Maria "Mary" Delfinia Martinez.

Jim's father, George Trujillo, was the third renowned hunter and trapper in this frontier family. "My dad was an excellent marksman," says Jim. "He could kill a deer on the run."

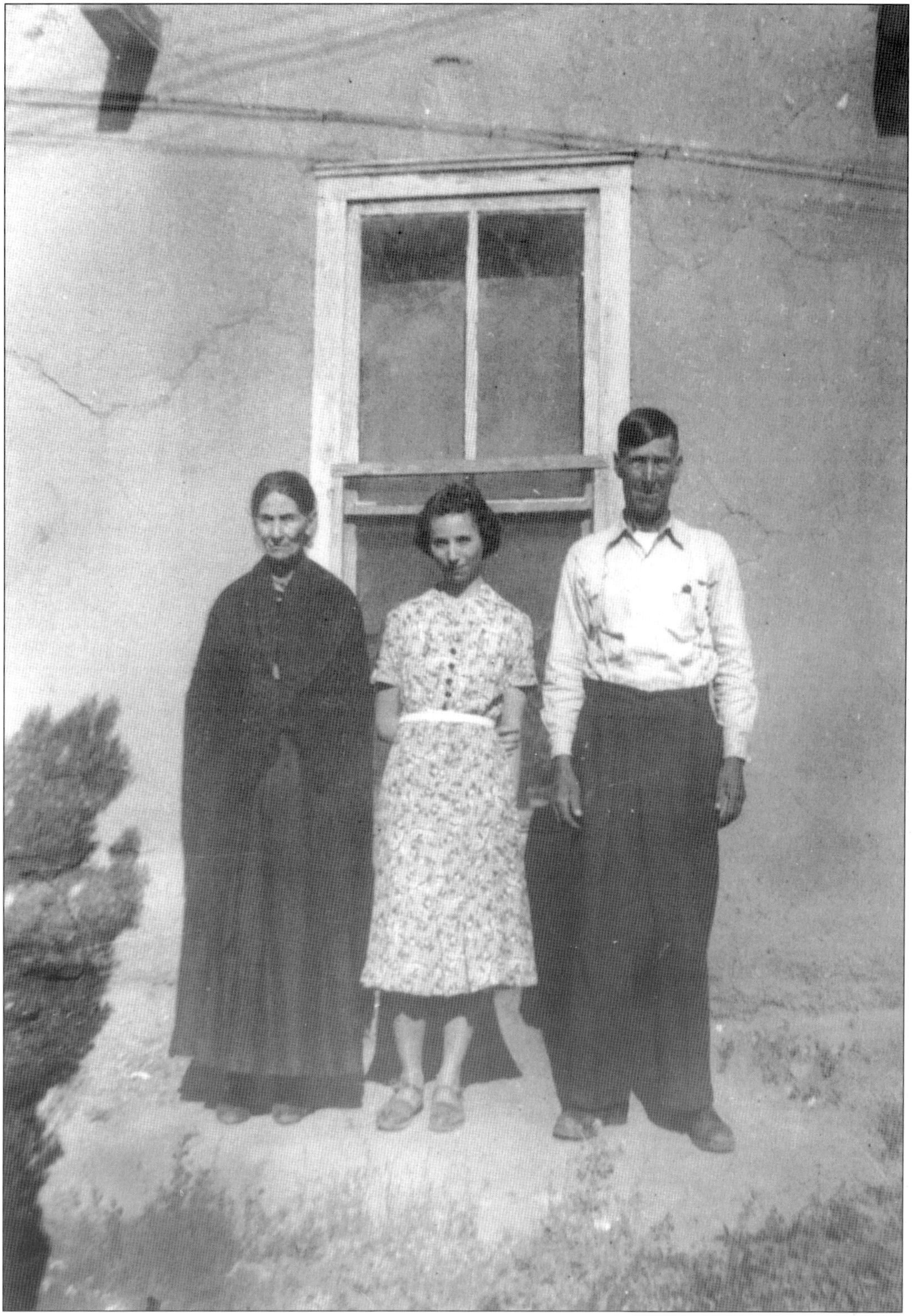

Jim's grandfather, Raymundo Trujillo (right), poses here with his sisters in front of their family home in Chimayo, New Mexico.

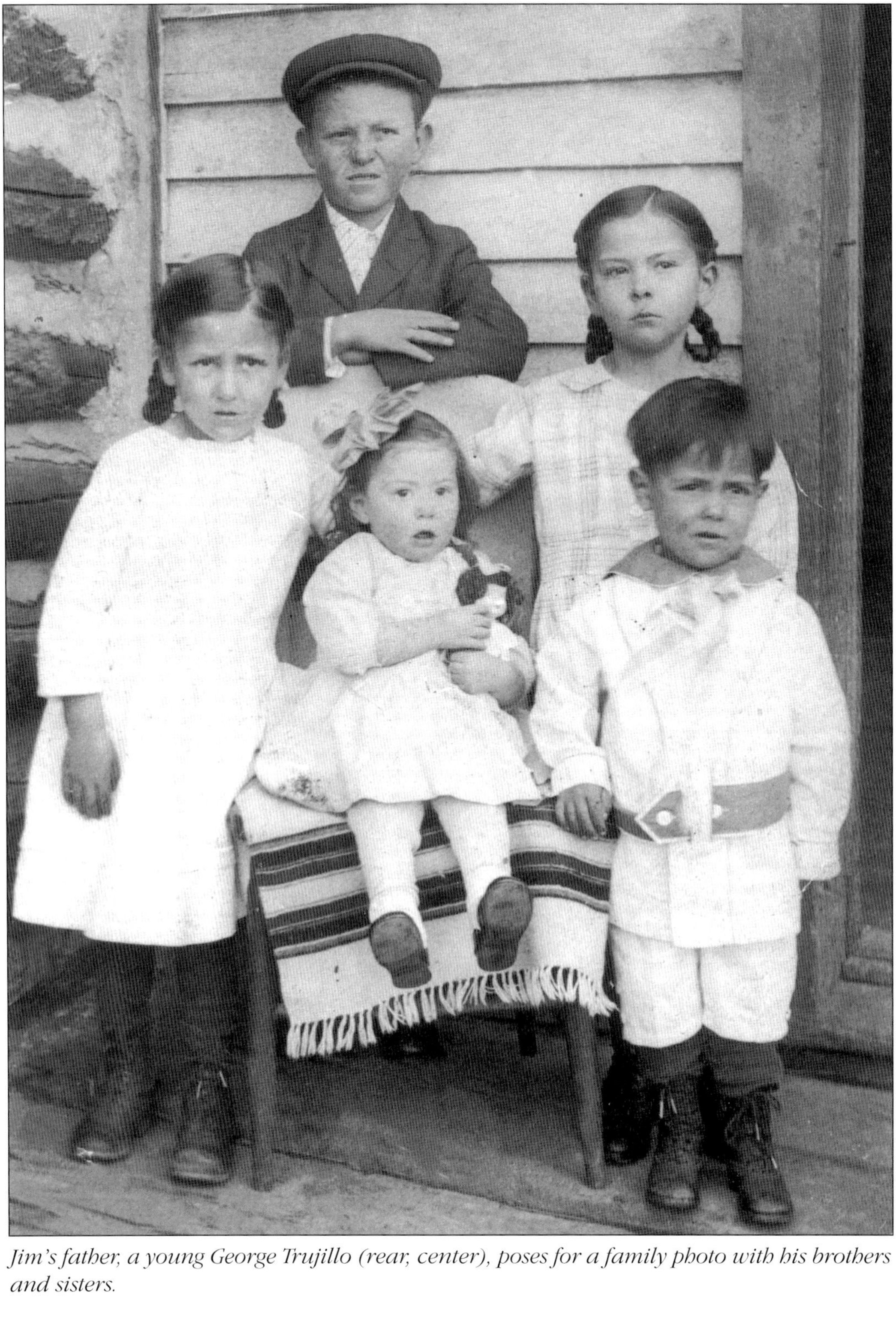

Jim's father, a young George Trujillo (rear, center), poses for a family photo with his brothers and sisters.

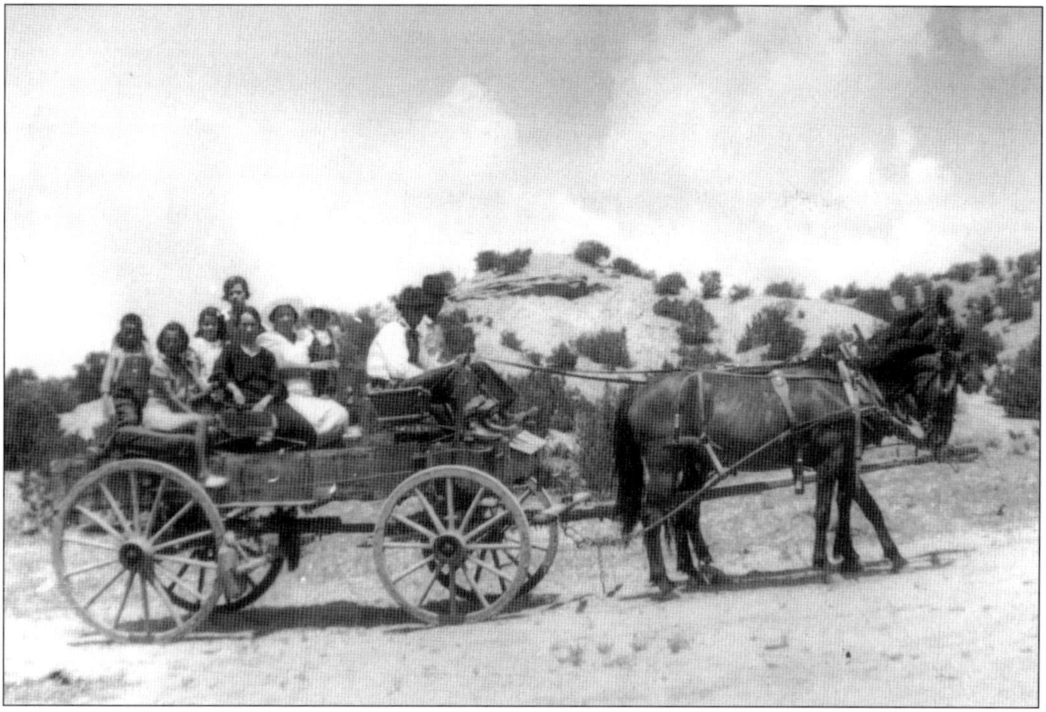

The Trujillo family heads for town in a buckboard wagon.

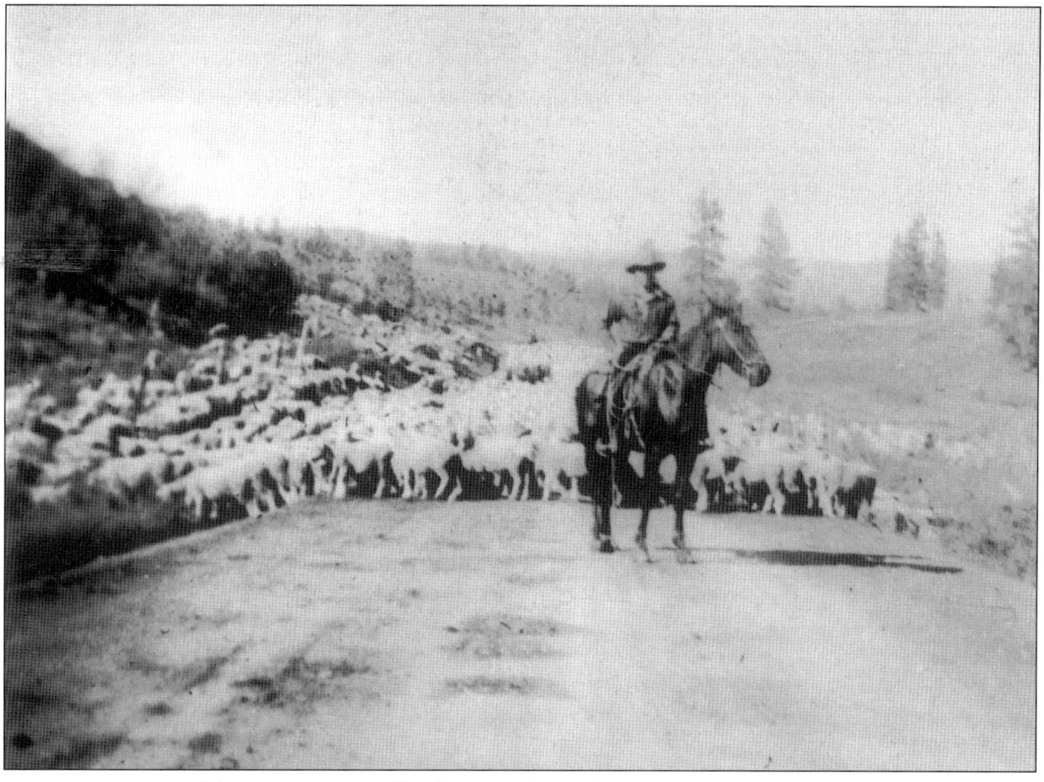

Here we see an older George Trujillo driving sheep down the road.

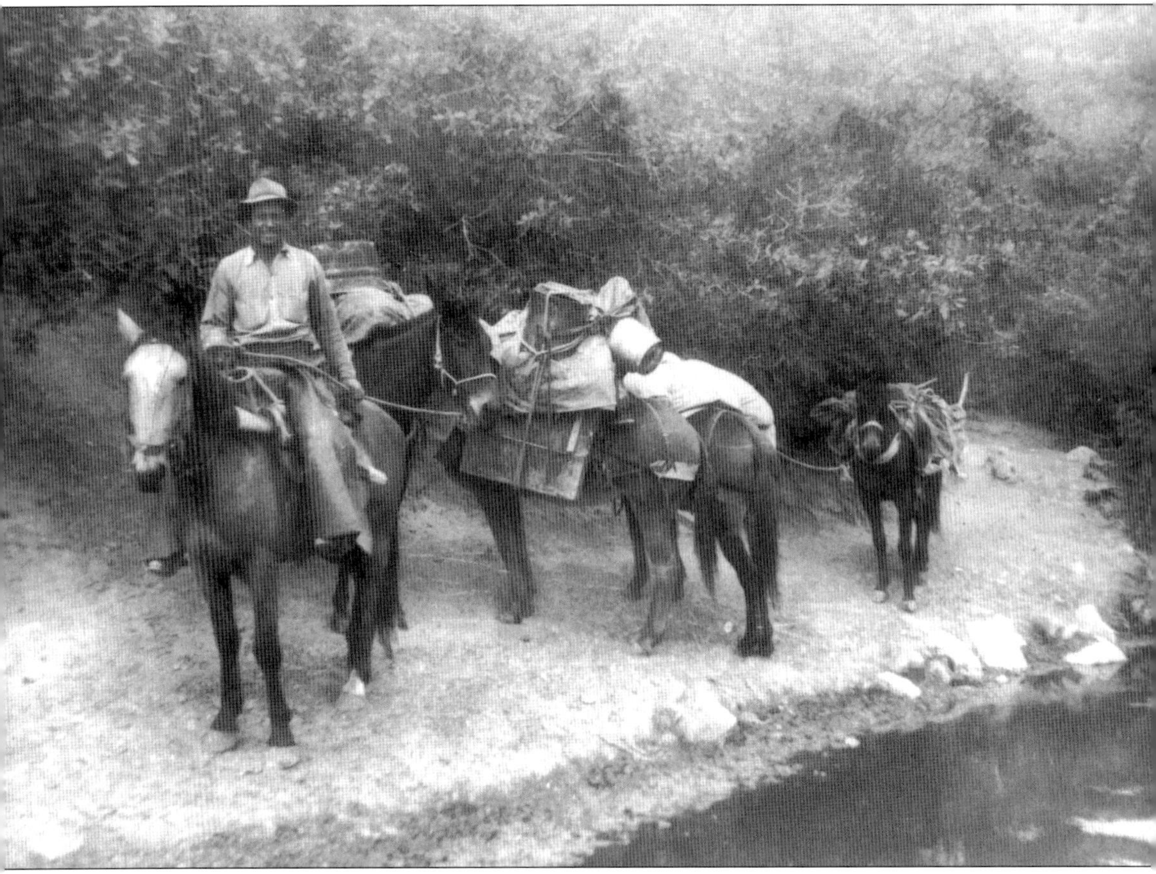

George Trujillo heads out into the mountains on a pack trip.

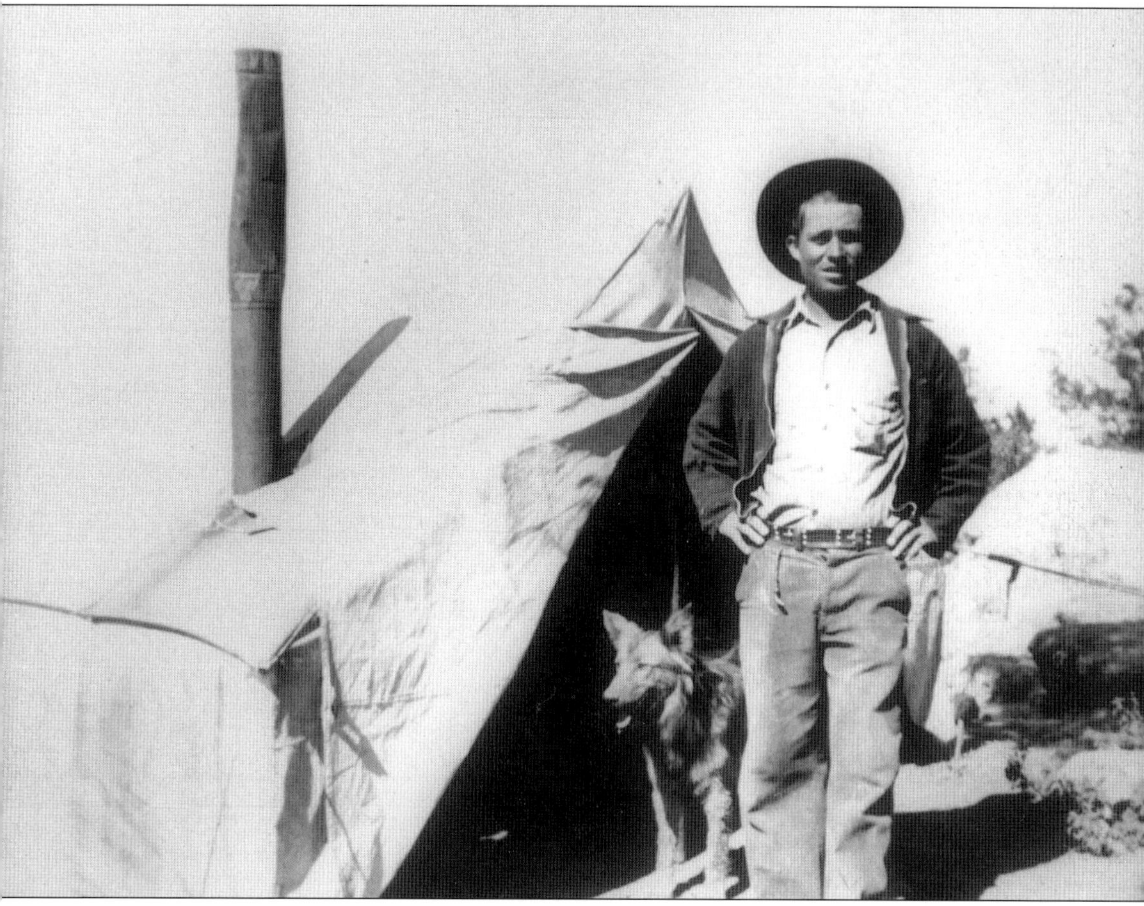

George poses with his dog Laddie at sheep camp up in the high country.

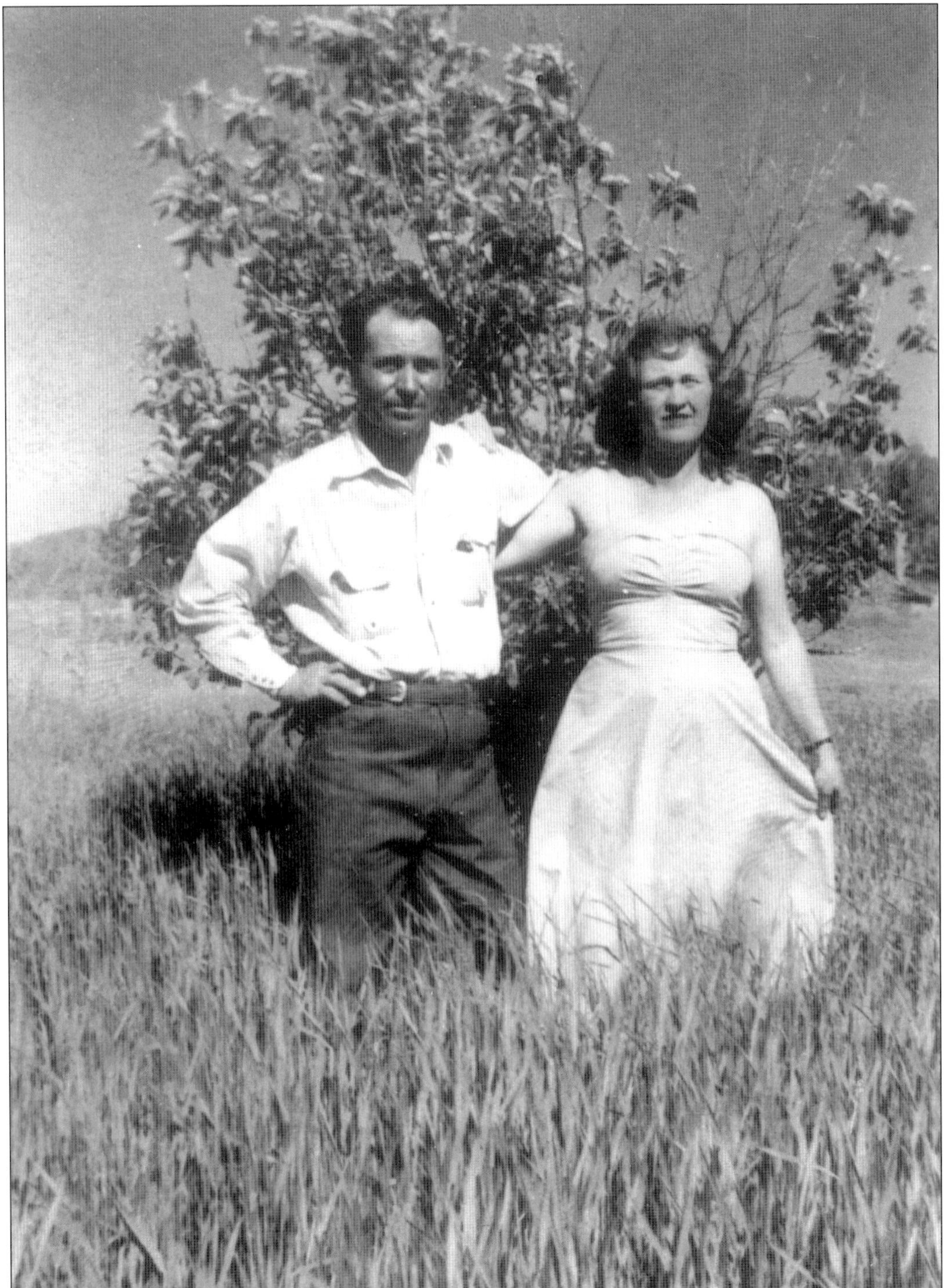

George and Mary stand arm-in-arm out in the wheat field on the old Trujillo homestead. "They used to combine oats and wheat," says Jim. "And the corn—for the pigs and cows—was higher than the top of your truck." "Before Mom and Daddy died," adds Joe, "we had about 75 cows."

George Trujillo steadies his young son Jim for a photo on the old Trujillo homestead.

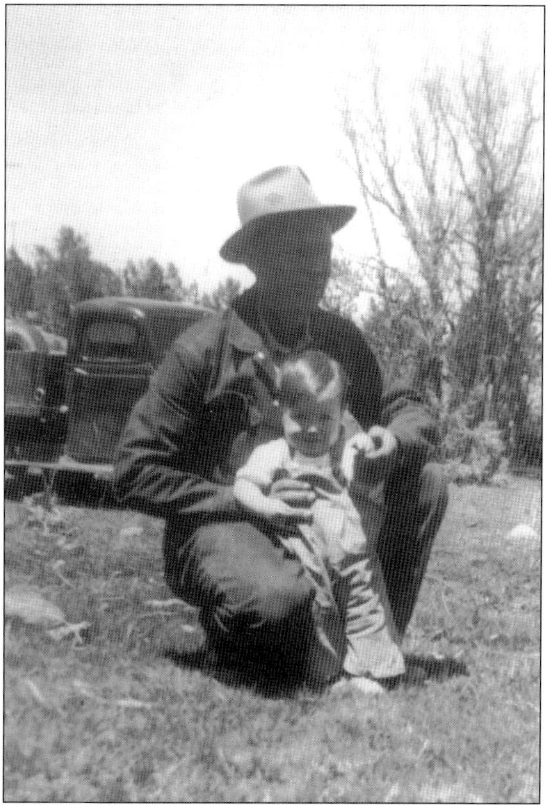

At bottom, George Trujillo (left) also worked for what is now the Durango & Silverton Narrow Gauge Railroad. "My dad worked for the railroad for 27 years," says Jim. "He was a section foreman."

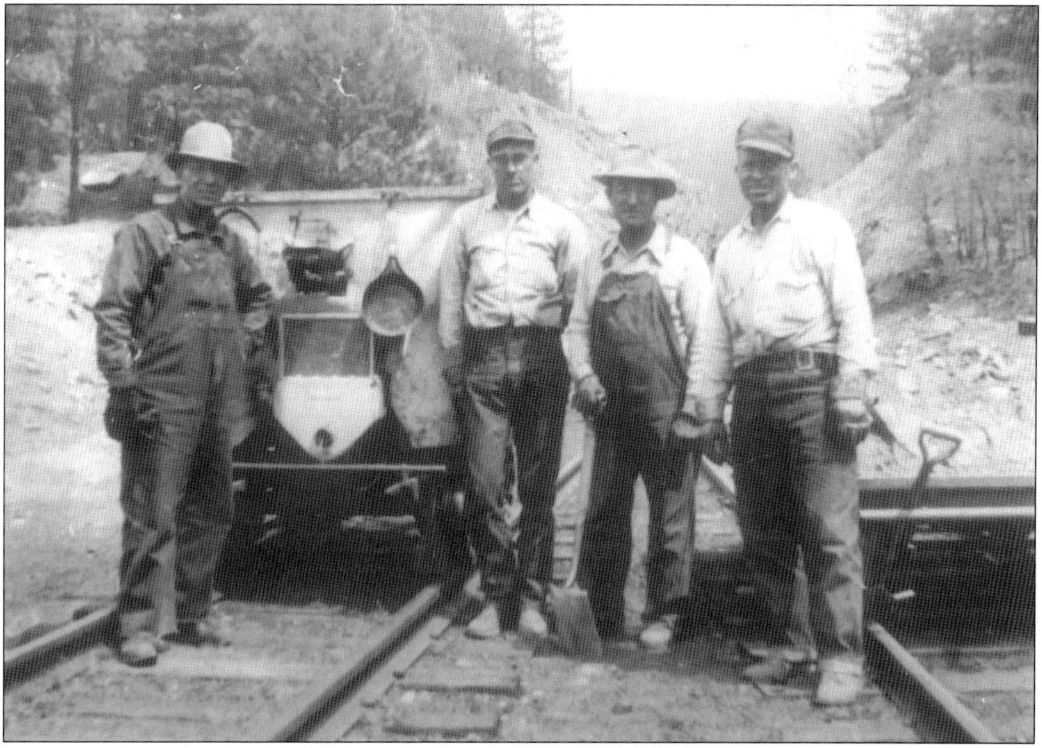

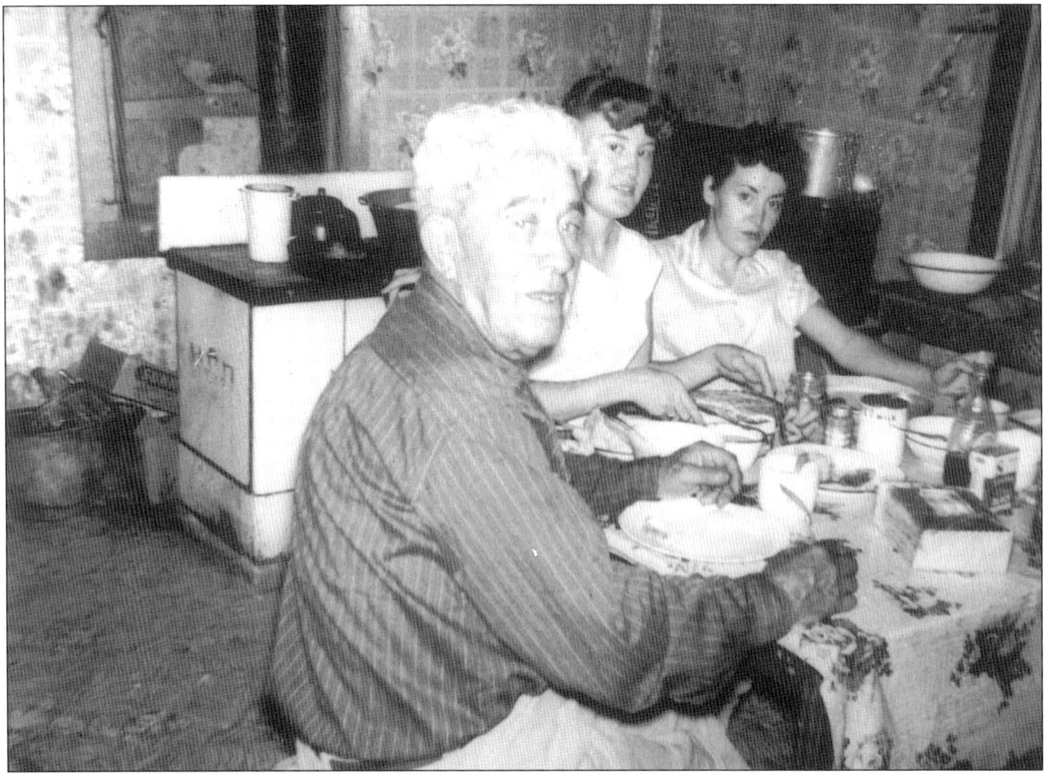

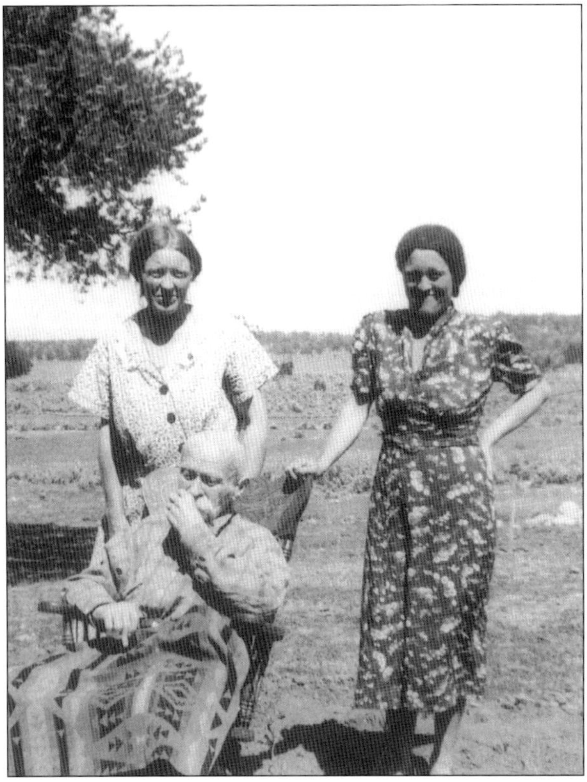

Virginia (center) and her grandfather, Delfido Martinez, finish dinner in the kitchen of the old place. Virginia's grandmother, Emilia, taught Virginia how to make tortillas in that kitchen. "You put flour, baking powder, shortening, a little bit of sugar, and milk or water in the tortillas," says Virginia, "and then she'd show me how to roll them out."

Jim, Joe, and Virginia's grandmother, Emelia Martinez (rear, left), their mother, Mary (right), and their great grandfather, Walter VonBuddenbrock (front), pose for a photo on the old homestead. German, Spanish, and English all used to be spoken before Emilia died. "Grandma Emilia spoke German fluently," Jim says, "but now we only speak Spanish and English."

Chapter 4

CATTLE*WOMAN* OF THE YEAR

STELLA MONTOYA

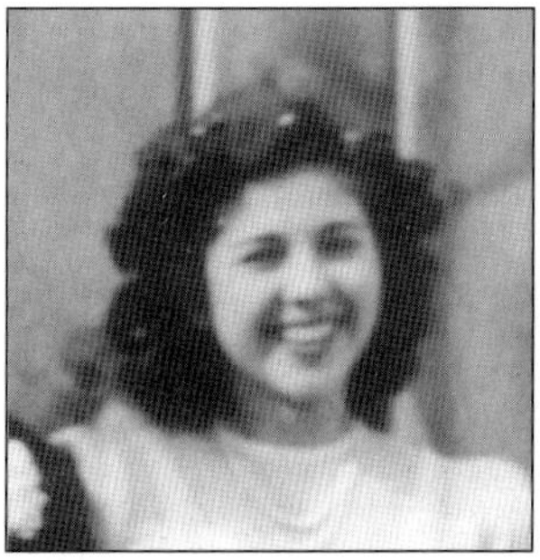

"My family started in the San Luis Valley in Colorado," says Stella Montoya, "and then they came over this way to Gallina, New Mexico. Some of them stayed down there but the rest of them came to Largo Canyon. And my aunt Sarah was born the day after they arrived. Can you imagine a lady coming down to Largo pregnant, bouncing in a wagon?"

Sarah was the oldest, says Stella, and her father Onofre was one of the youngest. He was born on January 6, 1895, in Blanco, New Mexico, where the family ultimately settled.

"My mother, Alvina Martinez, was from Clayton, New Mexico," Stella continues. "But both of her parents died when she was very small, so she came over here to Blanco to live with her sisters."

Growing up so close to each other, Stella's parents inevitably met and eventually married, homesteading a place near Cedar Hill, New Mexico.

"We had a small farm," says Stella. "We raised hay and had a garden. We had milk cows and we had pigs to slaughter for hams and bacon and lard. I grew up on the farm.

"The Animas River was below our place and we'd swim in the river. We could get under the railroad bridge . . . .

"We had to walk across the railroad bridge to go to school and sometimes the train would pick us up. That was a treat. The engineers would give us a ride on the caboose . . .

"One time we were going to school, and the train was coming and they blew the whistle. So I went on across and I turned to look to see where my little brother was and I couldn't see him. He had jumped off. And it was soft where he landed and so didn't hurt himself. But my mother was on the other side of the bridge and she was having fits. She just knew that he was dead!

"That was back when the Denver and Rio Grande Southern went to Aztec and down to Farmington. We had cream and the train would stop and take it to town for us. Then they'd bring a check back.

"That was our transportation."

***

As a couple, Stella and her late husband, Feliciano "F.F." or "Chano" Montoya, have been widely recognized as respected ranchers in northern New Mexico for many years.

"They started out down there below Farmington, by the mission down there in La Plata. And my father-in-law's dad was crippled, and he died before they moved, and they buried him down there. But during the 1911 flood, the cemetery was washed away and they lost him there."

Chano and his family bought property in a settlement called Greenhorn, on the La Plata River in New Mexico. Then Chano's dad bought a place across the river, where Stella lives now. "Actually, this was where his dad's house used to be," says Stella. "Chano lived here all of his life."

"And then there were some permits in Mancos that we bought and consolidated and pretty soon—with the permits we had up on the mountain—we had enough so we could make a living," says Stella.

"First we had sheep, but the coyotes came out here and killed them. See, we'd lamb out here—over on the hills out here—and one year they came in, them and dogs from town, they'd get in packs, and they'd come in and kill them. And then we went up to the mountains and the bears got them. Oh, they were destroying us up there! You know, we worked so hard all spring, herding them, lambing them, and mothering them, and we took them up there and the bears ate them. They got one bear, they treed one, and they killed him, and they did an autopsy on him, and his stomach was full of wool and bones from the sheep he ate. So we sold the sheep and went into cattle."

Stella helped out on the ranch. She went along with her husband on the round-ups. "But then I had babies," says Stella, "and I told him, 'I raised you five boys and one daughter, so *they* can help you now.' I had a lot of cooking to do. I baked bread; everything we ate I cooked. And I did a lot of washing and a lot of patching."

Stella was also involved in all the local organizations: the 4-H program, the Four Corners Association, the Steering Committee for the Center of Southwest Studies, and the Fort Lewis College Foundation. In 1994, the New Mexico Cattle Growers Association recognized Stella and Chano Montoya as the first couple ever chosen as the "La Plata Cattleman of the Year."

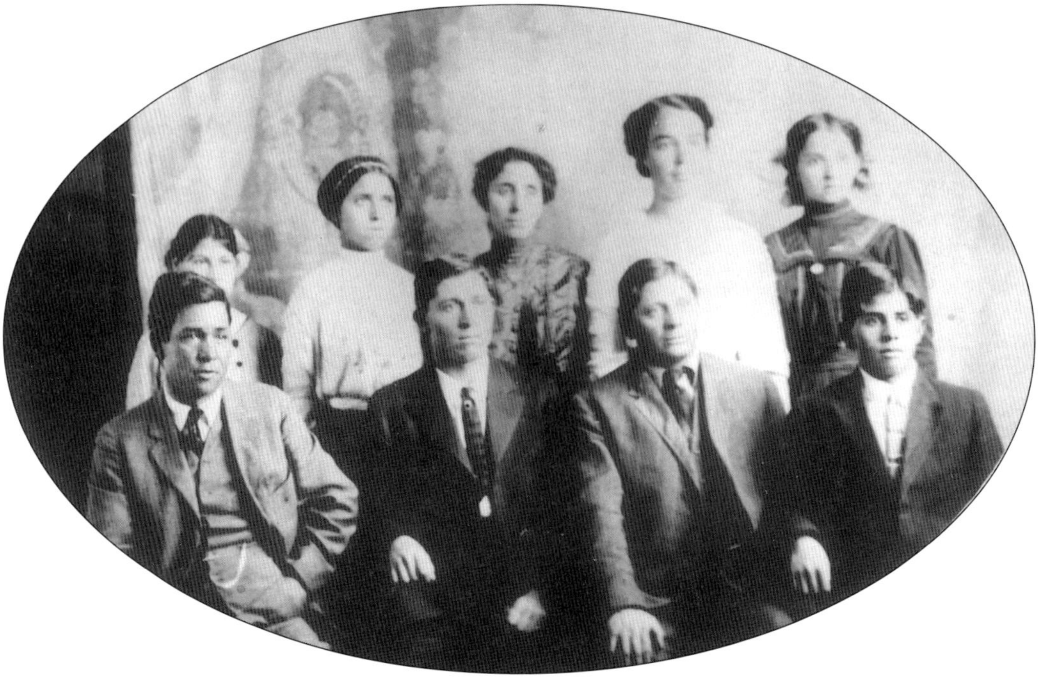

Stella Montoya's aunt, Sarah Jaquez (rear, center), and Stella's father, Onofre (front right), pose with the rest of the family for a family photo. Stella's Aunt Sarah is claimed to be the first Hispanic child born in San Juan County, New Mexico, born on November 1, 1878.

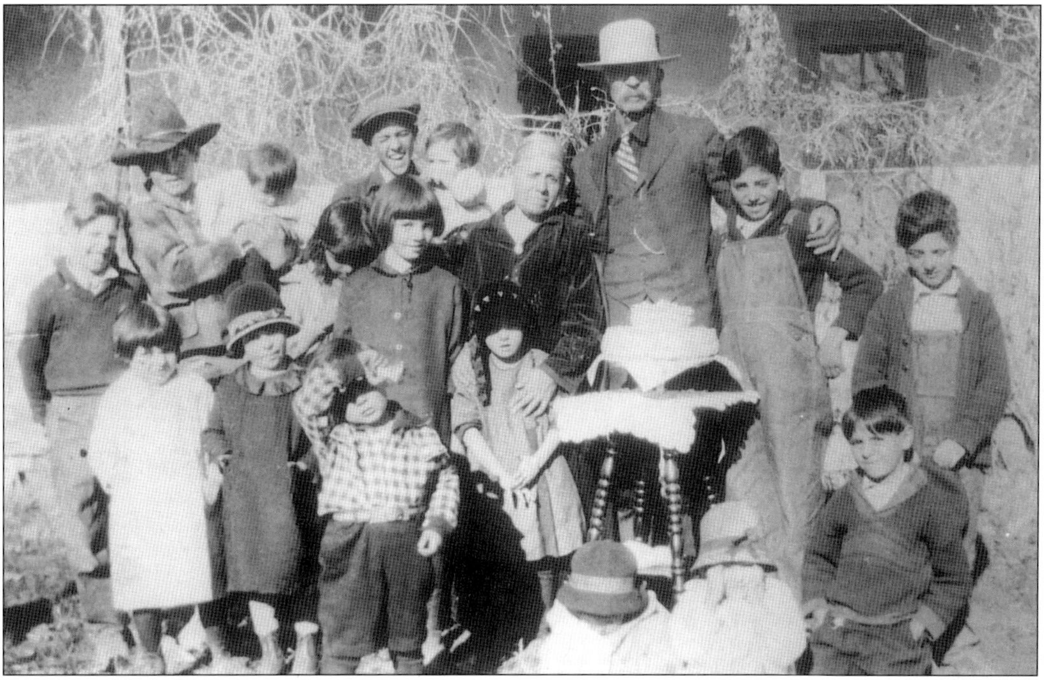

Stella's grandfather and grandmother, Juan N. and Anna Maria Jaquez (center), gather up their grandchildren and great grandchildren for a photo on their golden wedding anniversary. Juan N. Jaquez was once a member of the House of Representatives of the 32nd Territorial Assembly of New Mexico.

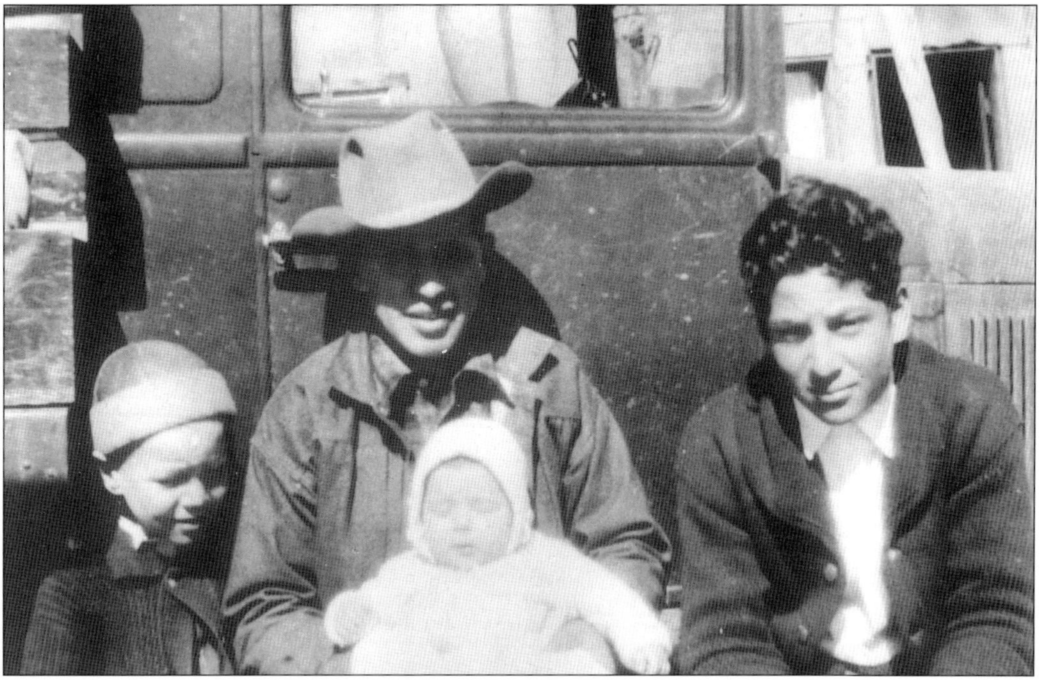

Stella's father, Onofre (rear, center), is shown here holding Stella when she was a baby. Stella was born in Silverton, where her parents were running sheep on their summer range.

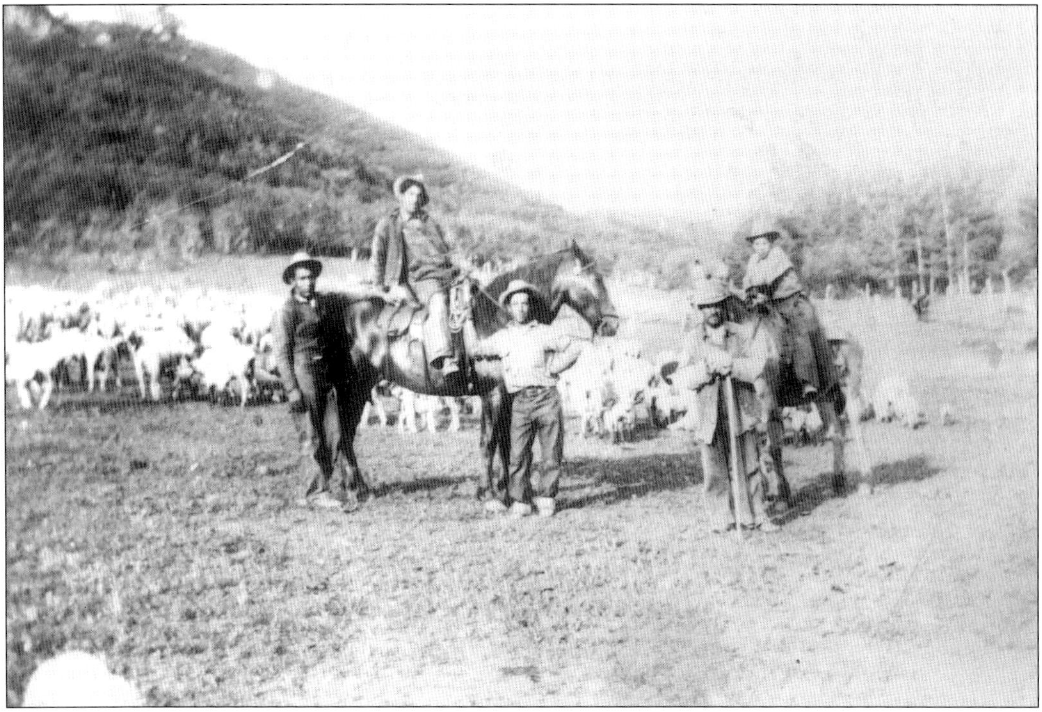

Here we see Belarmino and Chano (right), when Chano was a boy, herding sheep. Chano was the only living son of Belarmino and Rachel. The other son died when Chano was five years old. Chano's mother, Rachel, died when Chano was only three years old.

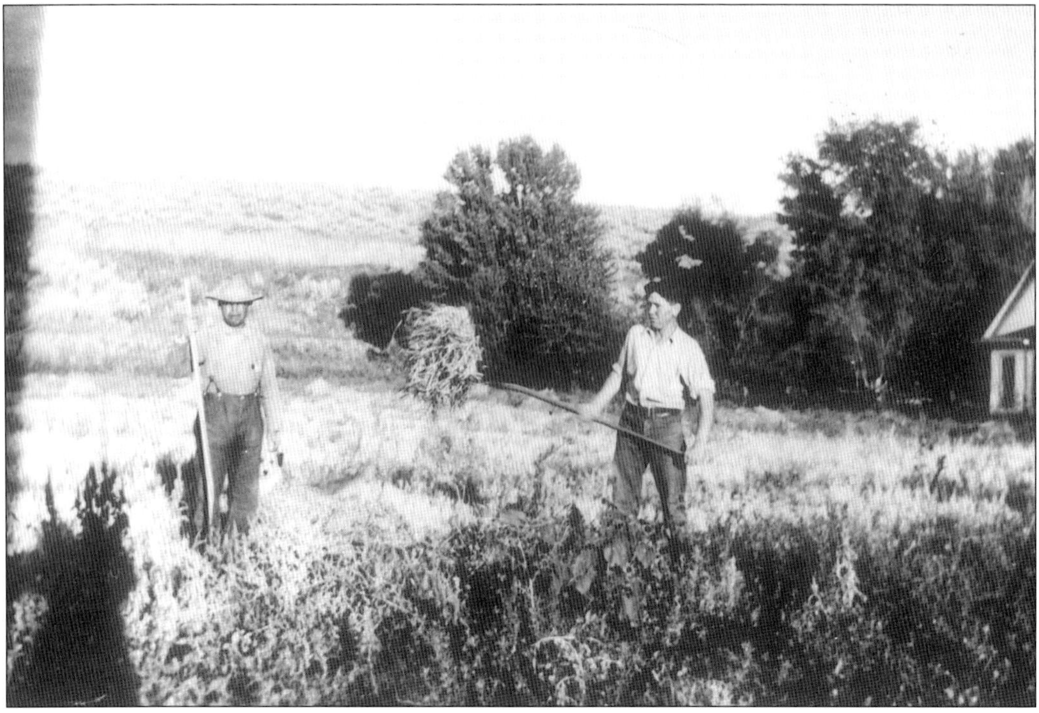

Pictured here are Belarmino and an older Chano working in a field together.

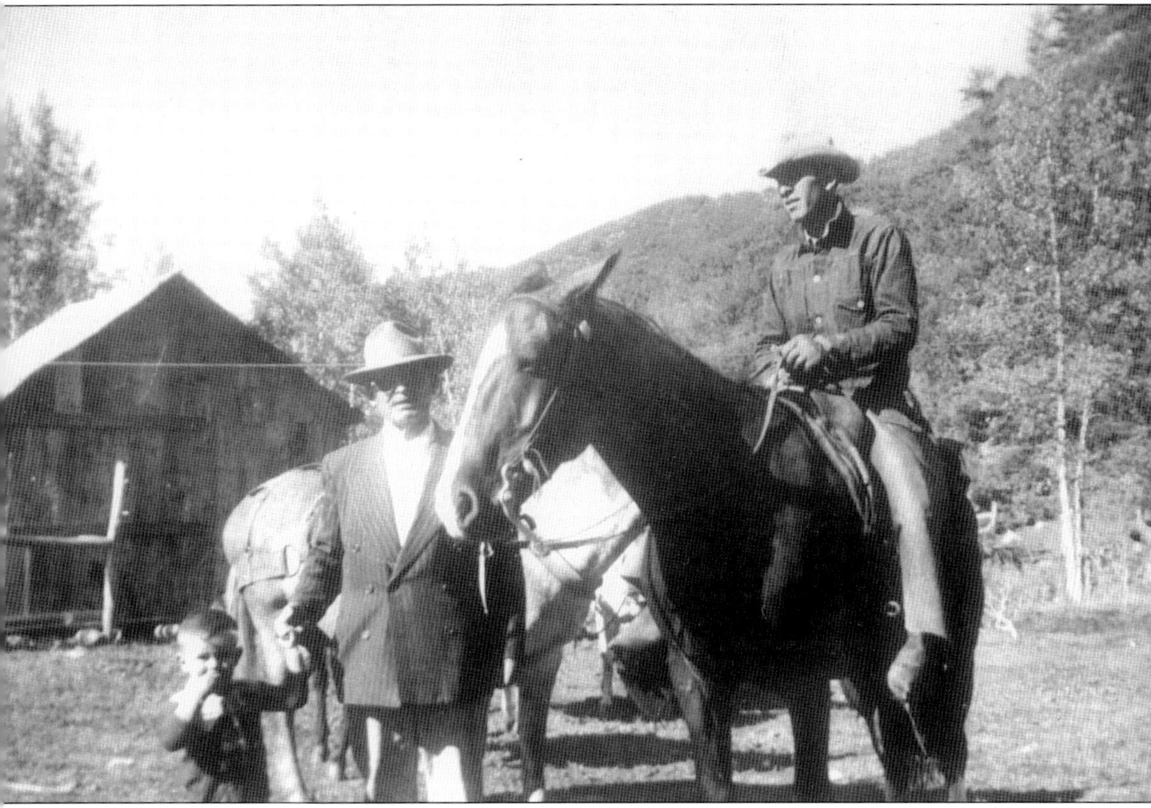

Belarmino (center) stands next to Chano (right), mounted up and ready to ride the range.

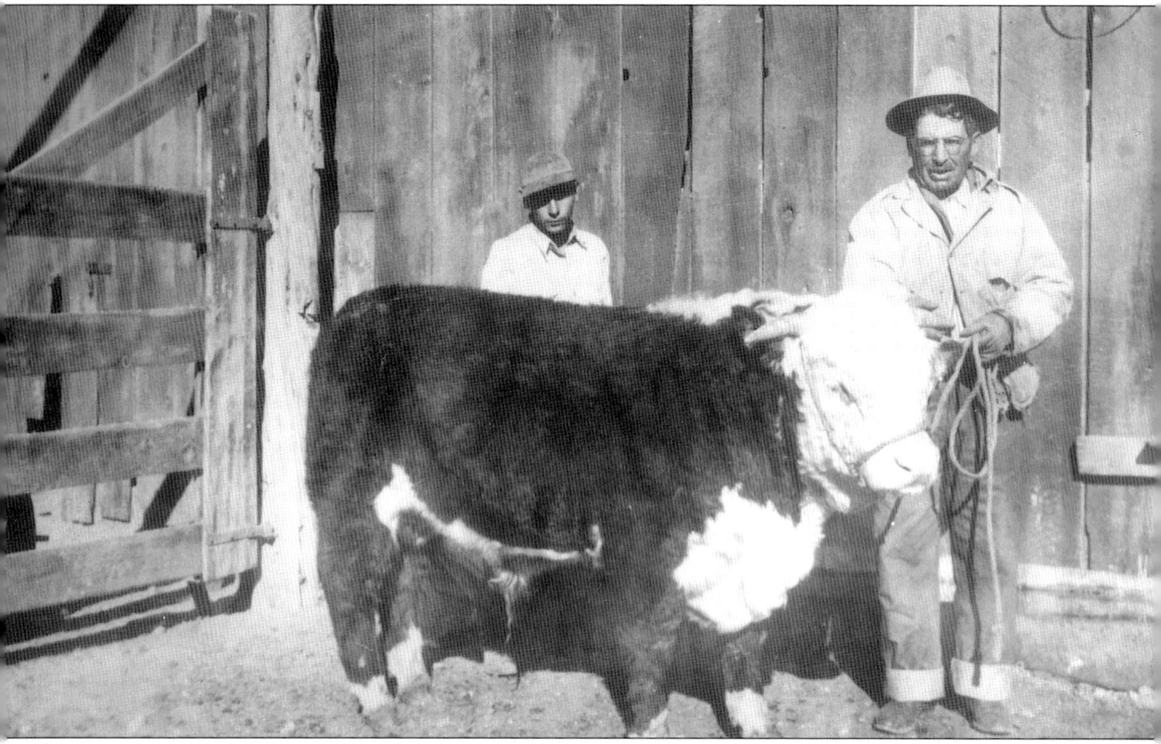

Belarmino (right) shows off his prize bull. The back of this photo indicates that in 1957 Belarmino paid $4,200 for this bull at an auction in Springer, New Mexico.

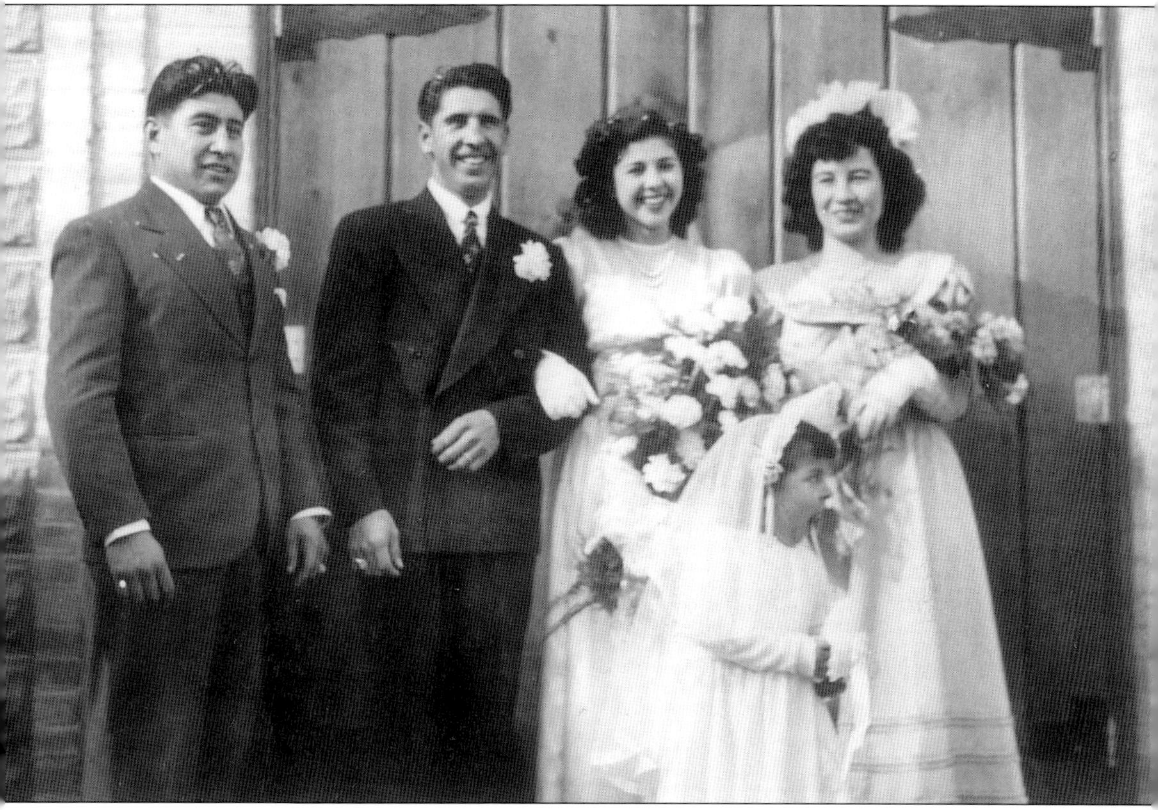

Chano and Stella (center) got to know each other when they were seniors in high school and were married on January 22, 1948. In 1960, they moved to the family ranch and built a house in the same place where Belarmino's house used to be.

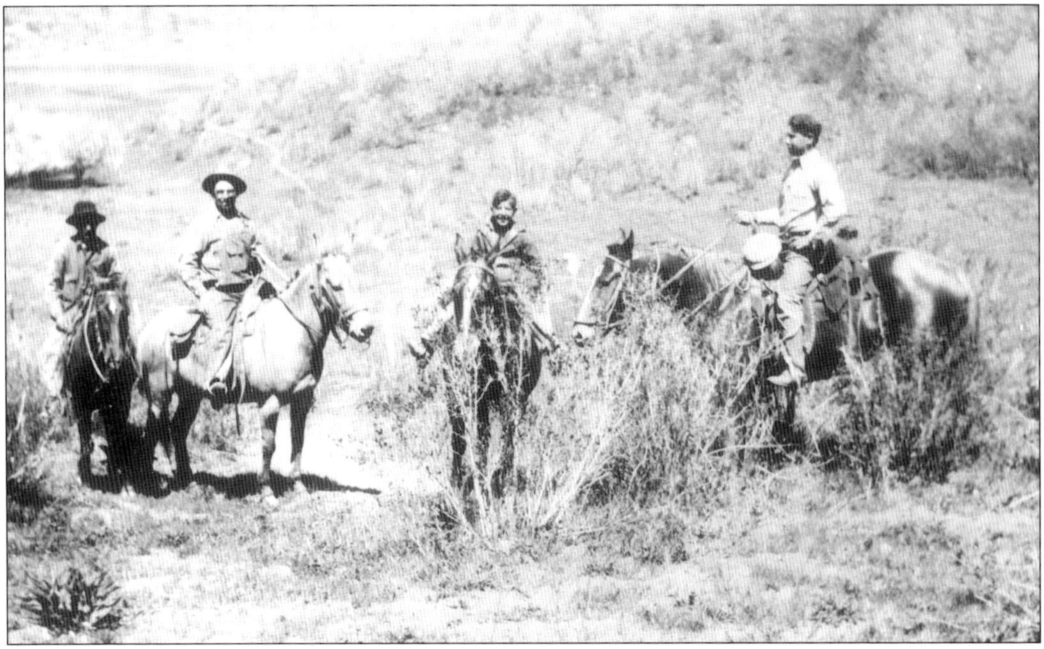

Belarmino (second from left), Chano (right), and Stella's oldest son, Anthony (center), interrupt a ride on the old ranch for a picture.

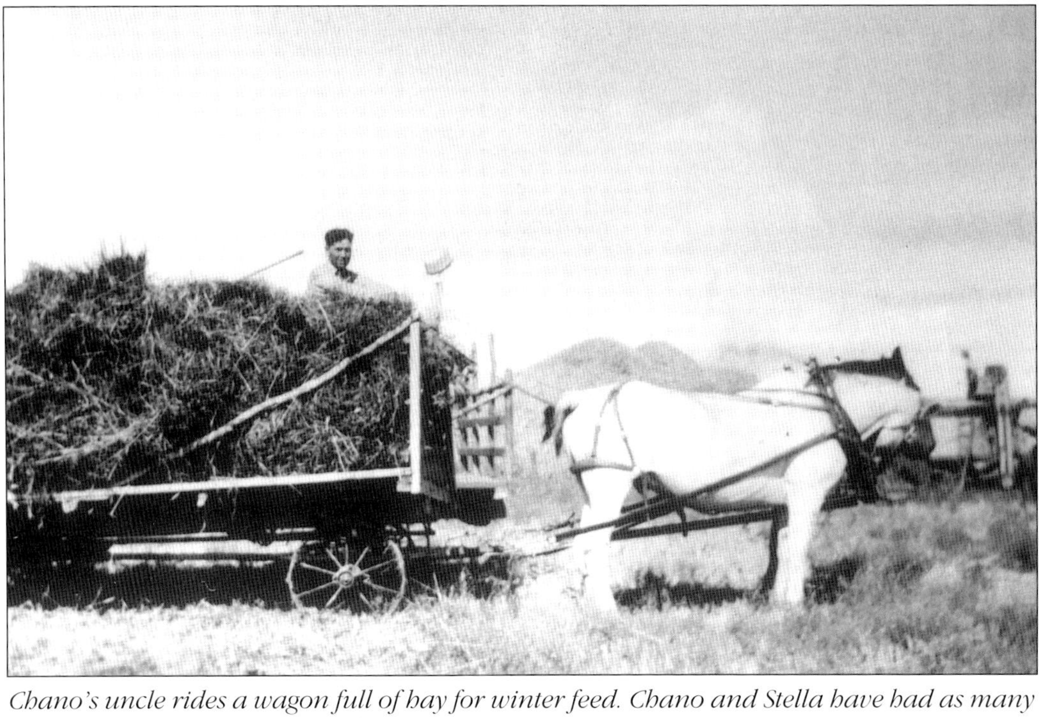

Chano's uncle rides a wagon full of hay for winter feed. Chano and Stella have had as many as 500 head of cattle on their place.

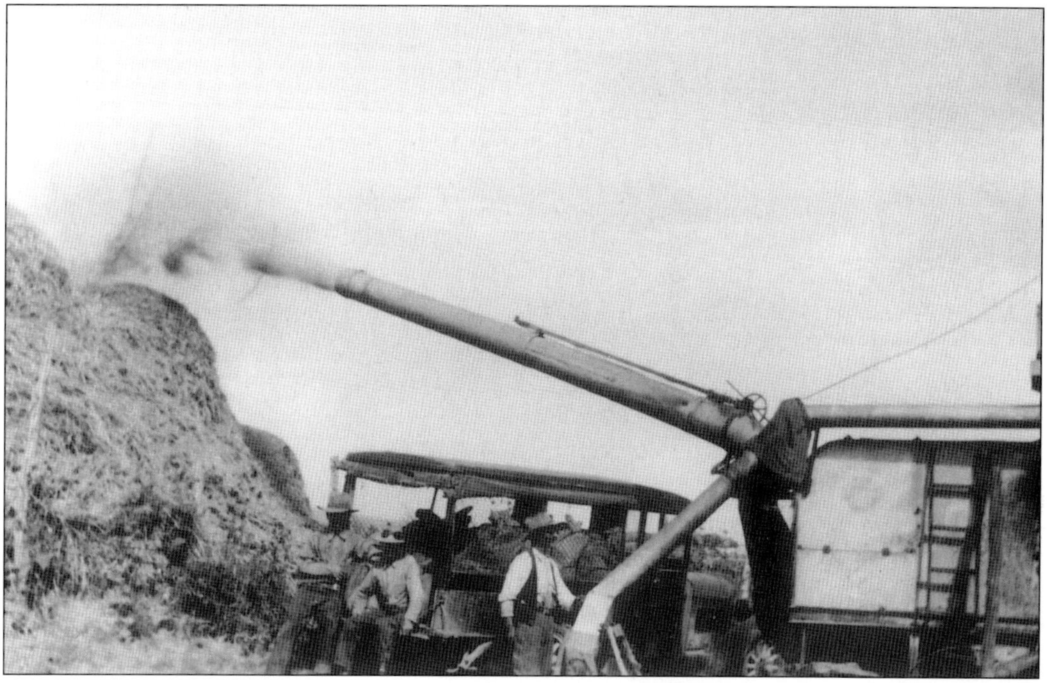

Captured here is a crew building a haystack.

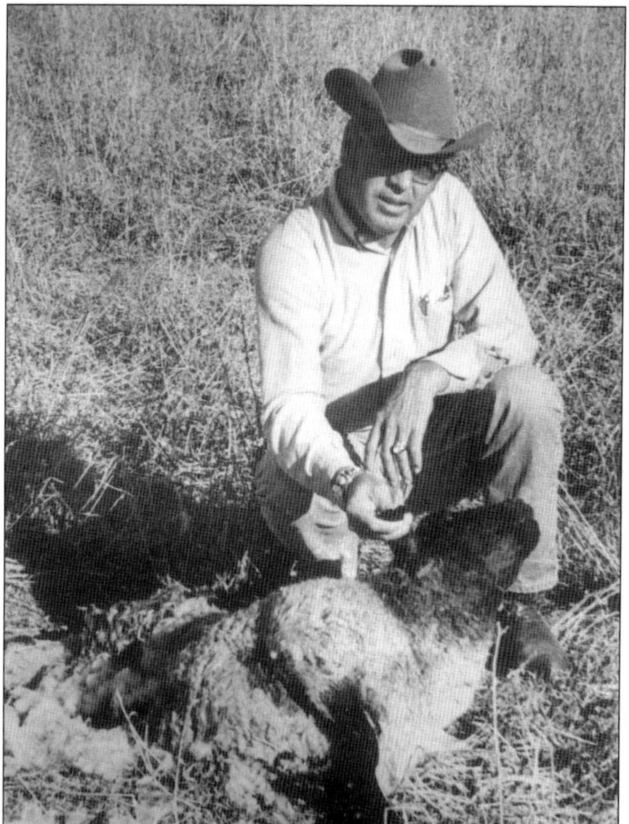

Before they ran cattle, Chano and Stella had sheep. This one, shown to us by Chano, was "eaten by a coyote," says Stella.

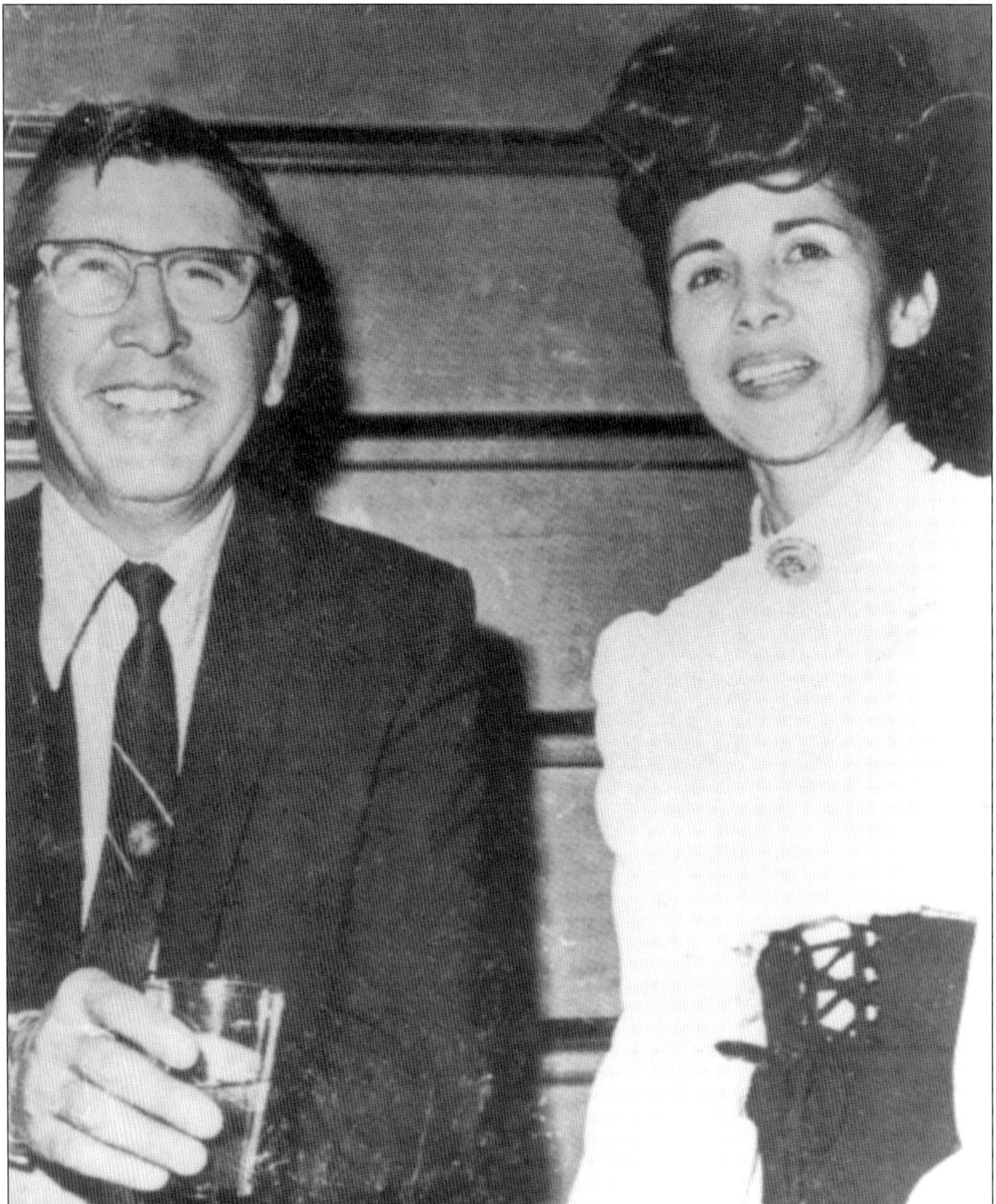

Mr. and Mrs. F. F. Montoya.

In addition to the "Cattleman of the Year" award, Chano and Stella have also been honored with the San Juan Soil and Water Conservation District Stewardship Award, the New Mexico Farm Bureau Leadership Award, and the Bureau of Reclamation Citizen Award.

Chapter 5

KEEPING IT STRAIGHT

THE CRAWFORD CHRONOLOGY

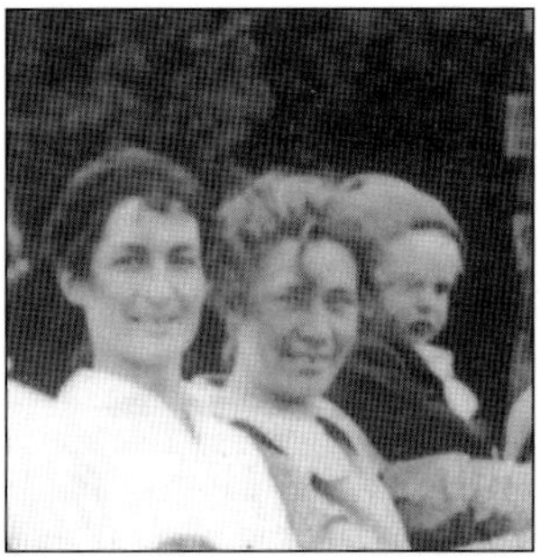

Ron H. Crawford is proud of his heritage. He comes from one of the oldest Anglo families in La Plata County. "My great grandad, John Marion Crawford, came in here in '74, '75, or '76," he says, following up with, "I want to do some more research and try to come up with the dates."

According to *The Crawfords of Adams County, Ohio*, John Marion Crawford was born on March 3, 1852, and died June 26, 1925. It is also known that John's wife, Dora Norwood "Tony" Norris, was born on December 19, 1853, and died in November of 1921. John and Dora had three children, one of them Ron's grandfather, Allen Hill "Pats" Crawford, born in Porter, Colorado in 1884.

John Marion, continues Ron, "homesteaded in west Alkali sometime in the mid-1870s and he moved into the Hay Gulch area in the mid-1980s. Then when the cavalry came in here, my great grandad cut the hay in Hay Gulch and sold it to the cavalry. That's how 'Hay Gulch' got its name.

"At the ranch in Hay Gulch, right inside the house, they had the post office set up and it was called Content, Colorado.

"And then, in about 1905, after they opened up the Southern Ute reservation, they came up there on top and built a house just west of Big Stick Mesa."

How about the Utes back in those days? How did Ron's great granddad get along with the Utes?

"Well, my aunt used to tell a story," Ron chuckles. "When they brought the Cavalry in here (in what, '88, '86?), they found my grandpa was already working them."

Ron's grandfather, Allan Hill, grew up on the old homestead. Ron's grandmother, Pearl Sealing, met Allan Hill after she came down from Denver to teach at the Rockvale School in Hay Gulch, just around the corner from the Crawford homestead. Allan Hill and Pearl were married in 1908 and the first child was born in 1909. Ron's father, Allen John, was born in 1912.

Ron's grandfather passed away suddenly when Ron's father was only eight years old. So it was up to Ron's great grandfather and Ron's father to continue running the Crawford ranch by themselves, which they did until Ron's great grandfather died. Ron's father ran the ranch by himself until he married Ron's mother in 1936.

Ron's mother, Olive Blanche Smith, came to La Plata County with her family from Broken Bow, Oklahoma in 1905, when she was about five years old. She was the oldest of 10 kids—5 girls and 5 boys.

"Grandad Smith homesteaded in east Alkali, just across the valley from Hay Gulch," says Ron, which made it easy for his mom and dad to meet.

Ron's mother, Olive, died in 1986. His father, Allen John, died in 1987.

"But we still got the ranch," says Ron. "The oldest brand in Southwest Colorado," he says proudl. "Three J's: J, J, and Lazy J."

Ron himself ran the ranch for 17 years, and then turned it over to his brothers. They still run cattle there on the ranch, Ron tells us, "100 to 150 head of yearlings." And they still put up a lot of hay, "something like 8,000 bales of hay last year."

"I still live in the old house," he adds. "I feel like I belong here, fourth generation and all. That's why I'd like to keep the history straight."

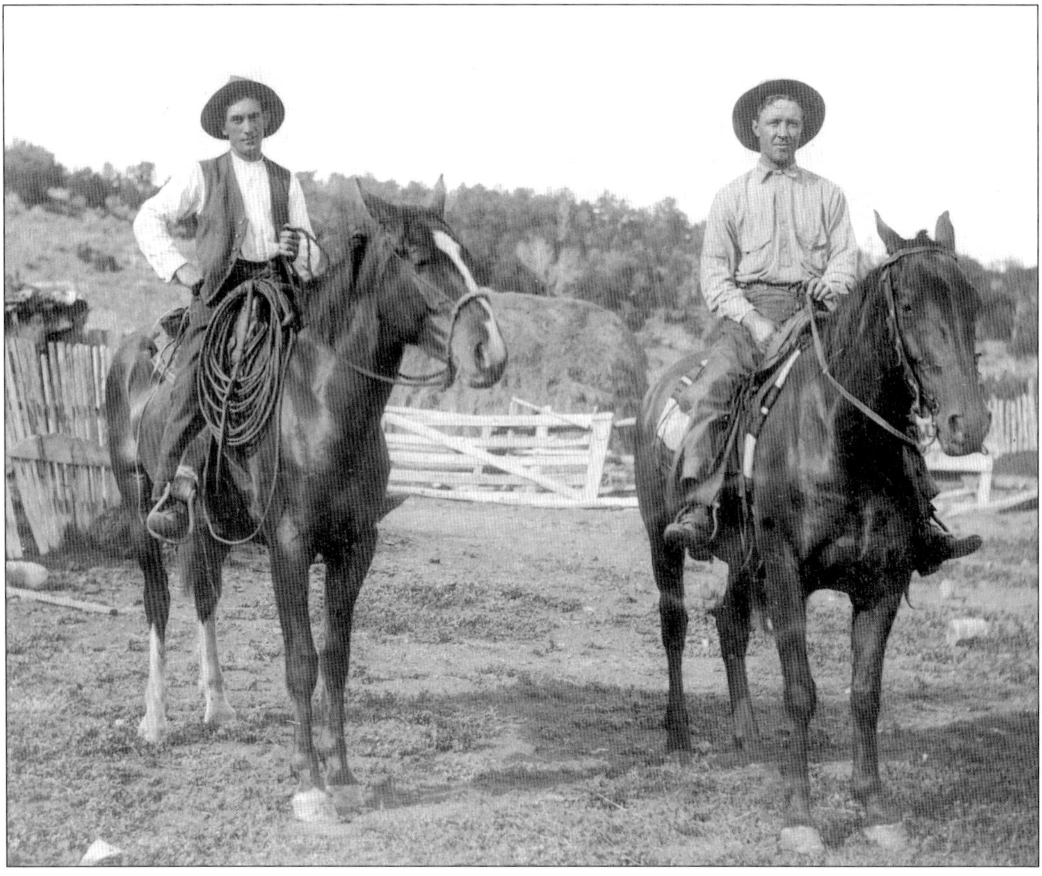

Ron Crawford's grandfather, Allan Hill "Pats" Crawford (right), was born in the mining town of Porter, Colorado, in 1884. Allan Hill died suddenly in Denver in 1920. "My grandad and my grandmother went to Denver for the stock show one fall," Ron explains, "and my grandad got pneumonia and never came home."

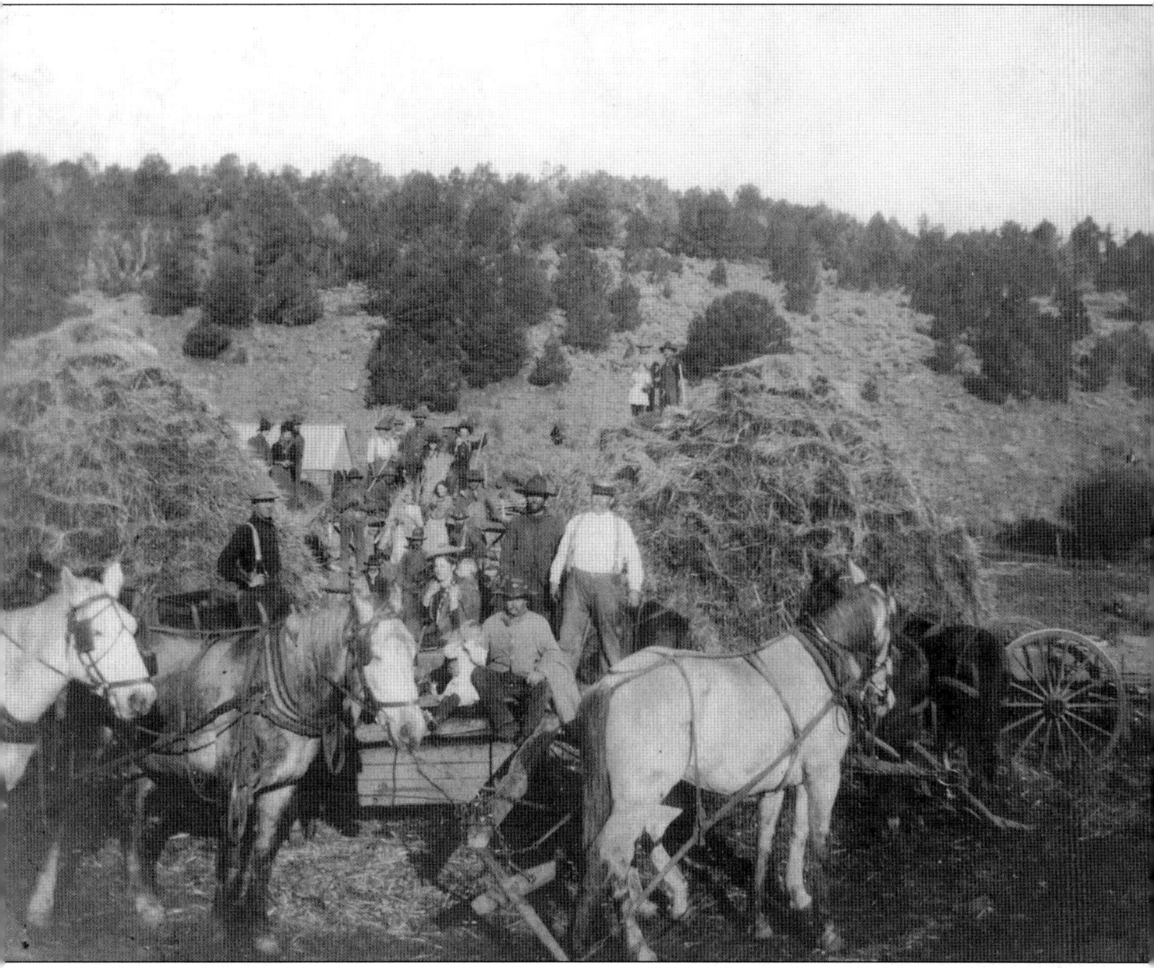

It is believed that Ron Crawford's great grandfather, John Marion Crawford (standing, center right), came to La Plata County, Colorado from Adams County, Ohio, in 1874. In this photo, John Marion is pictured with a threshing crew at the Old Stockham Place near the town of Content, Colorado, later known as Hay Gulch. Ron's grandfather, Allan Hill "Pats" Crawford, is seated in front of John Marion.

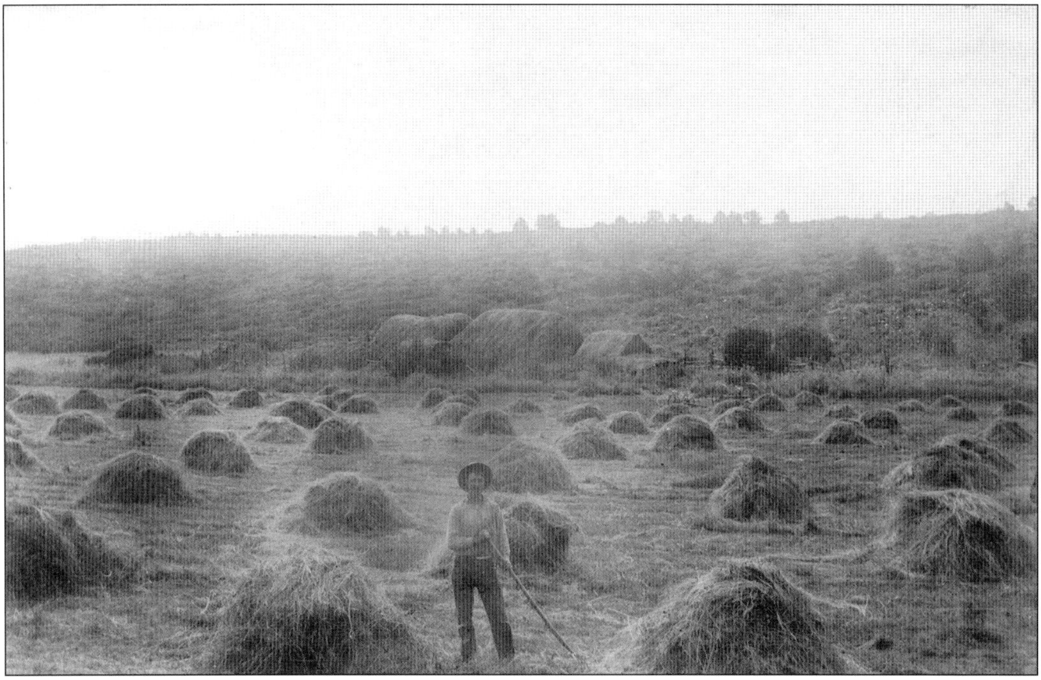

Here we see Allan Hill raking hay. "When they put up the hay in the summer time," say Ron, "they stacked it in the barn, loose. Then they'd pull this loose hay down and run it through a stationary bailer. The horses went 'round and 'round in a circle and they fed this stationary bailer. That made it a little easier to transport."

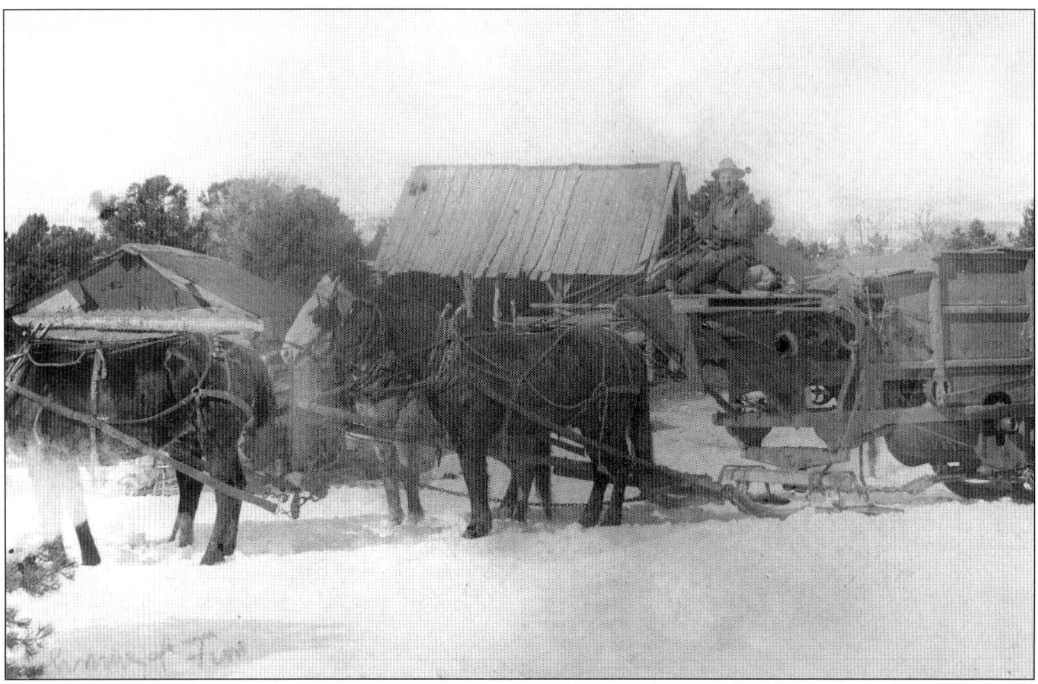

Pictured here is Allan Hill on a threshing rig mounted on a sleigh.

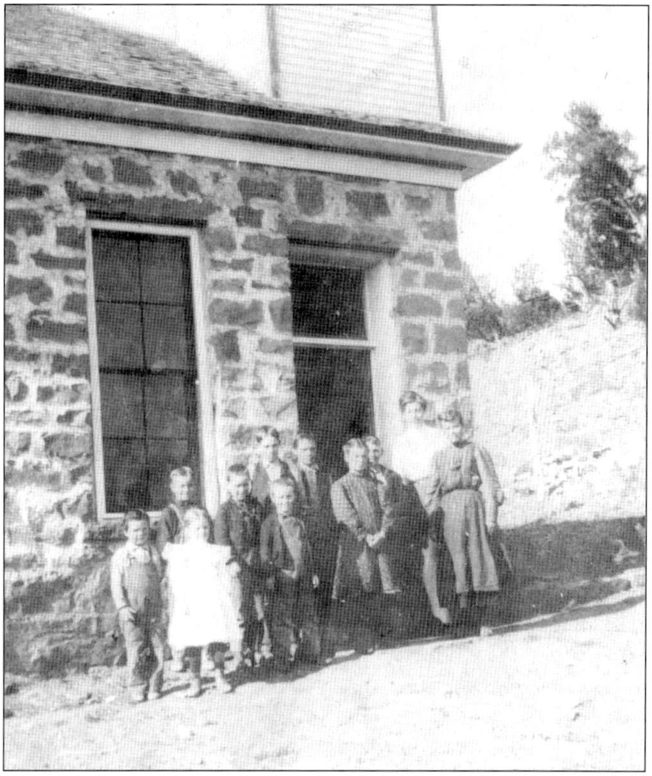

Ron's grandmother, Pearl Sealing (rear), came to La Plata County from Denver in 1907 to teach at the Rockvale School. The caption on this photo reads: "Rockvale School, Term 1907–1908." "My grandmother passed away in 1961," says Ron, "and I knew her pretty well. She was kind of a hard lady, hard but honest."

Pearl Sealing, sitting in the driver's seat in this photo, and Ron's father, Allen John, the child in the rear seat closest to camera, pose with other family members in front of the original old ranch house. "My dad was born in 1912," says Ron, "and is about five or six years old in this picture."

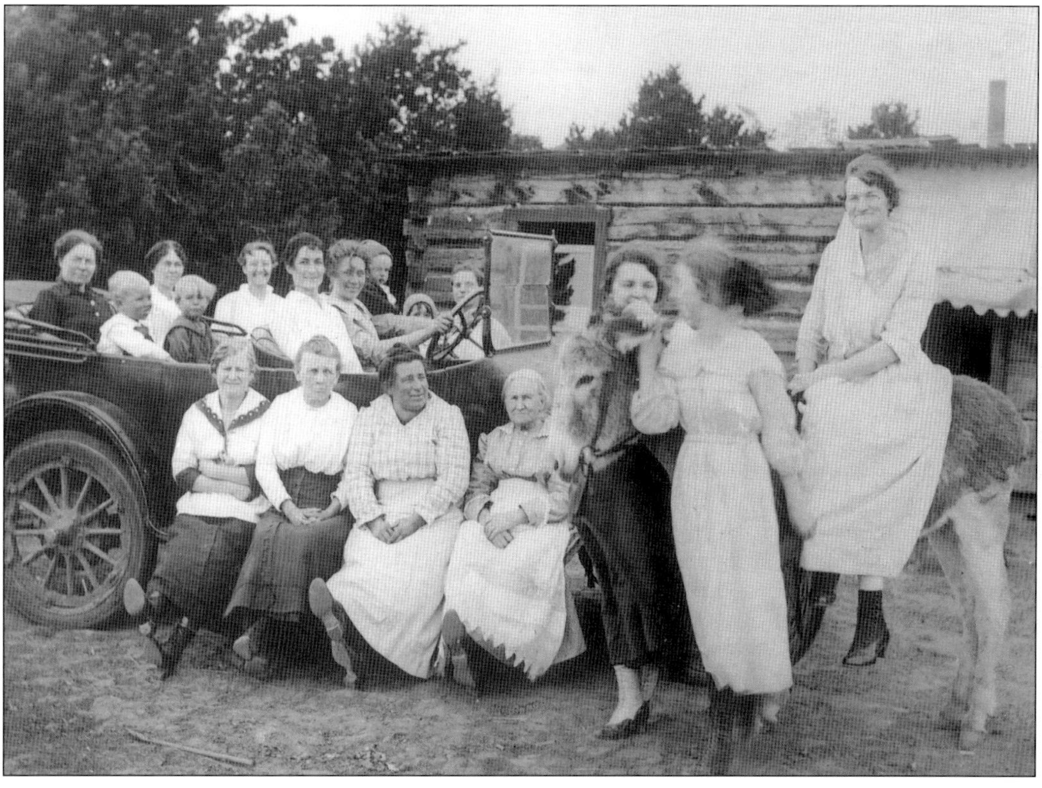

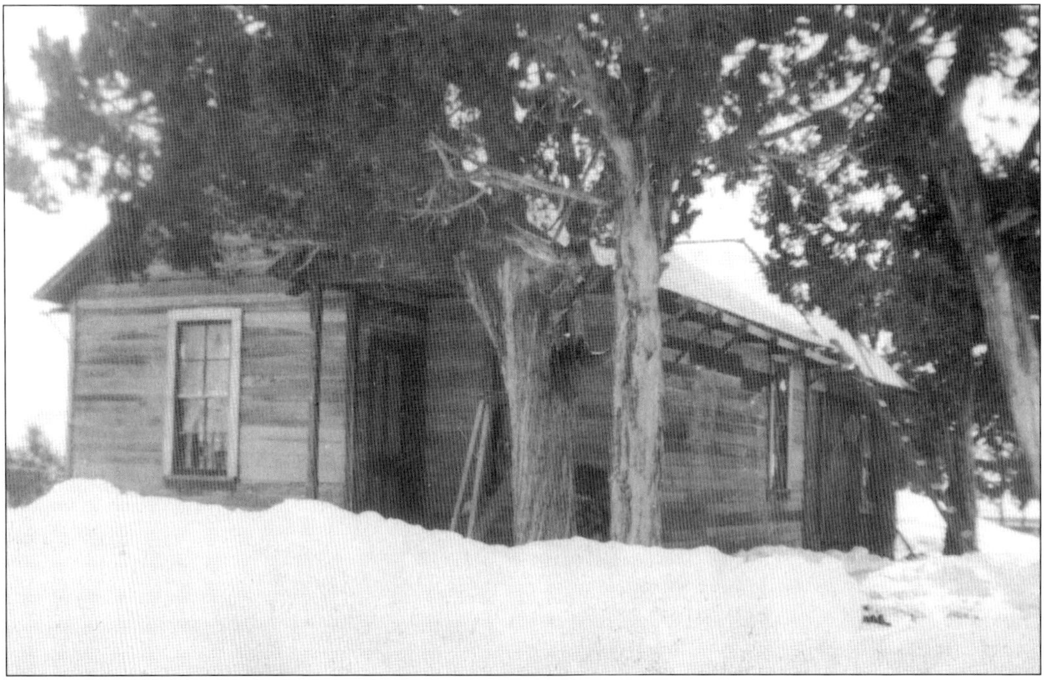

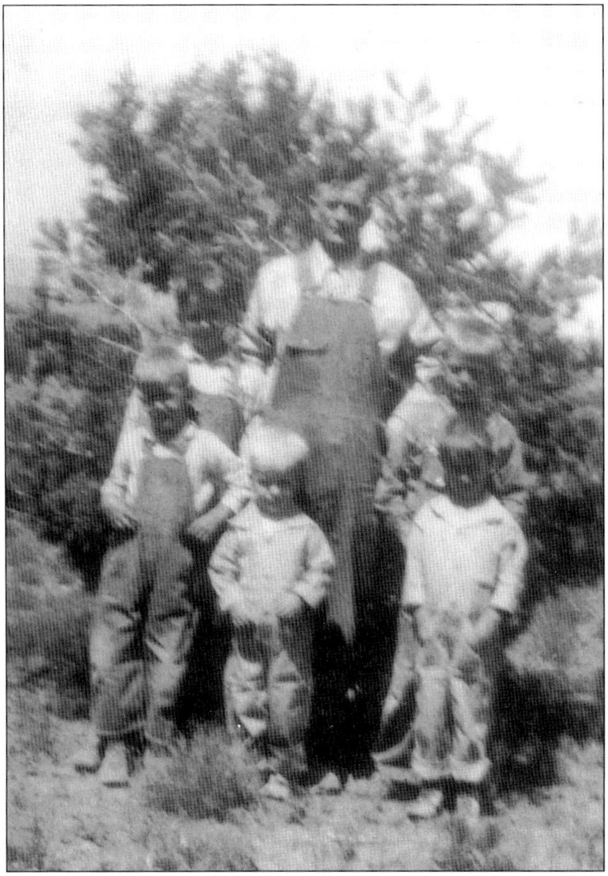

Ron's mother, Olive Branch Smith, grew up in this house on the old Smith homestead in east Alkali. Olive came to La Plata County from Broken Bow, Oklahoma with her family in 1905. She was the oldest of 10 kids in the family: 5 girls and 5 boys.

At left, Ron's granddad Smith (rear) stands with his five boys on the old Smith place.

Chapter 6

THE FAMOUS HARRIS BREEDING STOCK

DONALD C. HARRIS

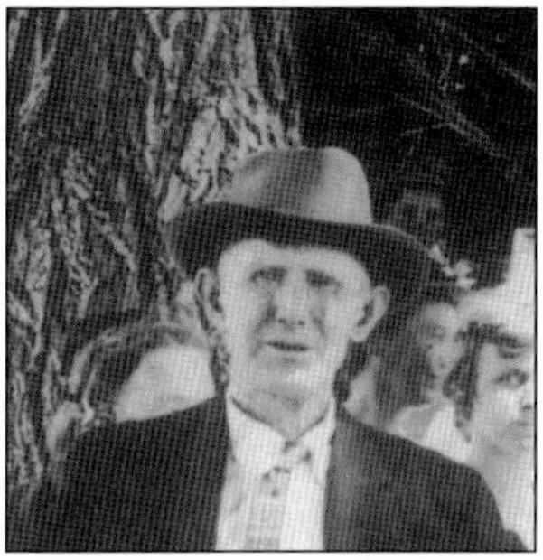

"I'll have to go back a little," Donald says, as he ushers us into the dining room. Donald C. Harris is a stocky, square-built man, barrel-chested, with a firm jaw and a wide slash of a smile. "The Harrises came from Iowa originally. But my dad was born in 1888 in Republic, Kansas. Then they were in on that land rush in Oklahoma and ended up in Pawnee. Well, a man named Charlie Tunnell traded some land he had here with some land my granddad had there. So my granddad left there and came out here."

"Charlie Tunnell—now this is true," Donald digresses, "I'm not a kiddin' you—he and another guy that lived up here east of Marvel traded wives." Donald breaks into a wide grin. "And the story is that Tunnell got a cow to boot."

"The old home place was a whole section, 640 acres, but it's all cut up now," Harris tells us. "My folks sold that to my younger brother and he cut it all up and sold it. So at the last minute, we jumped in and bought the 60 acres and the house to have some of the old homestead." We can see the old home place from the table where we sit, just a mile across the field. Russel Harris, Donald's oldest son, lives there now, three-and-a-half miles southwest of Marvel.

Donald Harris met his wife, Angelina G. Anesi, at a dance at the grange hall in Breen. He was 20 and she was 15. Angie's sister, Lilly Saunders, a schoolteacher in Durango, was Angie's chaperon. Donald tried to drive Angie home in his 1930 Chevy with a rumble seat in back, but Angie's sister wouldn't let him.

One year later, on June 22, 1942, Donald and Angie ran away to Aztec, New Mexico, and got married. "Had five flat tires on the way," Angie recalls. Her mother didn't say anything when they got back home. She just cried a little bit. "It was the first time I ever saw my mother cry," says Angie, "but I was the youngest, the last one out of 12 children, I was the baby."

Then Donald brought Angie out to visit his folks on the old homestead. "But we drove by this other place," says Angie, "and they had the place in pinto beans, a beautiful row crop. You could see it from the road. And I said I want *that*!"

Donald and Angie got that place—the old Sherman Place, a spread that Donald's aunt and uncle, Jim and Bessie Crane, homesteaded back at the turn of the century—fixed it up, and raised three children there.

There are three children, seven grandchildren, and one great grandchild in the Harris family tree now. Planning for family gatherings and being a mother, grandmother, and great grandmother—all this has been an important part of Angie's life.

They also did some farming and ranching on the old place. "We had a lot of irrigating water then," says Donald, "out of the La Plata River. That we don't have now, due to that compact with New Mexico. So that made these farms, which were really lush farms at the time, kind of dry-land farms now. We had haystacks all over, two or three crops a year, but now just one."

"And I also had cattle for years. You see that white bull right there?" he asks, pointing at a picture. "It was a Charolais, weighed 2,300 pounds. In 1970, I had five Charolais bulls. I crossed them with Herefords to get some size on the calves, 600-pound calves, rather than 400. I had the first Charolais bulls in the area, me and Ed Kennedy, and everybody laughed at us, even my cousins. But we brought home more money per head than anybody else."

A few years ago, Donald sold all his cows, but his sons still do the farming. "All three of the children—and seven grandchildren and five great grandchildren—are still right here in the Marvel area," puts in Angie, "and that's the important thing."

"What's important are the people who struggled and survived here and who are still here today."

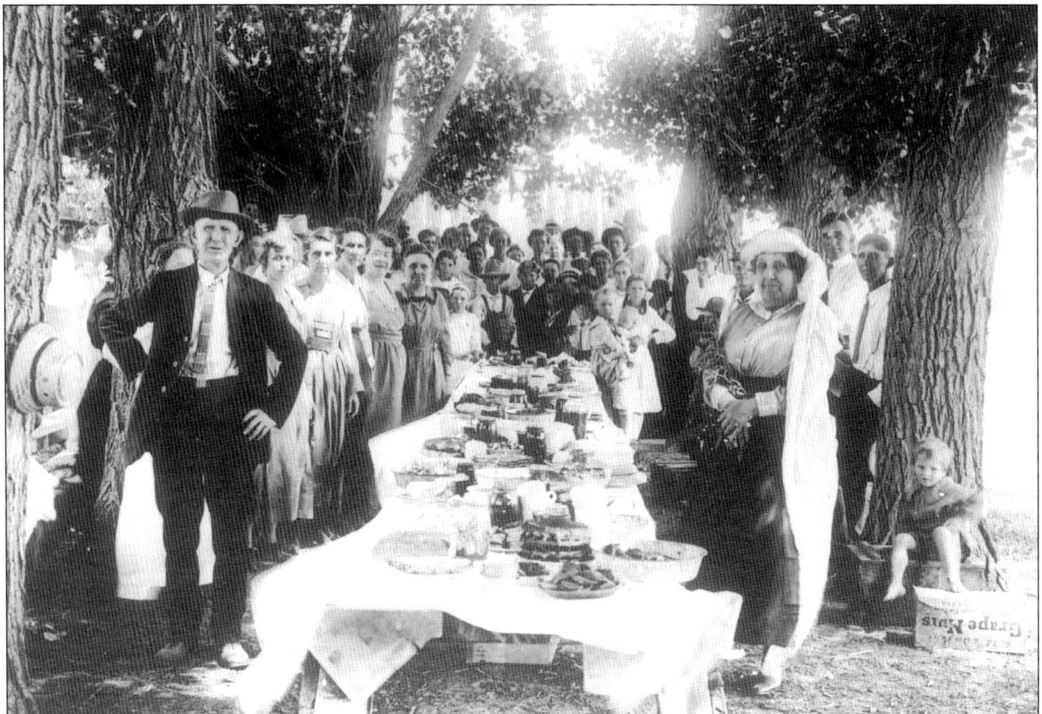

Donald Harris' grandfather, William Harris (standing, left), and his grandmother (standing, right) host a family reunion. After coming out west from Pawnee, Oklahoma, around 1912, William moved to Aztec, New Mexico, where he became the county assessor.

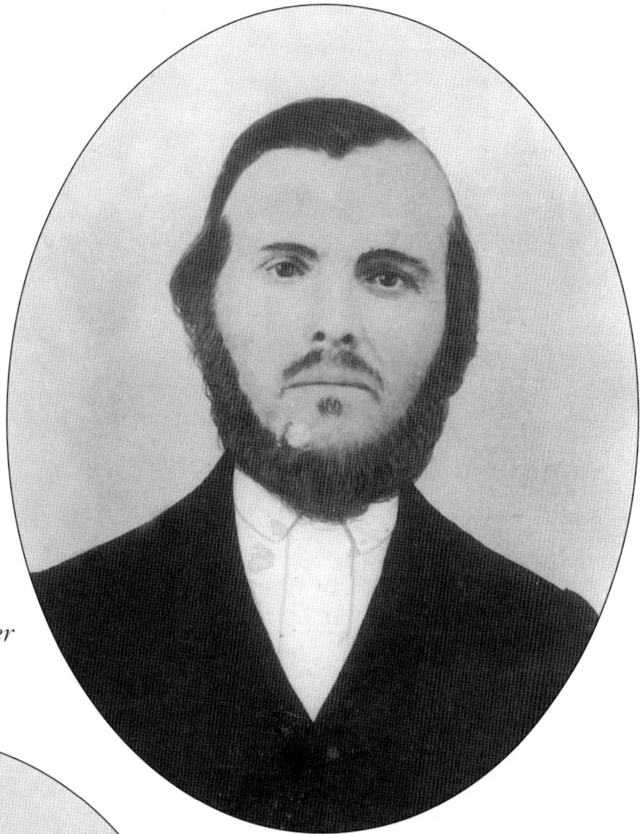

Donald Harris' great grandfather (1818–1872) and great grandmother (1821–1903) were originally from Iowa.

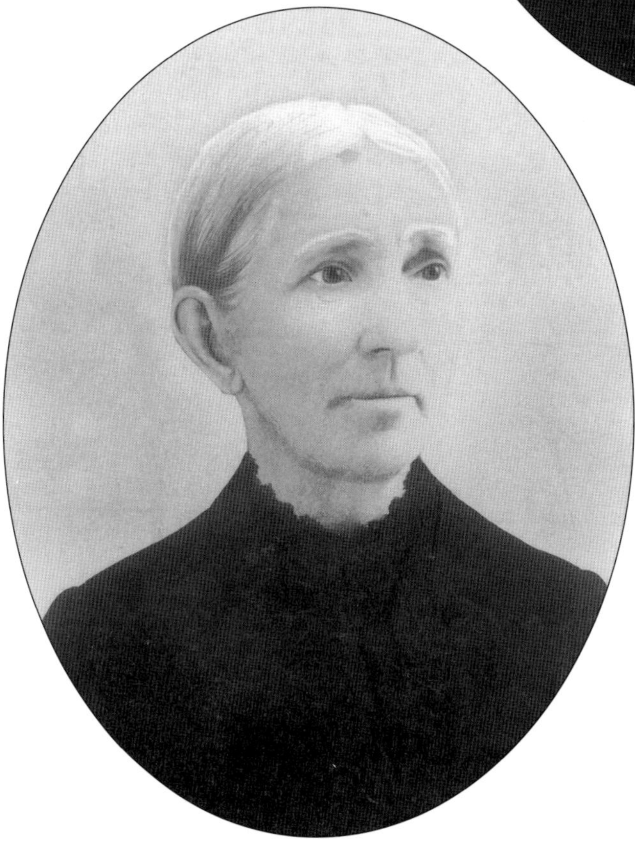

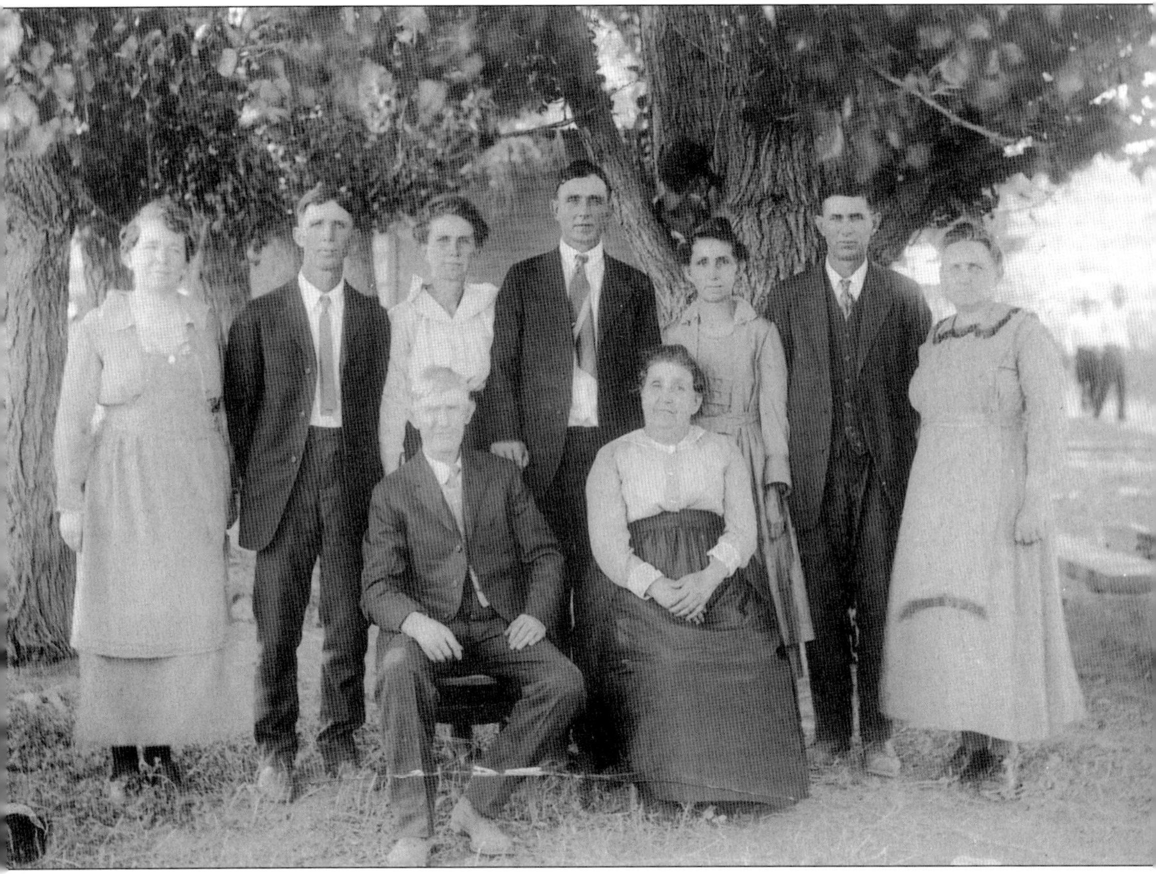

Donald's father, Chet Harris (rear, fourth from left), and his Grandpa and Grandma Harris (front) pose here for another family photo. "I went down there to Aztec when I was a little kid," Donald remembers. "My granddad sat me up on a camel one time, when they had a circus down there. And, then another thing, I'd never seen a woman smoke and I looked through the window and my grandmother was sitting in there smoking a pipe."

Donald's father, Chet Harris (right), and his buddy Burt Brooks pose for a studio photo, c. *1912. "My dad came out here in 1910," says Donald, "and was here awhile, then went back to Oklahoma. But it didn't take long until he came back to La Plata. Said he didn't like it in Oklahoma anymore after being out here."*

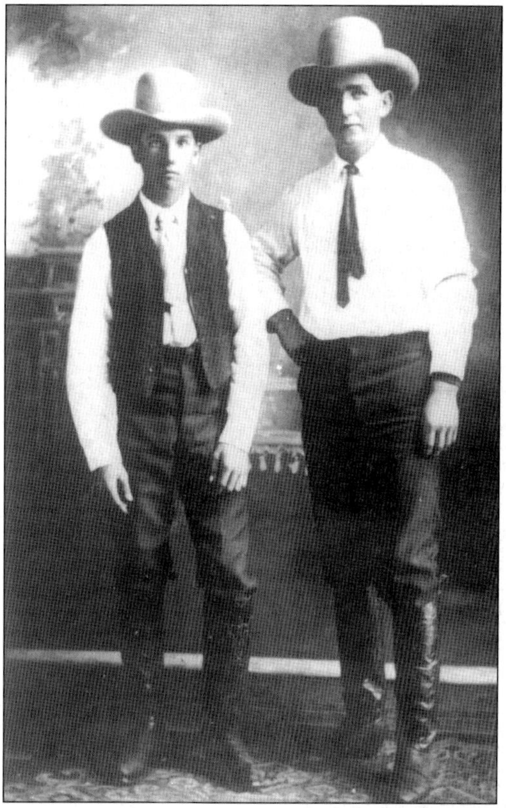

In this photo, Chet Harris sits mounted on his horse at the old home place near Marvel, Colorado. In 1912, Donald's grandfather, William, traded some land he got in the Oklahoma land rush for this 640-acre section of land near Marvel in La Plata County, Colorado. The old homestead was vacant, though, until Donald's parents moved there from the town of La Plata, New Mexico, in 1920.

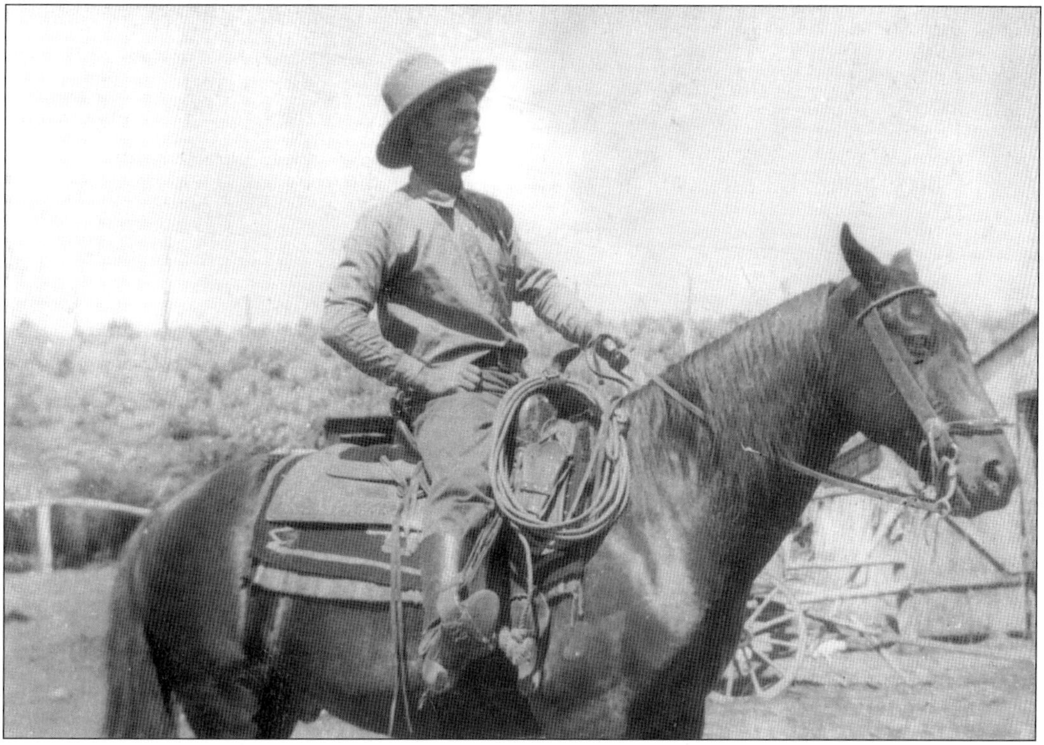

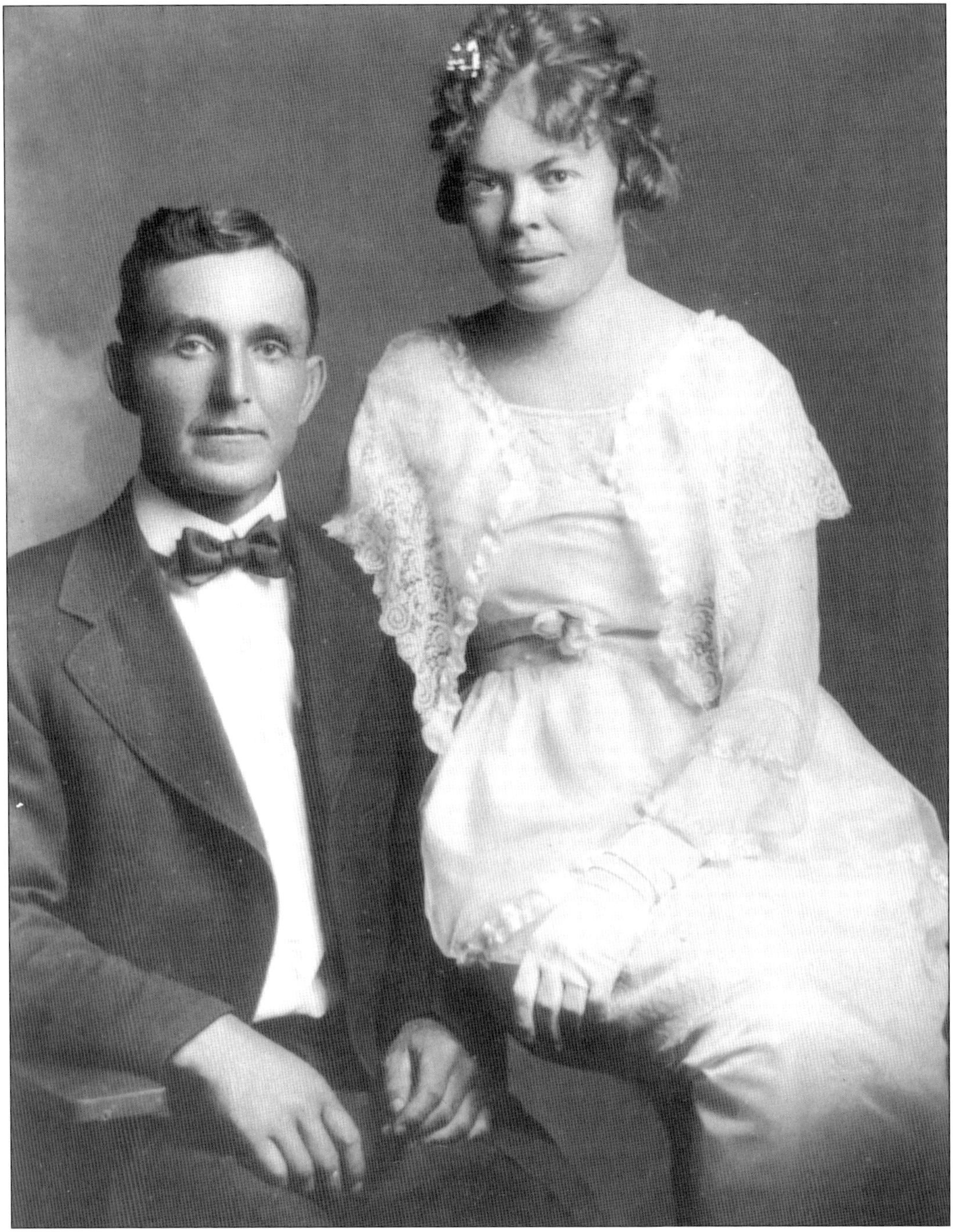

Donald's parents, Chet and Irene Harris, were married on July 10, 1920. "My father was in the cow business when he was real young," says Donald, "but I grew up on a sheep ranch, of all things. We had 1,000 head for years and years. We lambed and wintered down here on the old home place and summered up in the mountains, on the south fork of the Hermosa."

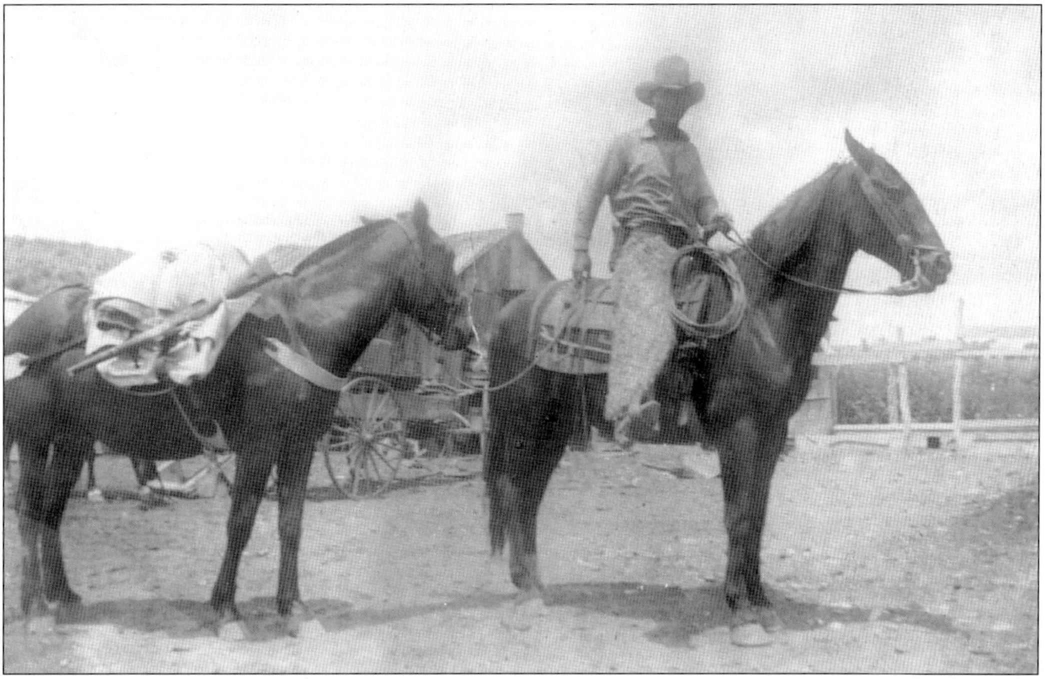

Here we see Chet Harris headed up to the summer pasture. "One time when I was real young," Donald tells us, "we were camped up there and for some reason my dad decided that I was going to come home. So I climbed up to the Highline Trail, came down through Hesperus, dropped down to the river, and got to Breen, where I stayed overnight at my aunt's. The next day I got home. My mother really got mad at my dad over that. 'Send that kid down the road only nine years old?' she said."

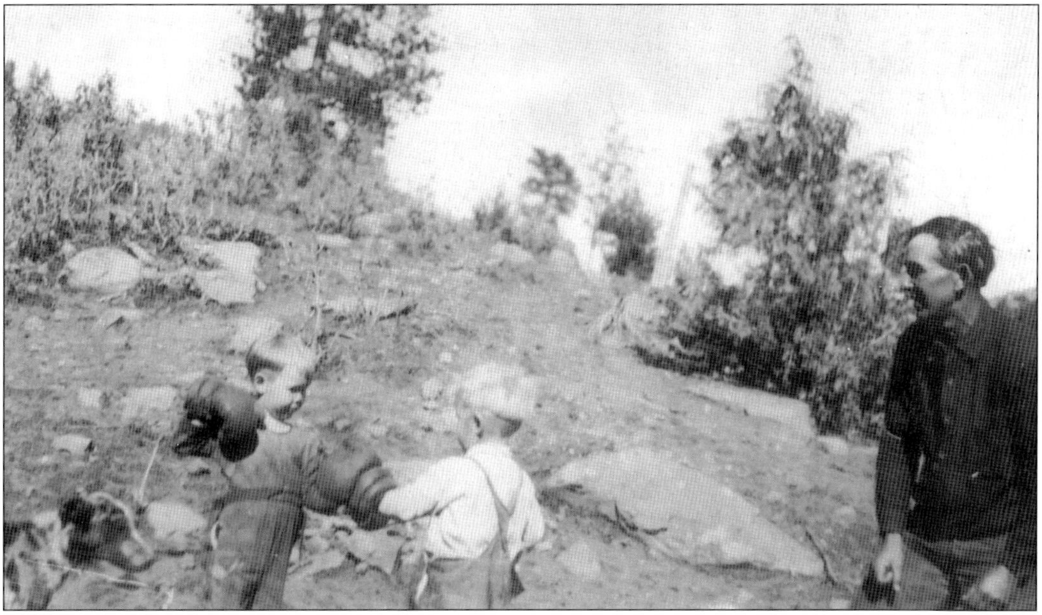

A young Donald Harris (left) engages in a boxing match with his cousin, supervised by his uncle Chet.

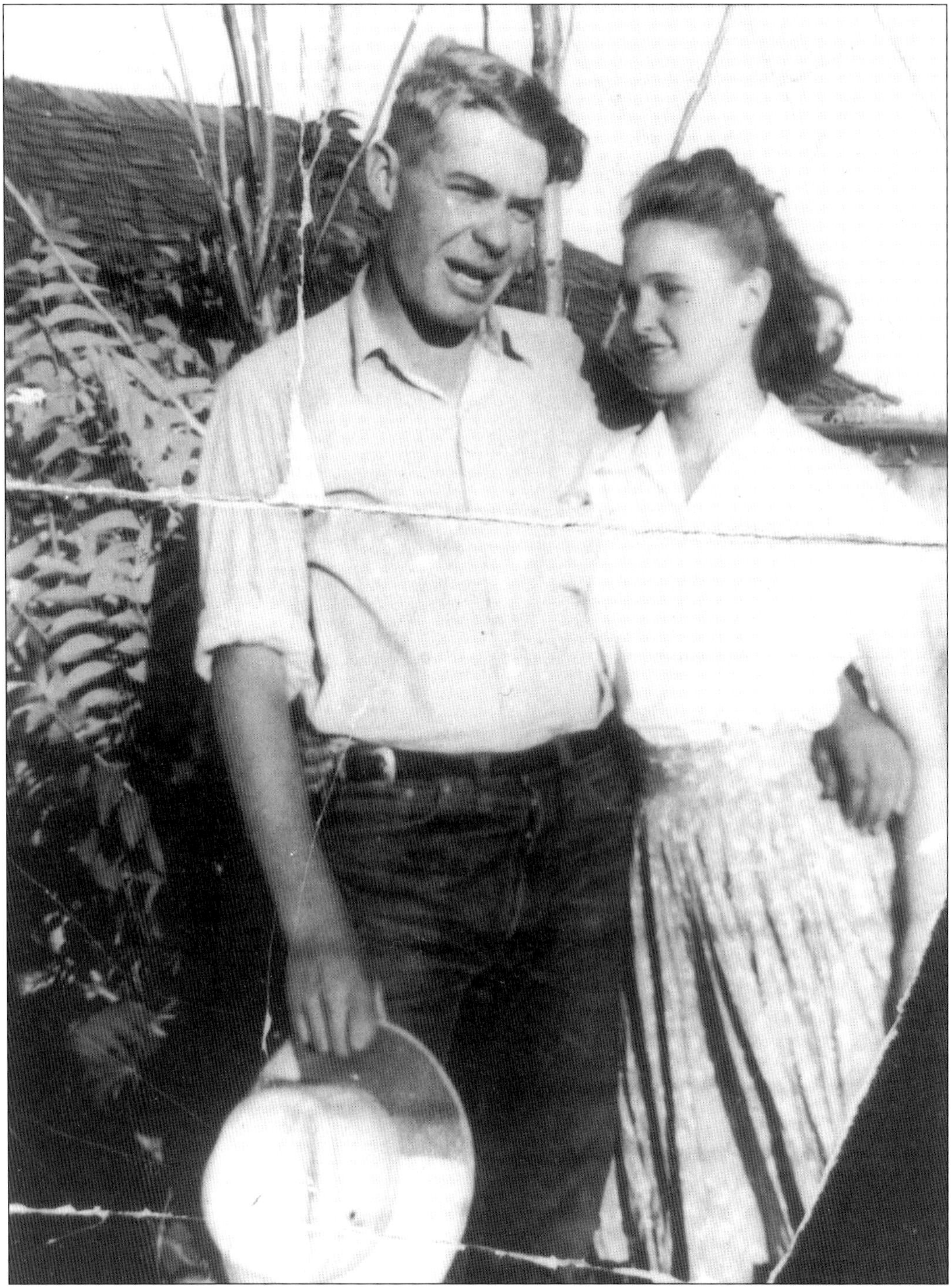

Donald and Angelina Harris pose together in front of the old house they fixed up and lived in on the old Sherman place, where they raised hay and ran cattle for over 40 years. During that time, Donald also had a good job with the Hathaway Oil Company, retiring in 1992. Donald still has an interest in some oil and gas fields. One whole series of wells is named after Angelina.

Chapter 7

"Sturdy Stock? I'll Give you Sturdy Stock!"

Angelina G. "Angie" Anesi Harris

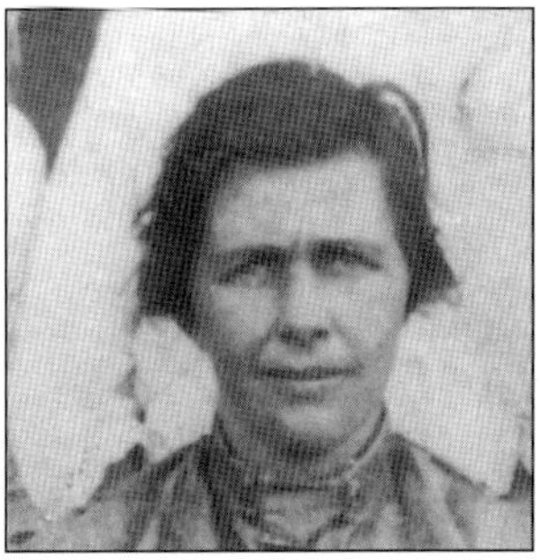

"Sturdy stock? I'll give you sturdy stock!" says Angelina G. "Angie" Anesi Harris, wife of Donald Harris. Her point is well taken. Angie's mother, Domenica Moser-Valentine-Anesi-Anesi, survived three husbands and raised 12 children, all by herself.

Sometime around the turn of the century, Angie's mother Domenica came to America from Trentino in the Val de Pine area of the Tyrolian Alps in Austria, that part of the Alps which is now part of Italy.

Upon her arrival, she and her father moved to Central City, Colorado, where Domenica married an Austrian miner whom she had known in Trentino, Amadeo Valentine. That marriage produced three children, but Amadeo died when the children were still quite young.

Thereupon, Domenica met and married another miner from Austria, Pietro Anesi, and they had two more children. In 1916, Domenica and Pietro and their family, now with five children, moved to Durango, but then Pietro also died.

Domenica was married once more, this time to Michele Anesi, yet another miner from Austria, who already had three children of his own. Then four more children were born to Domenica and Michele, including Angie. Tragically, Michele also died, leaving Domenica a widow once again.

"When mother was widowed for the third time," says Angie, "she was still a fairly young woman.

"The children ranged in age from 1 to 19. Even though she had very little formal education or special training, she was able to keep the family together. As soon as the children were old enough, they found jobs and were able to help out."

Angie and her closest sisters stayed home in "Webb Town"—an enclave of families situated along the Animas River just south of Graden's flour mill in Durango—and tended their large garden, irrigating and weeding, and delivering the vegetables to local grocery stores.

Domenica lived long enough to see all of her children grow to become responsible, productive adults. "We all attended Durango schools," says Angie. "Richard, Lillian, and Rose all went to Ft. Lewis College, when the campus was still at Hesperus. Lena and Ida were both nurses at the Old Ochsner hospital. Richard was with the Bureau of Reclamation in Durango when some of the earlier reservoirs in the area were being built. Lillian was a well-known teacher in the area. She taught at the old Whittier school in Durango, at Ignacio, La Boca, and on the 'Dry Side.'"

And when Domenica died at age 60 in 1945, she was still living in her family's little house in Webb Town. She had lived there since Durango was a quiet little town that only came to life on weekends, when the farmers came to sell their cream and eggs on Saturday afternoons, and the miners came to spend their weekly wages on Saturday nights. She had lived there through two World Wars and the Great Depression. Domenica Moser, says Angie, epitomized "the important part European immigrants had played in shaping the character of the town of Durango, as well as of the nation."

"Pa Needham, a long-time teacher and administrator in the Durango school system," Angie remembers, "spoke in my class, and used my mother as an example of how many of them had persevered in the face of extreme hardships.

"At the time, I was somewhat embarrassed about the attention he was drawing to the family, but now I realize he was paying a tribute to her and to others like her."

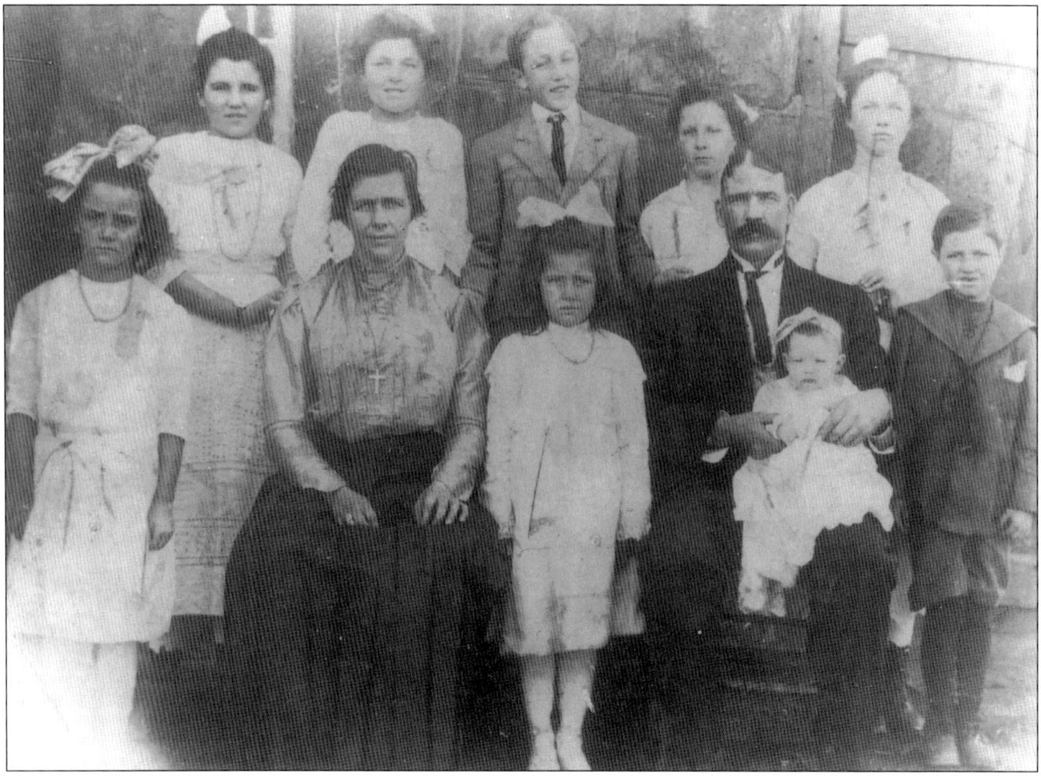

Angelina Anesi Harris' mother and father, Domenica and Michele Anesi, pose for a family portrait with nine of their children taken in 1921. Angie was the last of 12 children in the family, born on September 30, 1925. When Michele died, Domenica was widowed for the third time, leaving her to take care of the 12 children by herself.

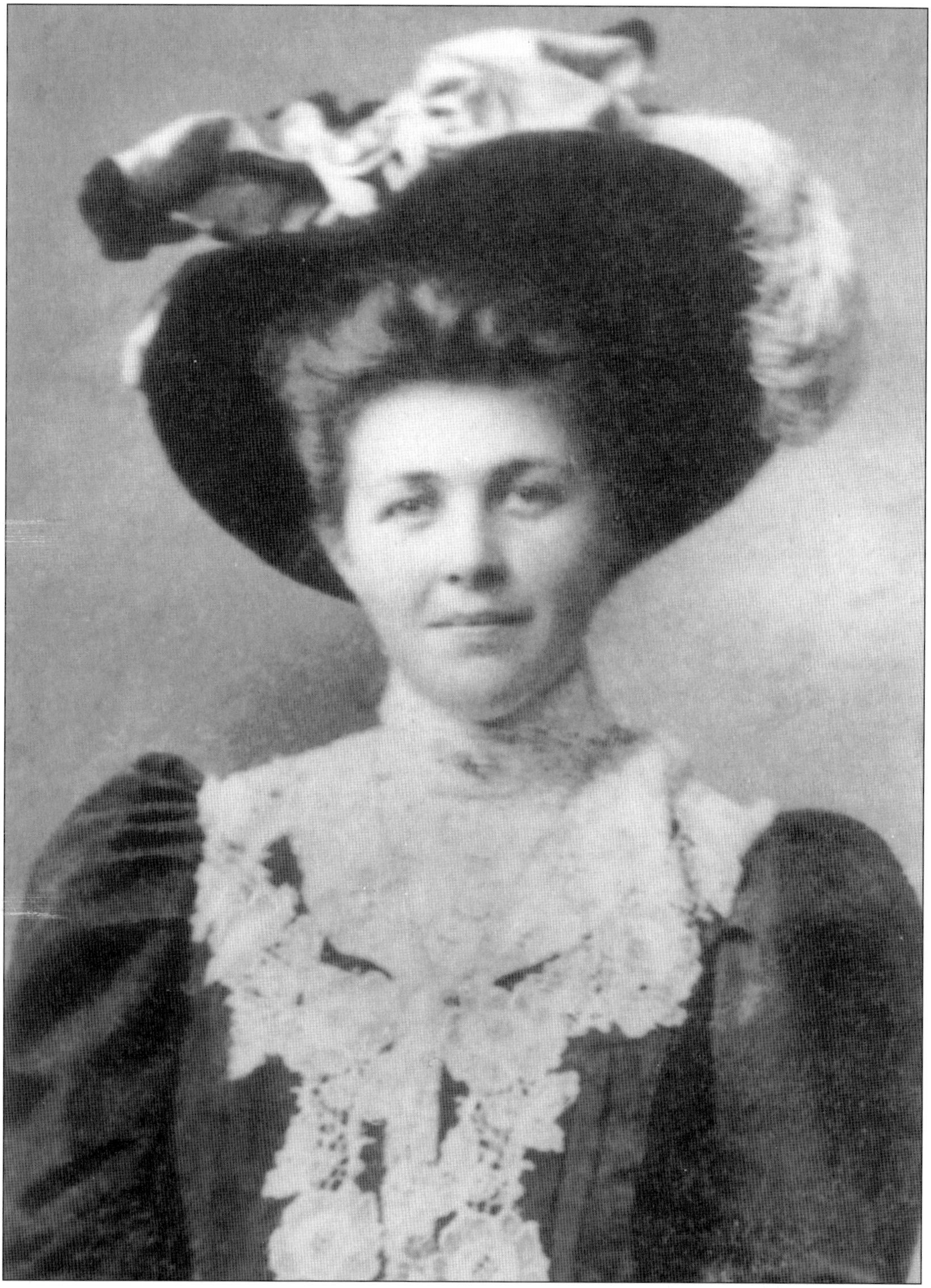

Here's a photo of Angie's mother, Domenica Moser, age 22, shortly after she arrived in Central City, Colorado, from Trentino, Austria, in that part of the Alps which is now part of Italy. Dominica came to America to marry Amadeo Valentine, whom she had known before in Trentino.

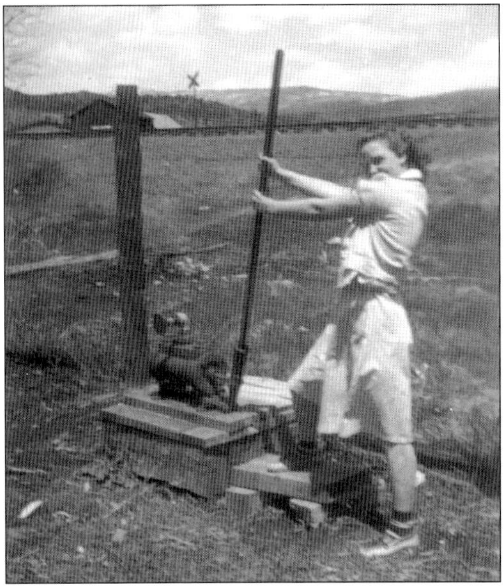

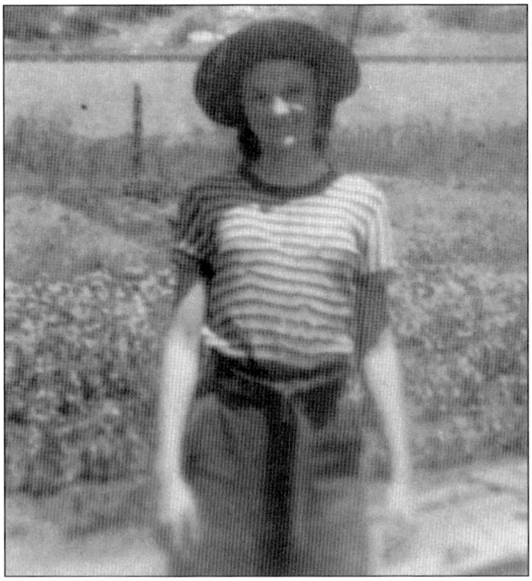

Here we see Angie as a teenager, hand pumping water to irrigate the family garden. "Before we could go roller-skating or to a ball game," says Angie, "our boyfriends had to help with the evening watering."

Pictured below is Angie (sixth from left) with some of her sisters and her brother after Domenica's funeral in 1960.

Angie helped support the family by raising vegetables in their garden, near Graden's flour mill. Angie and her sisters also took turns herding their goats. "One day when I decided to go swimming," Angie tells us, "the goats wandered over to the mill and got into the wheat. By the time I got there, the mill had already called the city and the goats had been impounded. It took a great deal of pleading on my part to get the goats released without paying the required fee."

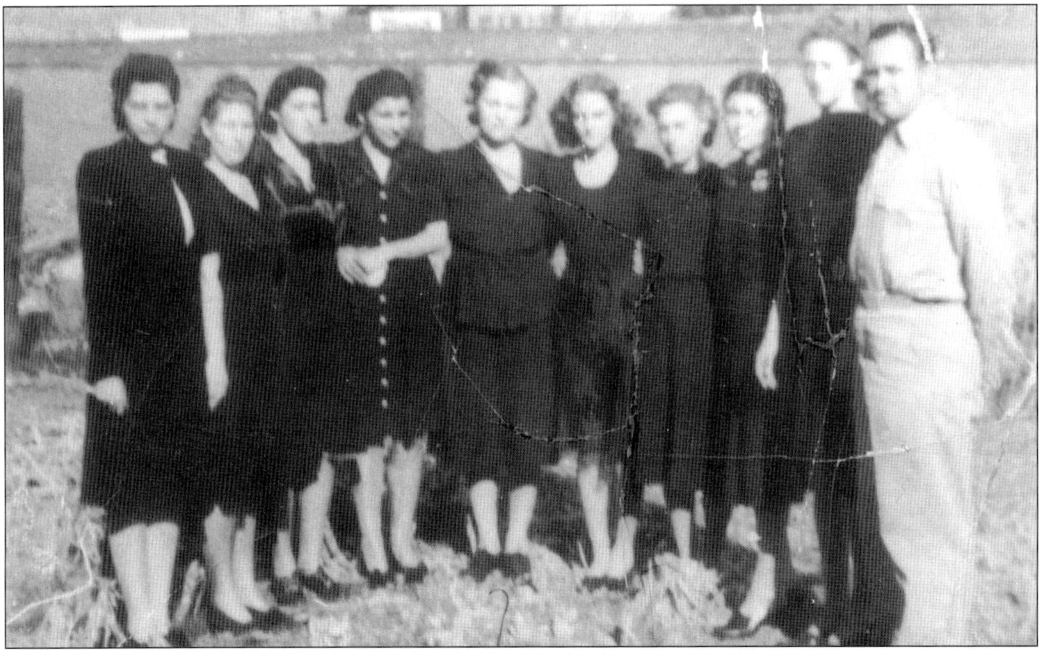

Chapter 8

BUSY MRS. MCBEE

GLADYS M. MCBEE

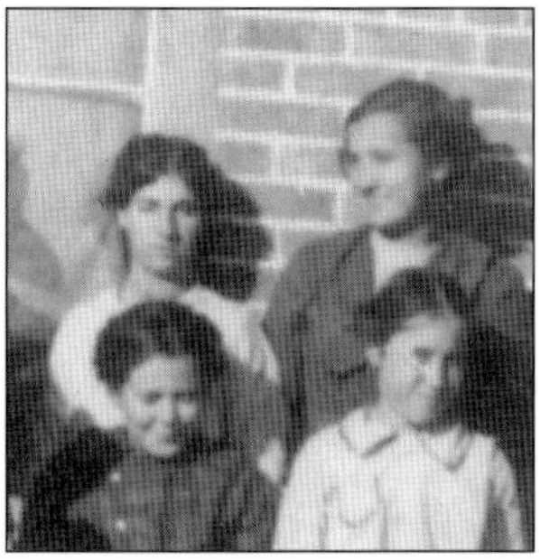

Mrs. Gladys McBee greets us at the door in a fuzzy, striped sweater—black and white stripes—reminding me of her name. But her maiden name is Hughes, she tells us. And her mother's maiden name is Hunt.

Mrs. McBee's grandmother, Ida Jane Hunt, came from Georgia to the Hesperus area in La Plata County, Colorado, by covered wagon with her son and her older brother in 1882. Then in 1884, her grandmother married her grandfather, William H. Hughes, in Aztec, New Mexico.

"In fact, when I was looking over...," says Mrs. McBee, suddenly buzzing off in a different direction. "Yes, here it is," she continues, pulling out a page of notes. "Bill Hughes came out from Illinois and he hauled freight for the Graden Company in Durango. Then he had a ranch in New Mexico and he ended up with three ranches, two in New Mexico and one in Hay Gulch, Colorado. He raised cattle."

Bill and Ida Jane Hughes had two daughters, Willa Elizabeth, and Mrs. McBee's mother, Mary Robert Hughes. And Mary Hughes married Mrs. McBee's father, Thomas Glenn Funk, in 1902.

"My mother was disinherited because she married my father," Mrs. McBee confides in us, her face growing perfectly round. "They were too young," she explains. "He was 18 and she was only 15. She left school and they ran to Hesperus. Grandpa knew that something was up and he chased them down there on horseback. But he had an asthma attack on the way, so by the time he got there, they were already married. Grandpa threw my father in jail and tried to talk them out of staying married. But they insisted, so he tells my mother, 'I'll never speak to you again. I won't stop you from seeing your mother,' he says, 'but I won't have anything to do with you.' And he didn't. So they went to live with my father's folks, the Funks."

"I was born in 1917," continues Mrs. McBee. "My father and mother were living at the Tenbroke Mine up in the La Plata Mountains. I was due in December, so Mother went back down to the ranch. And when I was six months old, we went back up to the mine . . . Well, then they had a mine explosion. One of the charges went off prematurely and it decapitated him . . . He was 24 years old.

"After Daddy was killed, Grandpa let mother come home."

"Here, look at this," she goes on, pulling an old photograph out from her hive of memorabilia. "That one gal said she thought we were related because our grandparents always talked about one another, the Fisherdicks and the Coppingers, the Hendersons, from out Hesperus and Red Mesa and out through there."

And, suddenly, Mrs. McBee is off again, antennae wriggling.

"I knew Mr. Henderson. He was in his 90s. And my mother knew him for years. He was always telling a story about when he first came here. He was, I think, three or five years old, and the land at Hesperus wasn't opened yet. So they settled down between Aztec and Colorado and they worked real hard. All the kids, even five years old, helped. And they had a real, real big crop because, you know, it's kind of like a 'banana belt' down there. They had all kind of squash and stuff.

"And one day a bunch of renegade Indians came. And Henderson and the wife went out to talk to them. They hid all the kids. But the Indians didn't harm them. They just took every bit of food they had.

"So the neighbors fed the family all winter, till they could get a crop the next year.

"Well, 30 years ago, Henderson got some of that land out at Red Mesa or Breen out there, and he ended up selling that back to the Indians. He said that's the only way he ever got even with them."

"Now these pictures I tried to place," says Mrs. McBee, buzzing off again, "but I can't. I was so upset when my mother died that we, just now, after all these years, are just now going through her things."

"When I look in here," she says, sifting through the photo box again, "I can recognize some of the names. I think that's the reason these pictures were given to my folks and they kept them. See, if Mother went through anything, she labeled it. I wish she had written more down.

"I've got boxes and boxes of these pictures," she says, circling, circling, "but I have no idea who they are."

And that's the stinger.

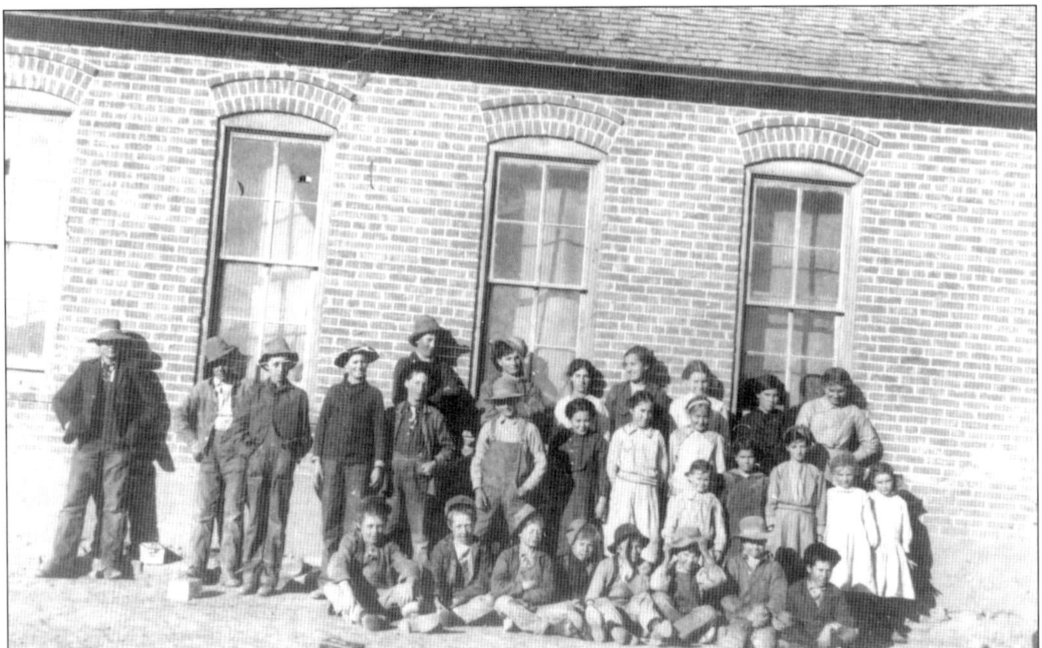

Glady's McBee's mother, Mary Robert Hughes, attended this school at Hesperus, Colorado. When Gladys' grandmother, Ida Jane Hunt, came to area, "Hesperus still belonged to the Indians," says Gladys. "So they went down to La Plata, New Mexico." Sometime after Ida Jane married Gladys' grandfather, William H. Hughes, in 1894, they moved back up to Hesperus.

Gladys McBee's aunt, Willa Elizabeth Hughes (left), and mother, Mary Robert Hughes (right), pose with their teacher, Emma Bowman (center), at Hesperus School. Mary's mother, Ida Jane Hunt, came from Georgia to the Hesperus area with her son Carl and her older brother, Robert Marcus, in 1892. Marcus was the son of Robert Rivers Hunt and Robert was a descendant of Judkin Hunt, who fought in the Revolutionary War.

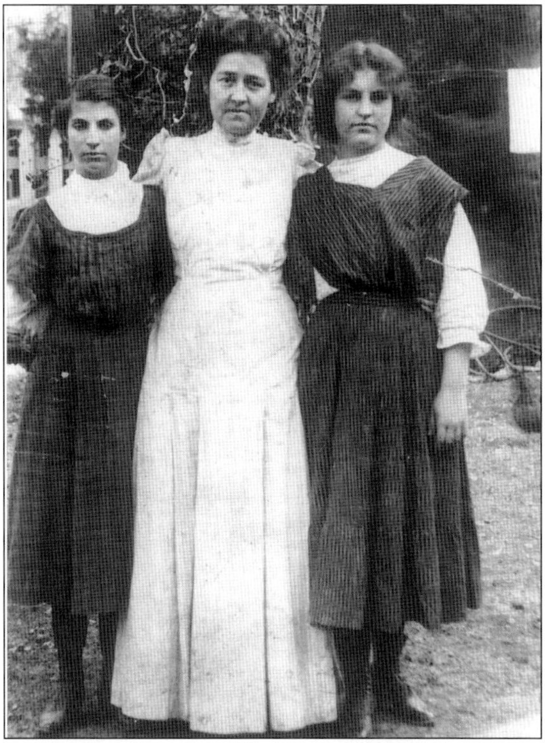

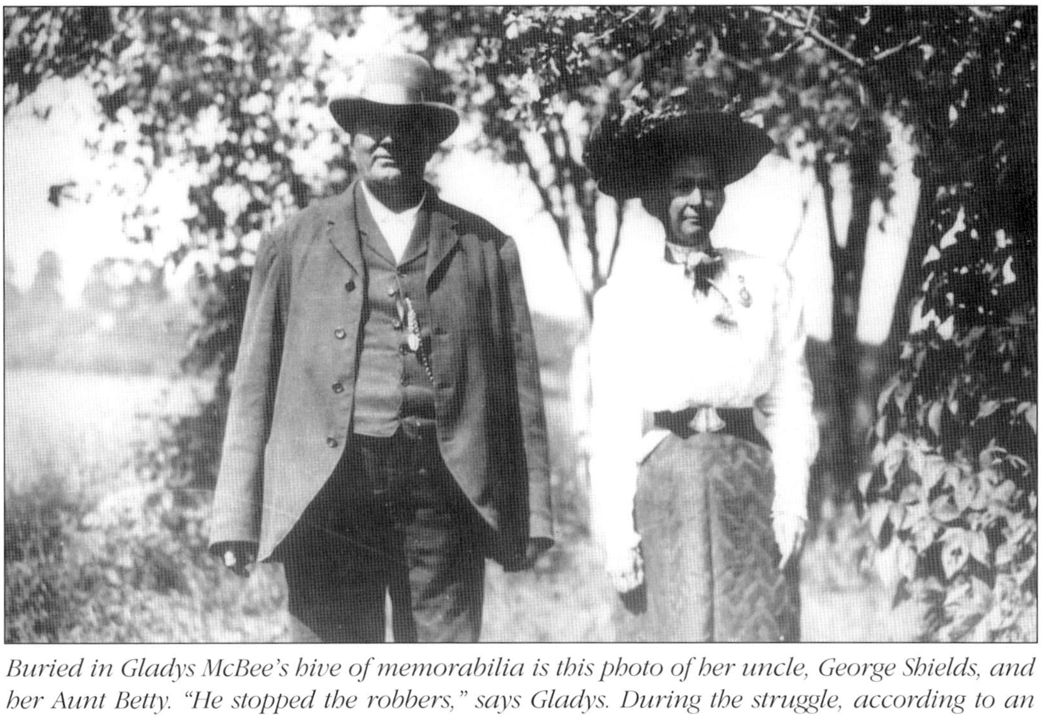

Buried in Gladys McBee's hive of memorabilia is this photo of her uncle, George Shields, and her Aunt Betty. "He stopped the robbers," says Gladys. During the struggle, according to an article in the newspaper, "The first bullet struck Shields high on the shoulder" but "the second shot missed....Wounded as he was, Shields was unable to retain his hold on the first robber and the two fled."

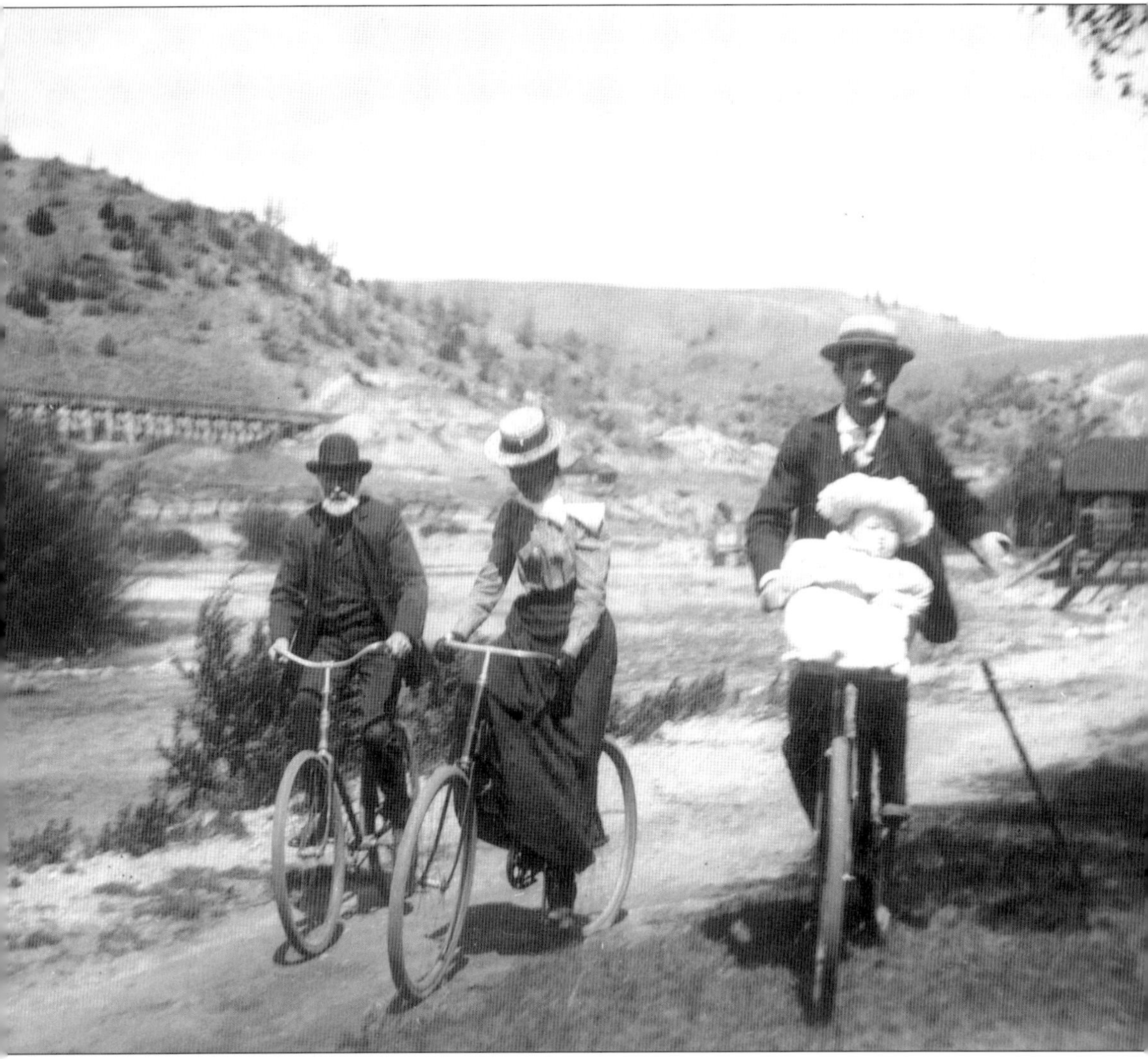

This is one of the unidentifiable photos from Mrs. McBee's hive.

Chapter 9

The Italian Connection

The Zellitti Family

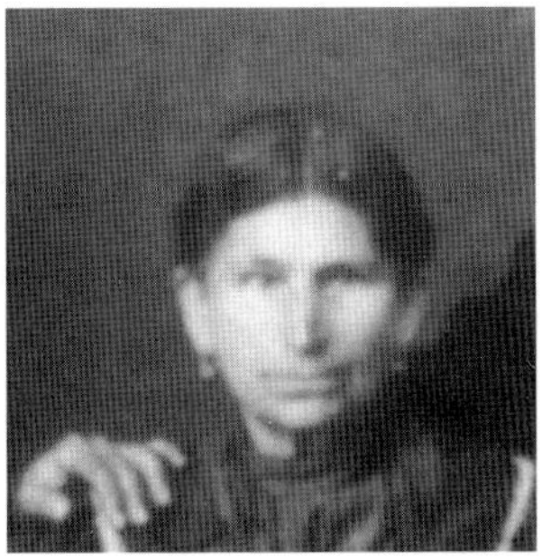

Dominick "Nick" Zellitti's father, Frank Zellitti, "came here in about 1900, when he was 17," says Nick.

"When he came over," says Nick's wife, Mary Sweitzer Zellitti, "he couldn't speak a word of English. He landed in Ellis Island, but he didn't want to stay in New York, so he was headin' west."

"First, he worked on the railroad...," says Nick.

"Clear across the United States," says Mary. "Papa, he was carrying these railroad ties, and the boss, he would say, 'Hey, Frank, take a five.' And Papa would take them down and he'd go back and get some more. And his boss would say, 'Hey, Frank, come on, take a five!' And Papa said, 'Hey, no take a five, I'm lucky I take a two!'"

Mary leans back laughing.

MARY (continuing): I just remember Papa telling me all these things. Oh, Papa, he was quite a character.

NICK: And then he came here to Durango and he went into mining...

MARY: And after Papa made his money and got a little bit ahead here, he sends for Nicky's mama, Concetta. And Mama says, 'I get on the boat, no speak-a English. It was Mary Cugnini and me and we meet this nice American man. And he says, 'Hey, you beautiful Italian girls, I teach you English.' So they're on the boat and these girls are learning English. And he says, 'Now, when you meet an American, this is what you say to every American you meet, and they like you, they love you, you speak good English, and all that.' So Mama says, 'Here comes a Mary and I off-a the boat. And we meet somebody and we say, 'How do you do, you somabitch, and go to hell!' And everybody she meets, she says that.

We all laugh raucously.

MARY (continuing): And she says, 'He teaches me this, and if I find-a this man, I'll kill him.' Mama was a character, too.

NICK: See, all the marriages were contracted...

MARY: Yeah, Nicky was contracted to marry Virginia Seroni.

Mary rolls her eyes.

NICK: But I told her I just didn't want to marry my cousin.

MARY: Yeah, all the Italians in this town are connected somehow either by marriage or otherwise. Everybody I meet downtown is a cousin, an aunt, an uncle, or whatever. Everybody's related in this town.

And how did Mary get Nick?

MARY: Oh, that was easy! We started dating. He found out where I lived, you know. And he'd wait outside the church there. I went to the Baptist church. He wouldn't go into church 'cause he was Catholic, right? So he'd be waiting out there for me. And Papa, I promised him I wouldn't get married until after I graduated. And you know when I was going with Nicky—my father was in the advertising business, he had an outdoor advertising business here—so he was in Albuquerque and my mother called on the phone and says, 'You better get up here, she's getting awful serious about this guy.' Boy, my dad came runnin' up here! He's a little German.

Mary leans back, laughing.

MARY (continuing): But you know, we were so much in love we used to stand out in the snow and kiss and neck until the snow was up to our knees. So we decided to get married, right? And Mama Zellitti says, 'Hey, watsa matter, you kids crazy? Whatta you gonna live on?' And I says, 'Love.'

Mary rolls her eyes again and folds her hands.

MARY (continuing): Nick was coming to pick me up that night. And my dad says, 'What's this I hear, what are you doin'? You're too young!' And I says, 'Oh, Papa, you'll just love Nicky!' So when Nicky got there my dad looked at him and he looked at me and he said, 'What kind of foreigner is he?' I said, 'Dad, he's Italian.'

Nick reaches over and squeezes Mary's knee.

MARY (continuing): Oh, I was so embarrassed. So we eloped. Nick and I caught a bus to Aztec. And we left notes for our parents. It said we were going on a picnic. But Nick was only 19, too young to get married. So Nick had to call his mother and get permission. She says, 'You no go on a picnic?' He says, 'No, Mama, I'm gonna get married.'

Nick laughs.

MARY (continuing): So then we got home and we moved in over the grocery store.

NICK: In 1921, Dad opened up the European Grocery and Meat Market right across from the depot, in the Italian section of town.

MARY: Yeah, and it was rough. Right next door Rose Fanto had a bar...

NICK: And, you know, she was the most wonderful, giving person that you could ever meet...

MARY: And then there was Blue Moon Lil.

NICK: She worked out of The Southern Hotel.

MARY: Right next door to Papa's store.

NICK: And then there was the Linmor Hotel.

MARY: Now that was a whore house.

NICK: From Sixth Street down...

MARY: It was a rough part, but those were the best people in the world. Everybody helped each other. It was wonderful!

(opposite, top) *Domenick Zellitti's grandmother, Patronella Delpagio Zellitti (front, left), and grandfather, John Zellitti (rear, right), pose for a formal portrait in their hometown of Campli, Italy. In 1930, after Nick's grandmother died, Nick's grandfather came to America to live with Nick's father's family in Durango,Colorado.*

(opposite, bottom left) *After Frank (right) arrived in Durango, he went into mining, opening the mine that was under the famous "Moving Mountain."*

(opposite, bottom right) *Nick Zellitti's grandfather, John (rear right), poses with his family, including Nick's father, Frank Zellitti (front, right).*

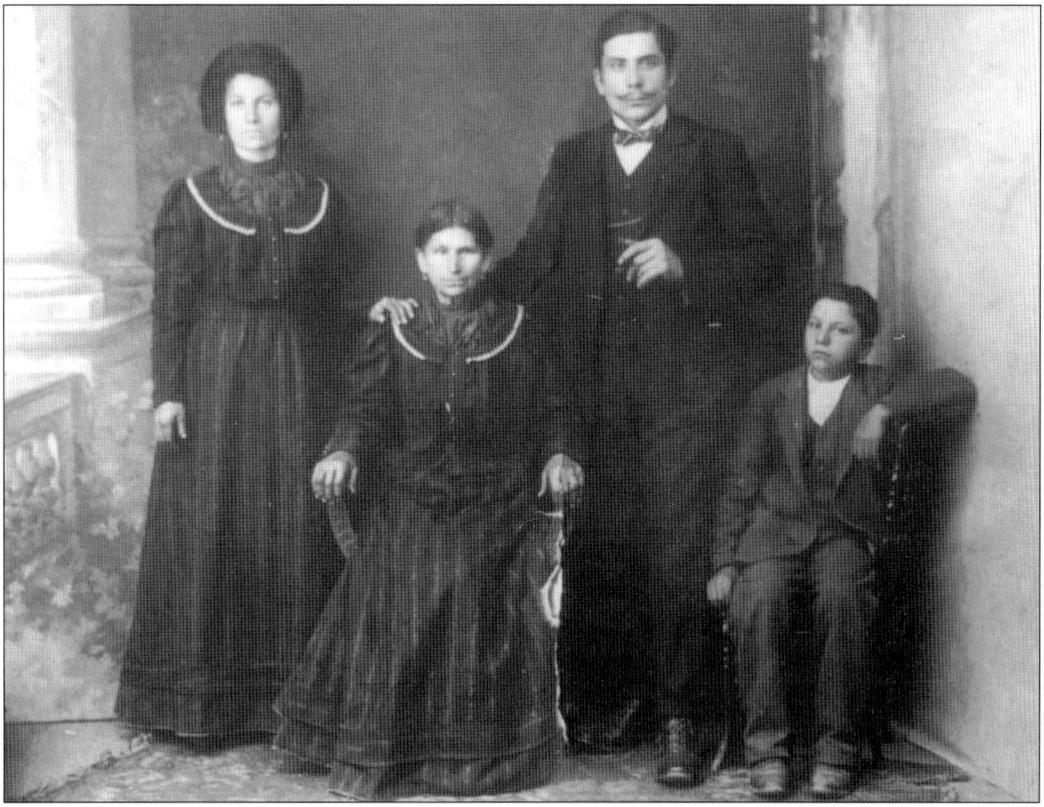

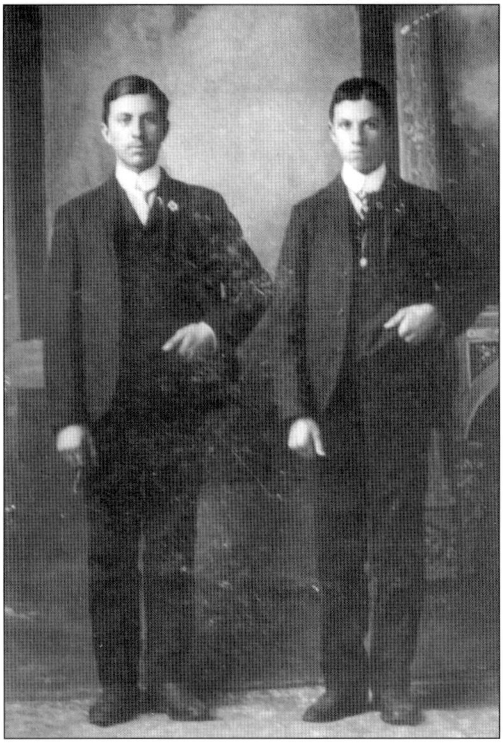

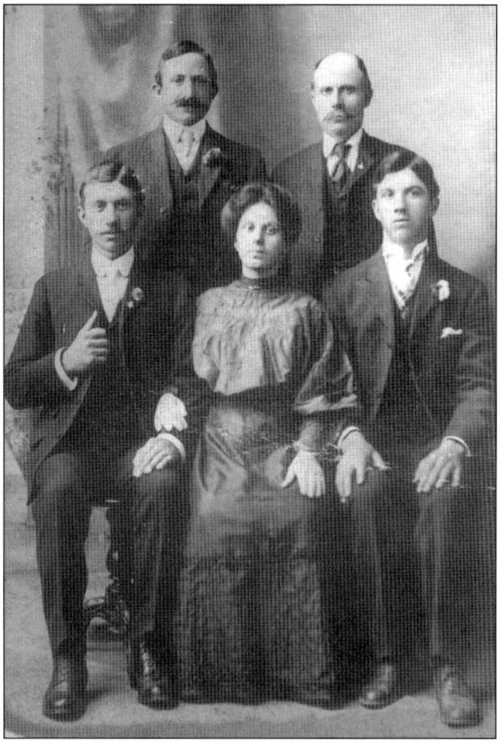

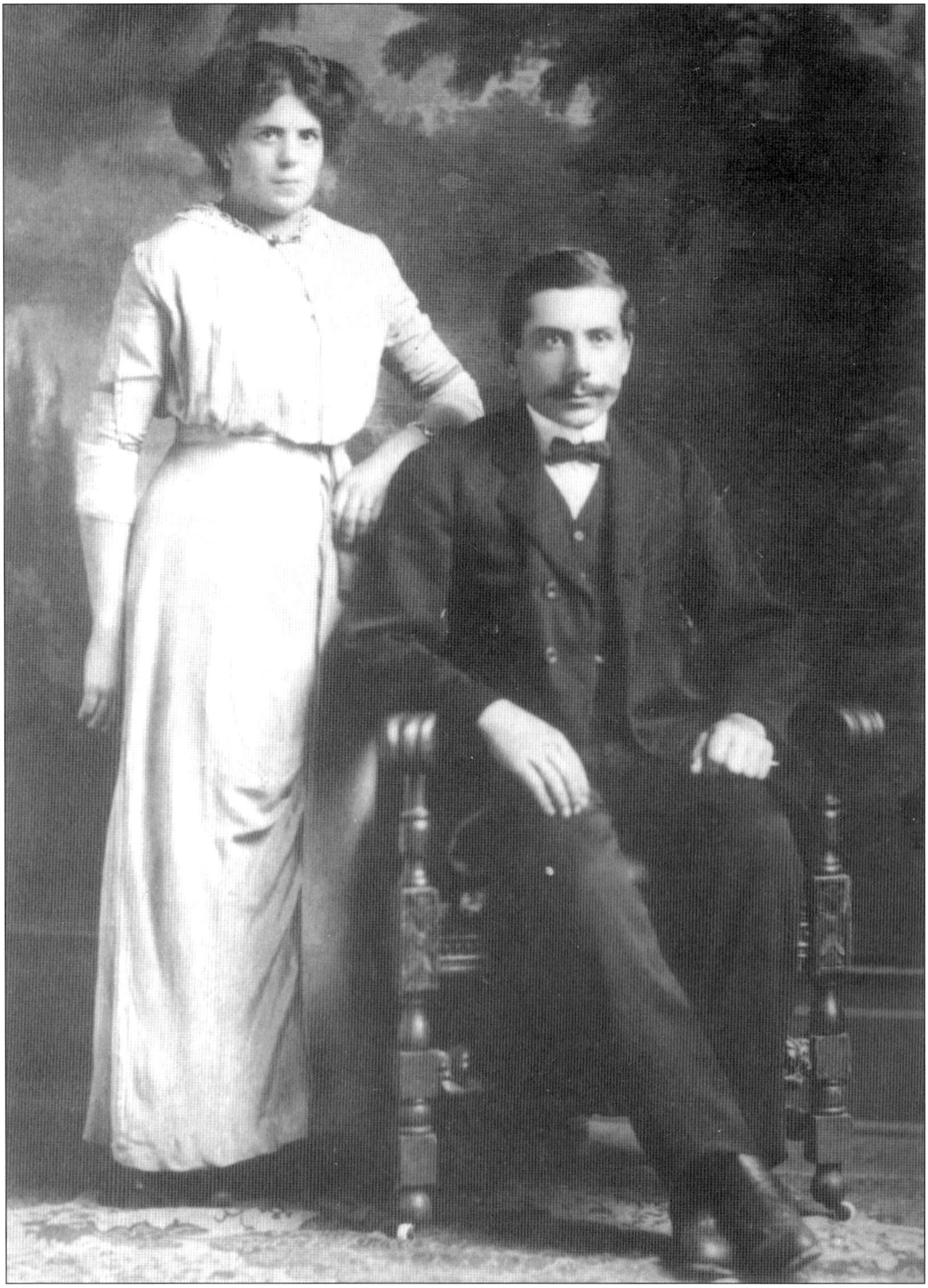

After Frank made enough money in the mines, he sent for Nick's mother, Concetta Faragalli Zellitti (left), to come to Durango and get married. Concetta came to America with her friend from the old country, Mary Cugnini, who acted as her chaperon. Mary Cugnini later also married into the Zellitti family.

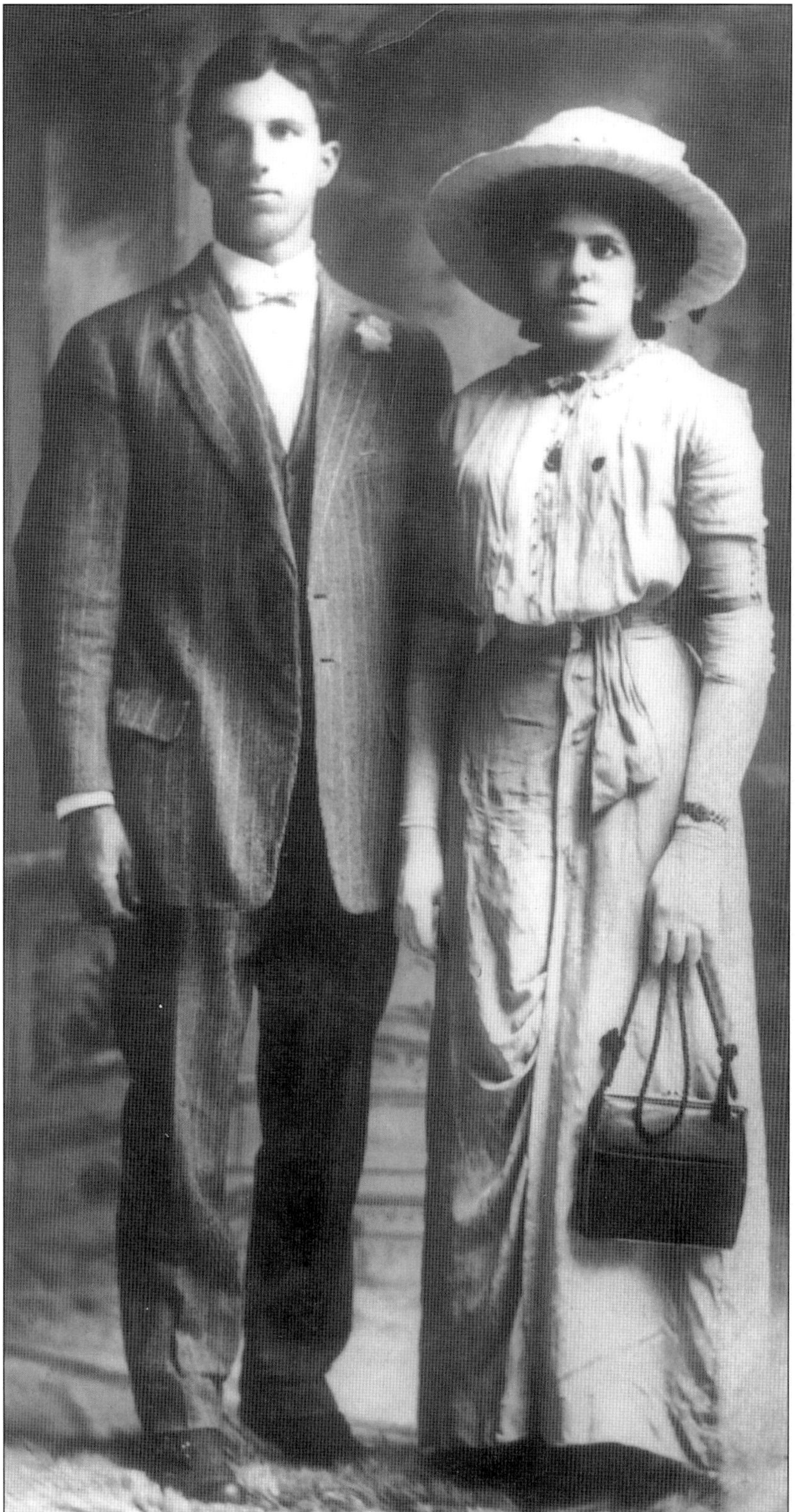

Nick's parents, Frank and Concetta, pose here for their wedding photo, c. 1909. In the old country, Frank and Concetta were contracted to get married when Concetta was six years old.

"This was the way the old families did," says Nick. "They send one of the boys over, and then he works, and then he sends for his wife, and then they send the money back, and they bring over the other brothers, and they bring over the sisters."

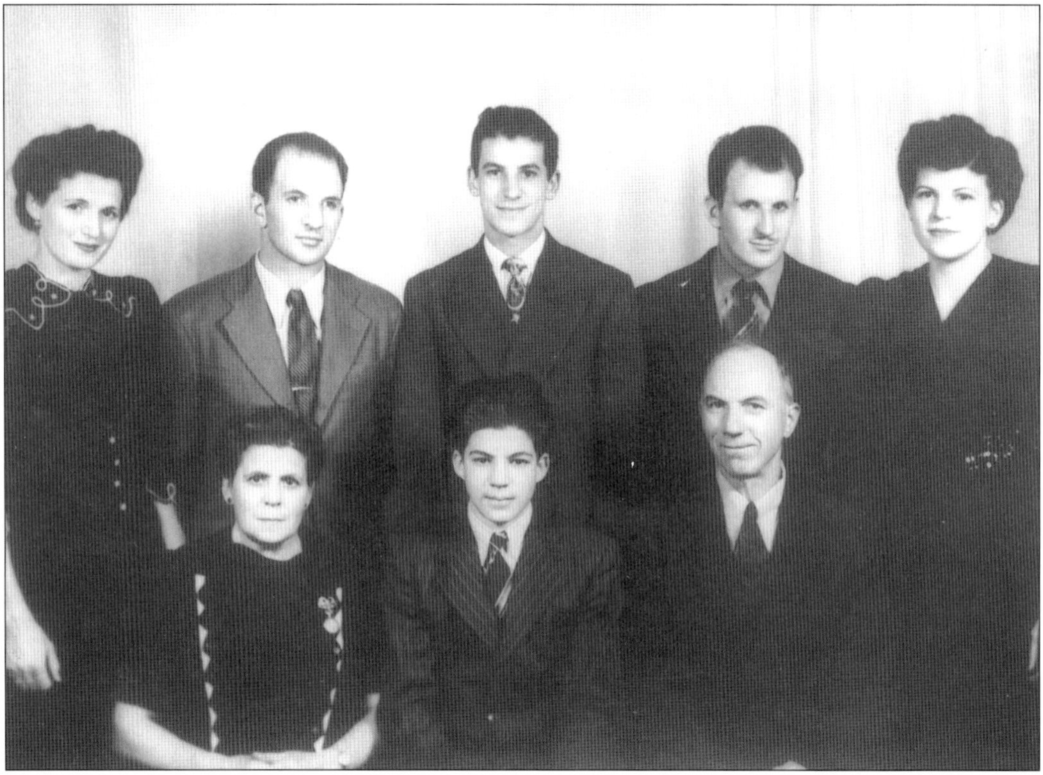

Nick (rear, center), stands behind his mother Concetta (front, left) and his father Frank (front right) in this family photo. After he was married, Nick's father Frank successfully operated the European Grocery and Meat Market in Durango, until it failed during the Depression. Then he went back into mining.

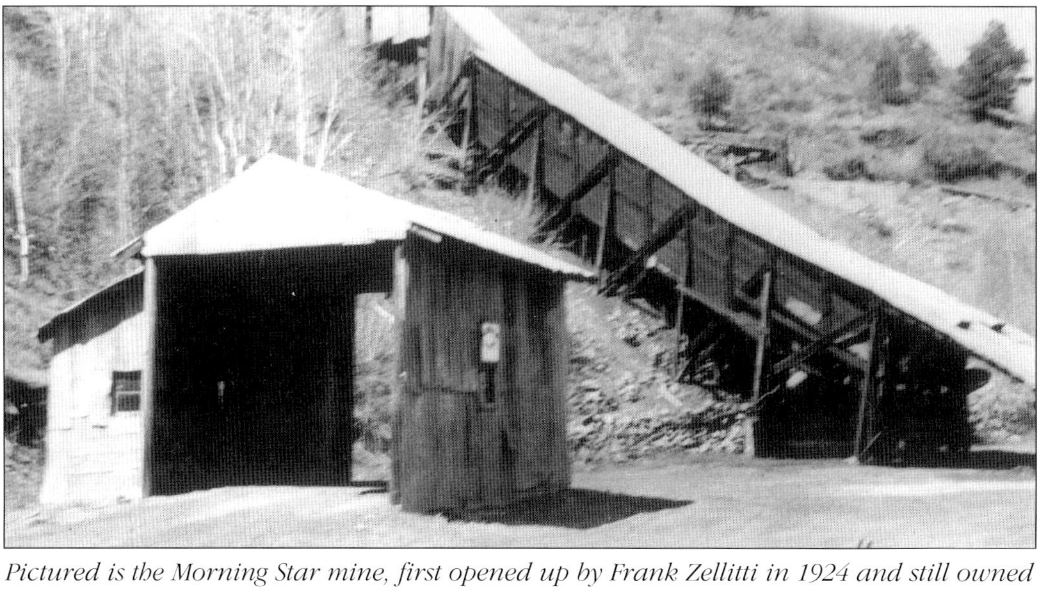

Pictured is the Morning Star mine, first opened up by Frank Zellitti in 1924 and still owned by the Zellitti family.

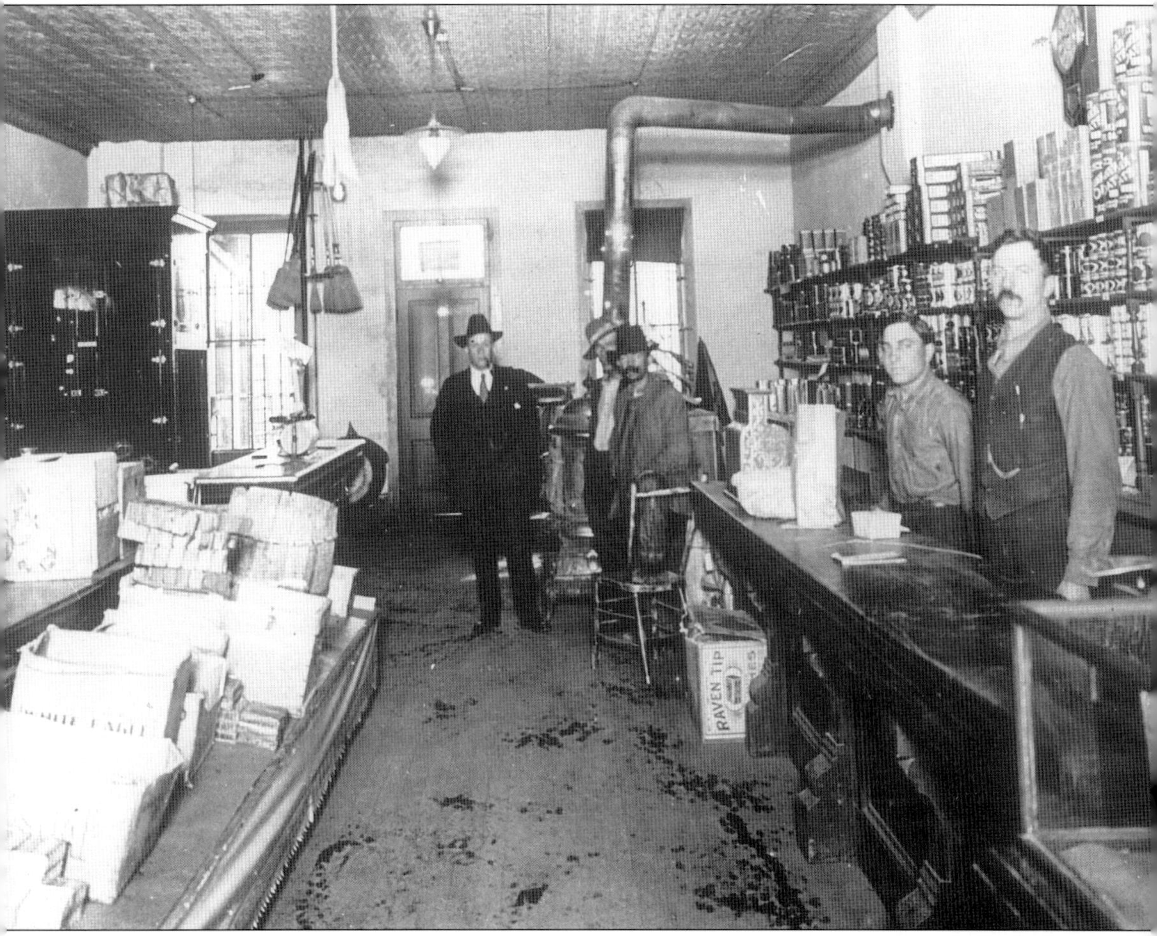

This is the interior of the European Grocery and Meat Market, opened by Frank (right) in 1921 and lost four years later during the Depression. "Poor Papa," says Mary, "he had such a heart of gold. He'd say, 'That's all right, you don't have to pay, that's OK, next week, next week, I understand.' So after going $50,000 in debt, he had to close up the store."

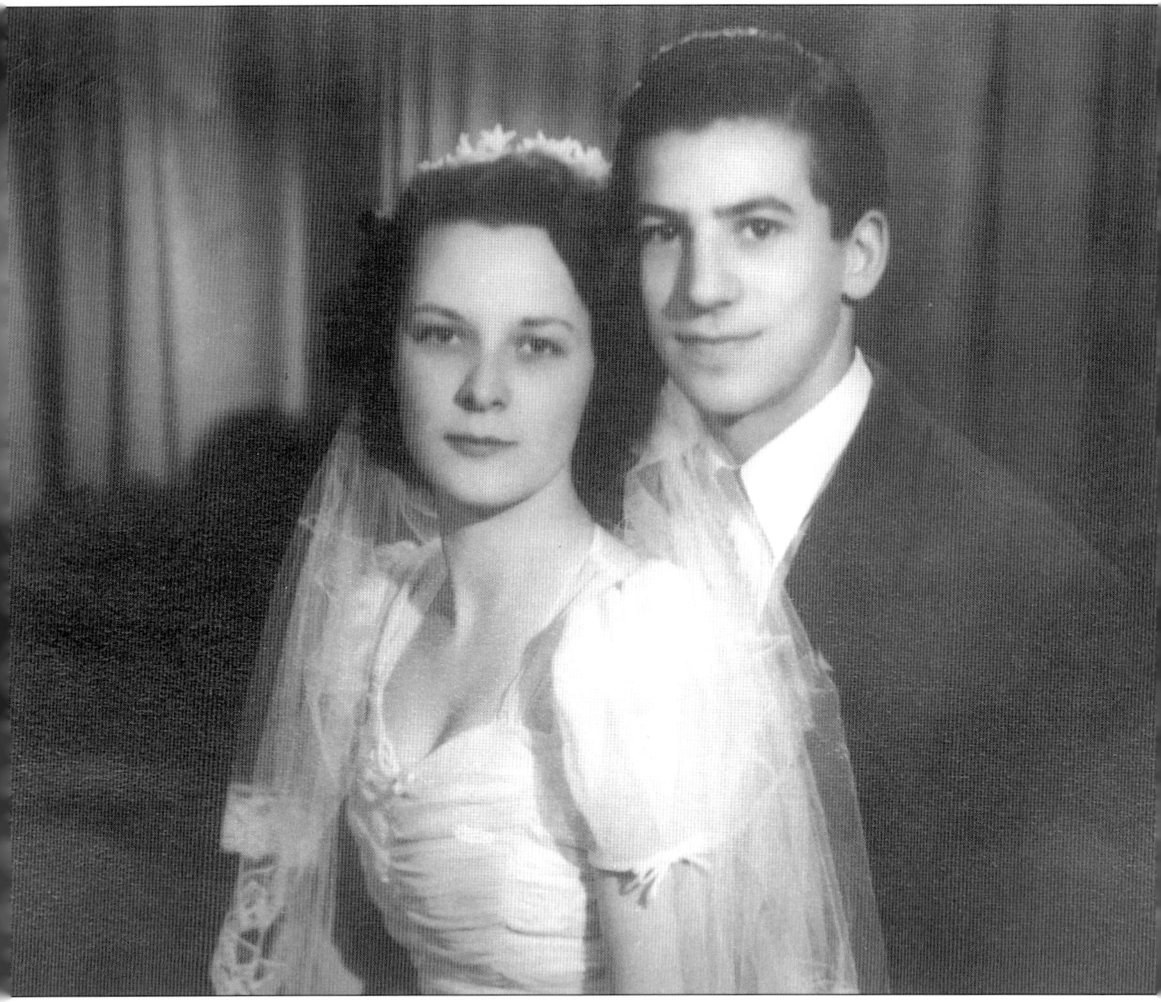

After Nick and Mary were married in 1943 they moved in above the European Grocery. When he was a boy, Nick had delivered groceries for the store, "for free," says Mary. "People would do anything for money." "Like my cousin," says Nick, "he would sell his dad's shoes, he'd sell his mother's canned goods just to make a little money."

Chapter 10

ARCHIE BODO STORIES

ARCHIE AND HAZEL BODO

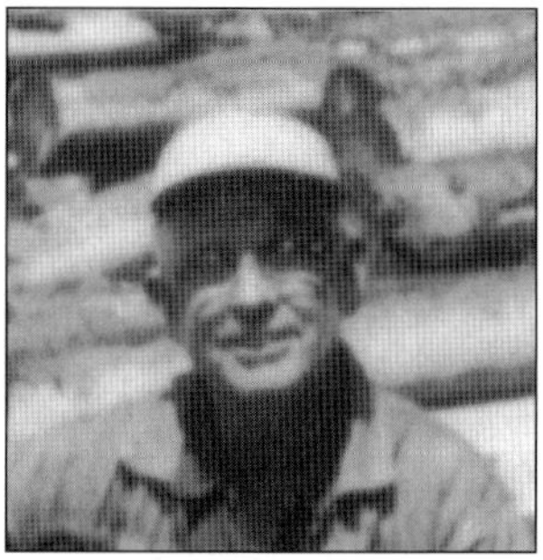

Archie Bodo's father, Michele Bodoira Sr., was born in 1882 and came with his parents from Torinio, Italy, to Durango, Colorado, right around 1900. Michele worked in several mines, Archie tells us, and then went into farming.

"The old man's name was Bodoira," Archie tells us. "He cut the 'ira' off when he went to work at the smelter and from then on we went by 'Bodo' ever since. And my mother's maiden name was Ballesio, Rosalia 'Rosie' Ballesio. My mother was from a little town outside of Torinio by the name of Cirie."

Archie launches into a story about how his father and his mother, met and got married.

"Dad got a paycheck from the Porter Mine and, of course, his mother would always take care of the money. She would give him a few dollars to go to a saloon and have a few drinks and play a little pool.

"So one night when Dad found out he only had a nickel left in his pocket, he threw it on the roulette wheel—and it hit. It hit about four times in a row, all on the same number. He went home that night with better than $7,000.

"So the next morning he quit his job, got a ticket to Italy, and went back there to get married. But he didn't have a girlfriend, so he had to find one.

"Well, my mother's folks had a restaurant in Cirie and Rosie was cooking in this restaurant. So Dad went in there to eat and saw her and they got married, May 1, 1905."

By the time that Archie was born, May 6, 1909, Archie's father had made enough money in the mines to get into farming. "This was the kind of work my dad liked," says Archie, "as he was a farmer back in Italy." First, "they rented a small truck farm on Junction Creek, where they grew vegetables and sold them to the mining camps and the stores in Durango." They then moved to the Florida Mesa and did the same thing. "That winter," continues Archie, "Dad took a job feeding cattle for Mr. Graden of the Graden Mercantile Company in Ridges Basin." In March of 1912, Archie's father and his two brothers rented the Morgan farm in Ridges Basin and his father continued farming by himself.

Eventually, Ridges Basin became the permanent home of the entire Bodo family, on what became known as the Bodo Ranch. But "Dad was never a cattleman," explains Archie. "It was my brother Mike Jr. who always wanted to be a cattleman. So, when he was very young, Mike got a cow and it had a calf. Then he got another cow and the next year he had five head, two cows and two calves and one two-year-old. Then the next year he had eight head. So, in this way, by the time he was fifteen years old, he had a little herd."

"My dad," continues Archie, "seeing Mike was so interested in cattle, decided to go in with him and they started a good herd.

"And in the spring of the year, we'd have to round 'em up, brand, vaccinate, de-horn, and take them up to the mountains for years up above where Lemon Dam is at. And then later we went up to Hermosa. Then, see, the doggone Forest Service started splitting them up—a little bit here, a little bit there, a little bit someplace else. So then we started buying more land down here. That's how we got 7,593 acres."

After Archie's dad died on April 13, 1960, Mike Jr. took over the ranch. "And then," laments Archie, "when Mike died, of course, I had to sell it, because nobody wanted to run it, couldn't depend on nobody."

Archie loves to tell stories.

"You know how I met Hazel?" asks Archie.

Archie's wife, Hazel Lemon Bodo, seems to enjoy these stories too. She sits there right next to Archie, smiling, her make-up perfect, dressed in shades of red, complementing her bright red hair.

"I was running the threshing machine," Archie goes on, "up on the Fort Lewis Mesa and . . . " Archie turns and gives us a wry grin, "you want me to tell you how she caught me? Well, all those girls were cookin' up cakes for the threshing crew and they wanted me to see which one was the best cake. So I picked hers. Hers was the best cake.

"When we got married, my brother was to take us to her folks' place up at Lemon Lake to get her clothes. Then we were going to go to Arizona, because her uncle had a job for me."

"Anyhow," Archie chuckles, "we didn't get up there with the car. My brother-in-law had to come down from the ranch with a sleigh and a team of horses. And we went up there and we got snowed in, didn't get out of there until March, honeymooned up there."

"We had fun," adds Hazel. "We went sledding and everything."

"In places where I dug down," says Archie, "the snow was over 10 foot deep.

"Hazel's folks had 200 head of cattle up there, but we couldn't get them out to the timber. And cows—if they can't get to the timber where they can bed down, out of the open—they'll get pneumonia and die.

"In March, when we came out of there and put them down here on my folks' place, we only had 90 head left."

(opposite, top) *Archie Bodo's father, Michele Bodoira Sr., came with his father from Italy to Colorado to work in the mines right around 1900. Michele's father made his money and returned to Italy, but Michele stayed and worked in the coal mines around Durango, eventually ending up at the Porter Mine, living in one of the small houses (upper left) shown in this photo.*

(opposite, bottom) *Eventually, Archie's father ended up owning a ranch in Ridges Basin. "The early years were hard," says Archie. "All of us kids worked. They give me a team of horses that nobody could handle—but they was good horses, old Bill and Blue, they'd do anything for me—and I cut all the hay, raked it, bunched it, and got it ready for the stacking crew. And I was only 10 years old."*

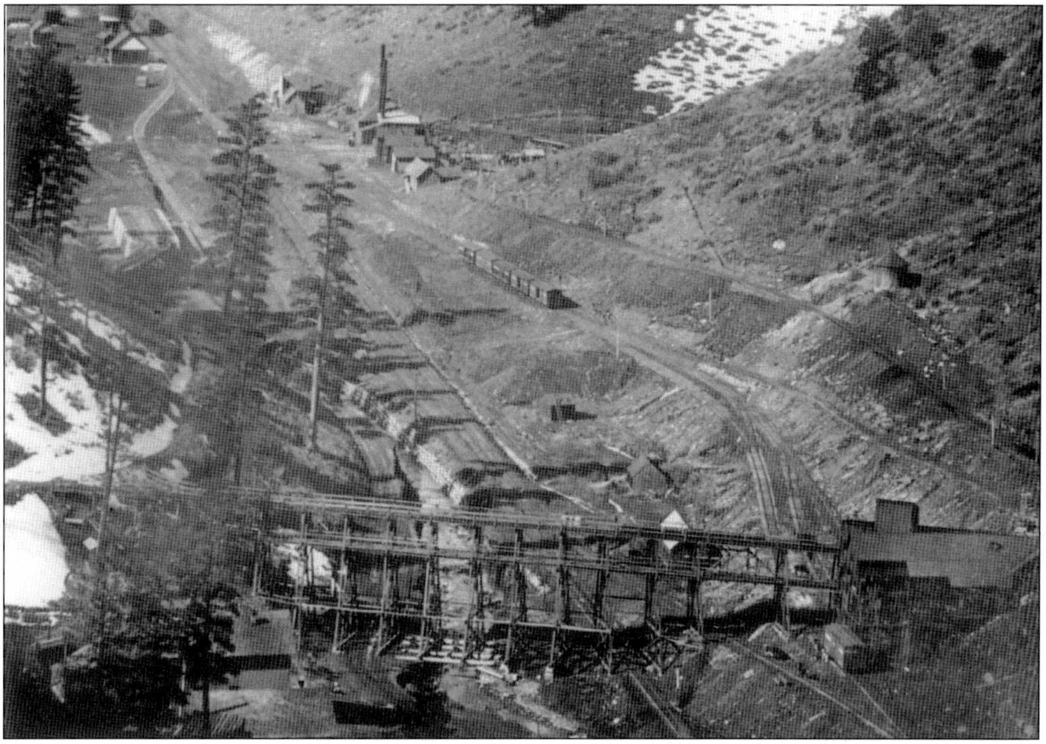

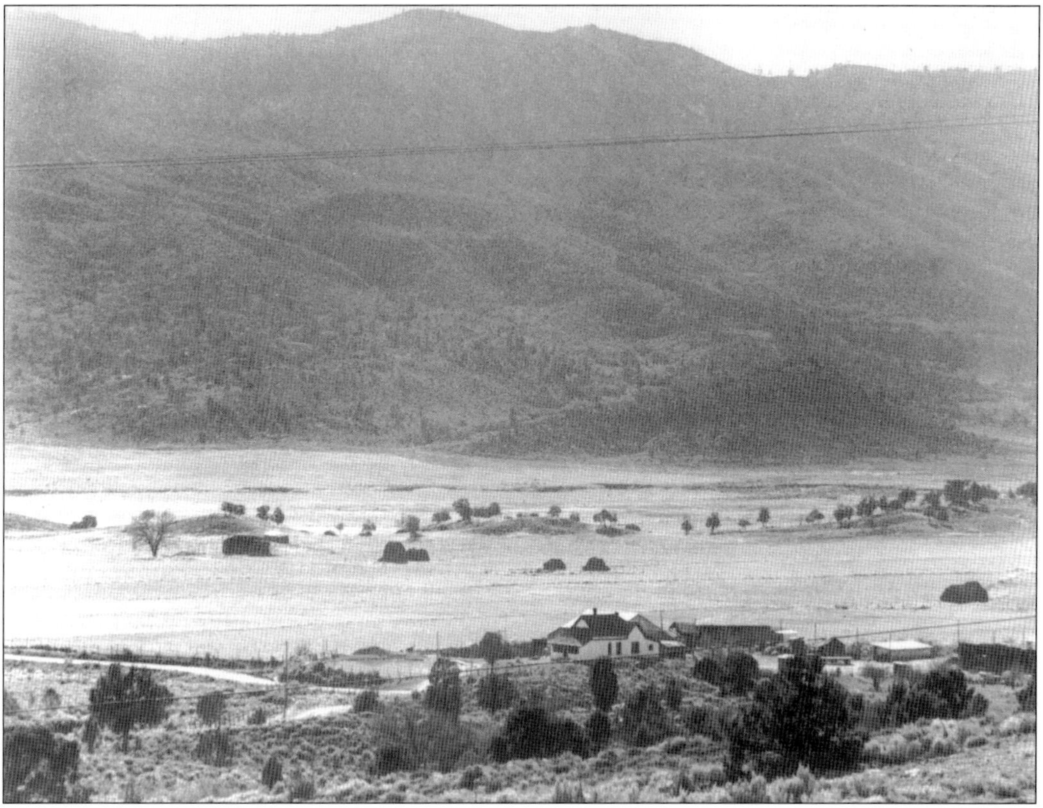

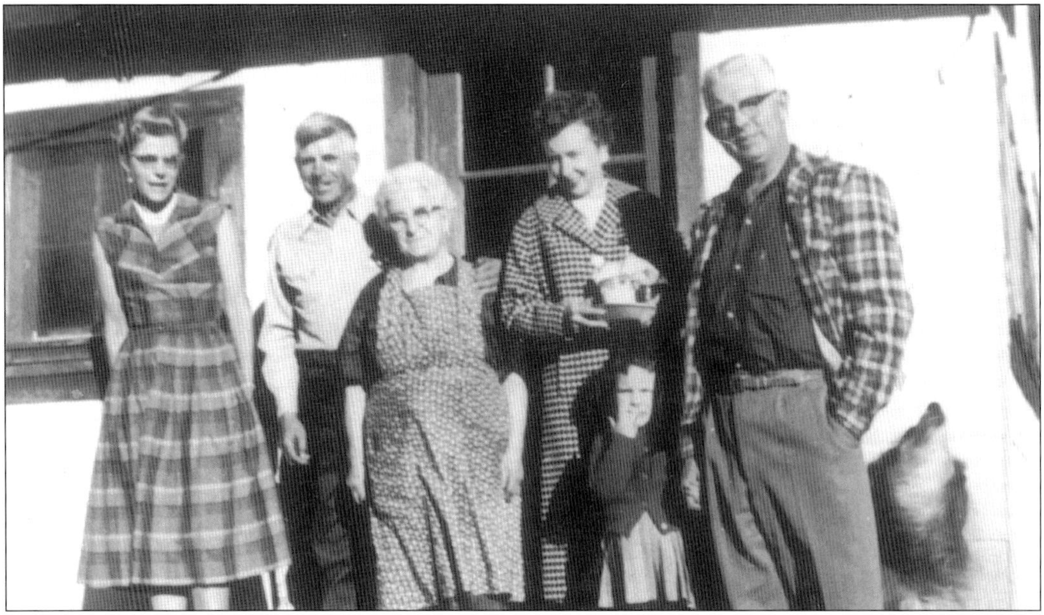

Archie's mother, Rosie (third from left), Archie's wife Hazel (fourth from left), and Archie (right) pose with other family members in front of the old Bodo house. Archie and Hazel were married on November 25, 1931, and spent their honeymoon snowed in on Hazel's father's ranch. "We had to kill five or six deer that were snowed in and butcher them," remembers Archie, "and we had venison every night. I never liked venison after that."

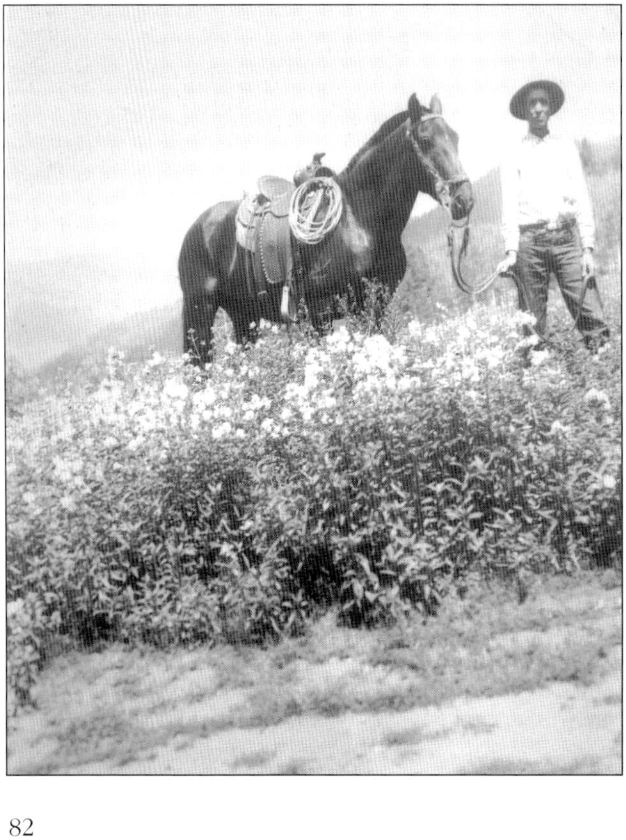

Hazel's father, Henry Lemon, stands out in the field with his horse on the Lemon Ranch. "My dad didn't like anybody else I went with," says Hazel, "but he liked Archie."

"Yes," says Archie, looking over at Hazel, "and she was my mother's pet."

"It didn't make any difference what I did," Hazel laughs, "even if it was wrong. Archie couldn't say a cross word to me because his mom would give him hell."

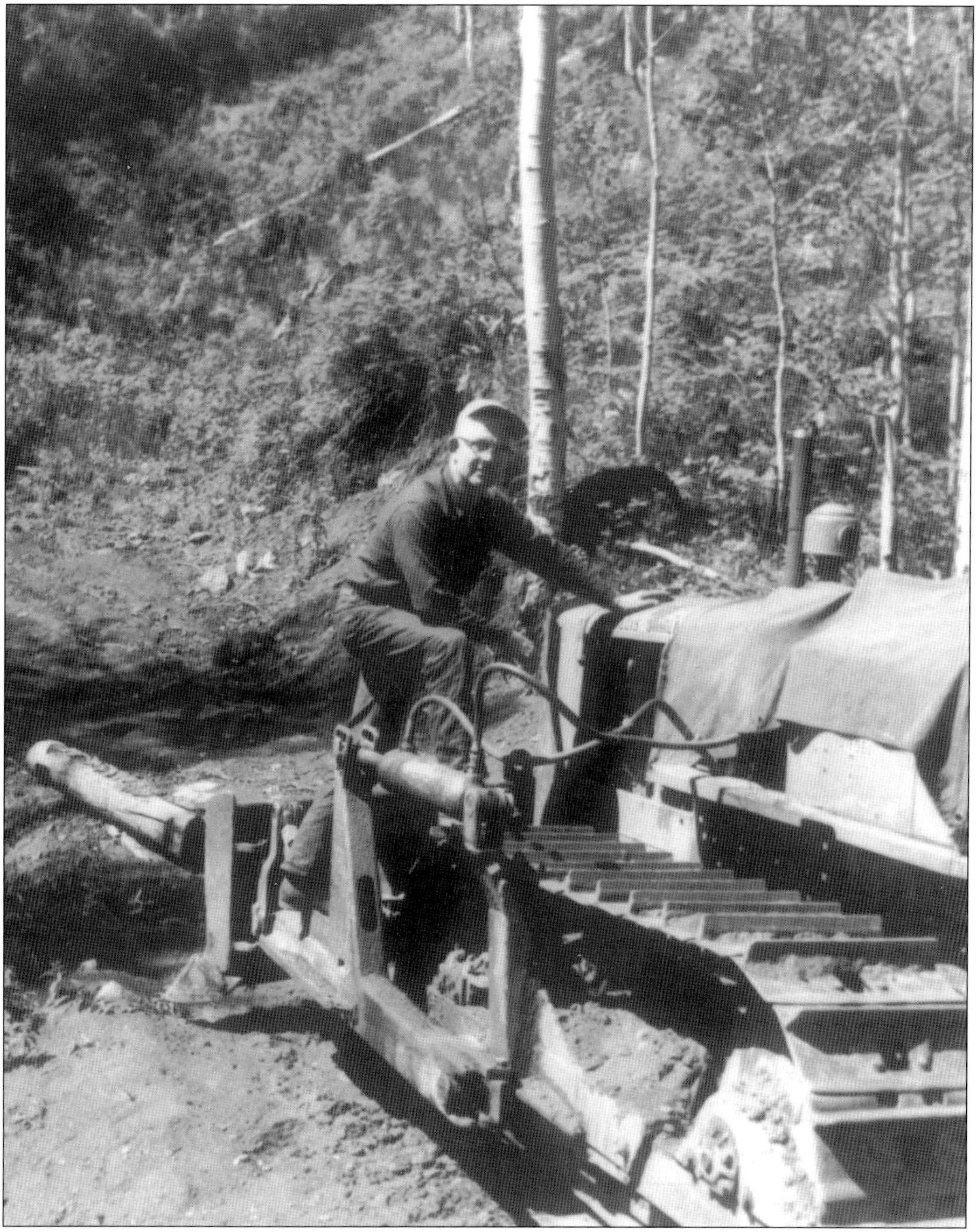

After Archie and Hazel were married, Archie went to work for La Plata County, driving a Caterpillar for 50¢ an hour. "But really I was an automotive machinist," says Archie. "I went to work for the Channel Motor Company, then for Motor Accessory, re-building engines." Then "in 1946," continues Archie, "I already had a building and was ready to go on my own, Archie Bodo's Machine Shop, and had it until I sold it in '83, 45 years." Since retiring when he was 73 years old, Archie still keeps busy. He still owns a couple of coal mines in the area, for instance.

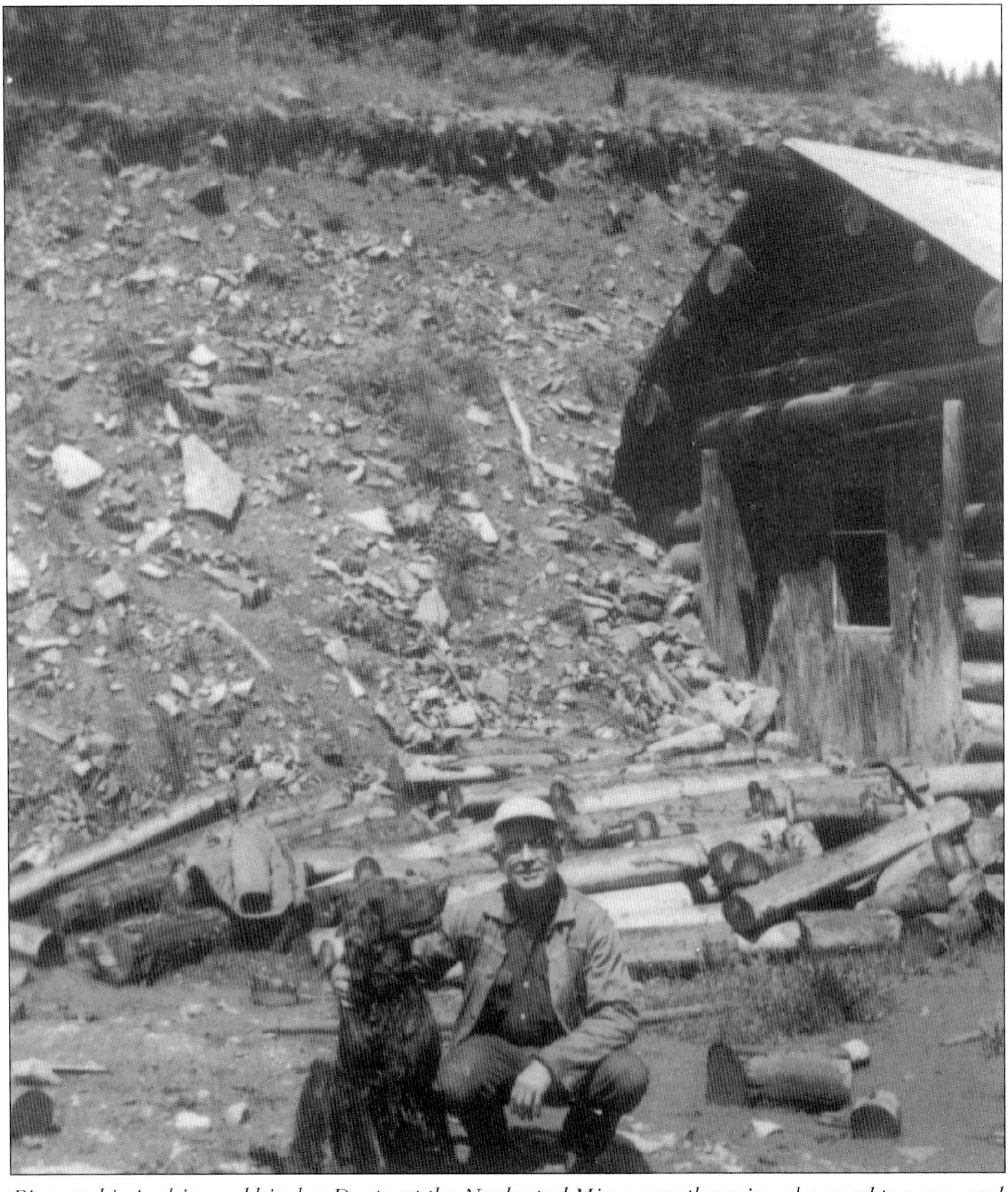

Pictured is Archie and his dog Dusty at the Neglected Mine, one the mines he used to own and work on weekends. "I had to go up to the Neglected and didn't have room for the dog, so I left him in the backyard. Well, every day at noon I'd buy him a hamburger, and come noon, there was Dusty sittin' at the eatery across the street. And Wade Hyatt, who run the eatery, says, 'Go on home, Dusty, Archie ain't here.' Dog wouldn't move. Little while later Wade went out and the dog was still there. Well, he took him all around the restaurant and he says, 'You see, he isn't here, now go home.' Dog sat down and wouldn't move. So Wade says, 'I think I know what's the matter with that dog.' So he fixed him up a hamburger and give it to him and then he come on home. That evening when I came home, Wade says, 'Hey, come over here, I got a bone to pick with you.' And he says, 'You owe me 35¢—your dog charged a hamburger.'"

Chapter 11

A Cowboy Courtship

Charles and Lolly Lemon

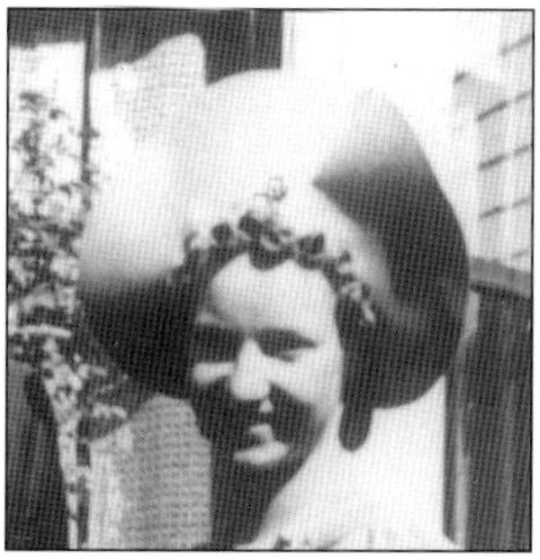

"I met my husband Charles in a potato cellar," says Lolly, "where the Lemon Dam is now." The Lemons bought into that country, up on the Florida Mesa, in 1931, she tells us. "Originally Charles' grandparents settled on Cherry Creek in Denver. Then they moved over into Paonia and the Crawford area. And then they came over to this country."

Charlie's father, Henry R. Lemon, used to work in a pack string when he first moved here as a young man, says Lolly, and then he drove the stagecoach from Silverton to Ouray, eight-head in front of the coach. "He said that there were times when he went over that mountain you couldn't see your leaders."

Henry met his wife, Vivian Slack, in Durango, Colorado, and moved onto the old Locke place in the upper Animas Valley and started farming and ranching there. After all the kids were born, they rented the Jarvis place, by Breen, on the dry side. "They hated it out there," says Lolly, "although they made good, raised good crops, and had a good bunch of cattle. But they hated that wind and they said that they all laughed when they left there and moved up on the Florida."

In about 1938, Lolly's family, the Kaimes, also moved up on the Florida.

"My parents had homesteaded down in the Largo Canyon in New Mexico in the early 1900s," says Lolly, "but we were dryin' up down there. So then my folks purchased approximately half of our holdings up there on the Florida, which worked out good because there was so much poison up there with the cattle that we could go up there with sheep and graze the poison off and then we could use it for cattle. So we rotated the ranges and that worked out real well.

"And so that's how I came to meet Charles. We went up there and they were sacking potatoes in early spring—and that's where I met Charles.

"We didn't really never court each other, though. We just rode horseback all the time. I grew up on a ranch and knew more about a horse and stock than I did about cookin.' So we just rode together and took care of the cattle. And in the fall we were married."

The courtship between Charles and Lolly was really courtship with life itself—the life of a cowboy. Lolly explains:

"Somebody said to Charles, 'Why don't you take a vacation and go somewhere?' And Charles said, 'Well, hell, I go every day on a vacation!' And somebody said to me, 'Don't you get tired of just a workin' on the ranch?' And I said, 'No, every time we go to the mountains to ride, that's our day off. That's what we enjoy."

"Our kids, for our 50th anniversary, wanted to do something special for us, and they said, 'Now you need to go someplace where you've never been and just take some time off.' 'Well,'

I told them, 'you know where I'd like to go, where I've never been?' And they said, 'Where, where's that, Mother?"

"'Picnic Flats,' I said. I'd never been to Picnic Flats."

"And they just about died. You know, it's kind of like the Hermosa up there. I always wanted to go up there and ride that range and never did get a chance to. So one summer we took a pack horse and our two horses and we went up there. We spent five days up there on that range, riding it, and it was great!"

But did they ever get a real trip, a real vacation?

"On the 17th of April in 1991," says Lolly, "after our 51st anniversary, we planned a trip to Hawaii. And we paid all our kids' expenses. And we spent about 12 days there."

But then, just a few years later, Charles suddenly died.

"Heart attack," says Lolly. "His legs were all wore out, you know. He got around with a cane. But he'd still get on that black horse, Spirit, and he'd go work cattle. All that week they cut out cattle, getting ready to go to the mountains, you know, doin' what he liked to do.

"And then, Sunday, he didn't feel like going to church. That was Father's day. And we had turkey and angel food cake. And he ate a little bit. And that night we went to bed. And midnight, he woke up, and he said, 'I'm sick at my stomach.' And I said, 'Maybe you should go to the doctor.' And I was just a kiddin.' I knew he wasn't goin' to any doctor. And he said, 'Well, I'm not goin' to any doctor.' And then he just laid back there in my arms and never said one more word, never moved a finger or nothin.'

"But what a wonderful way for a cowboy to go."

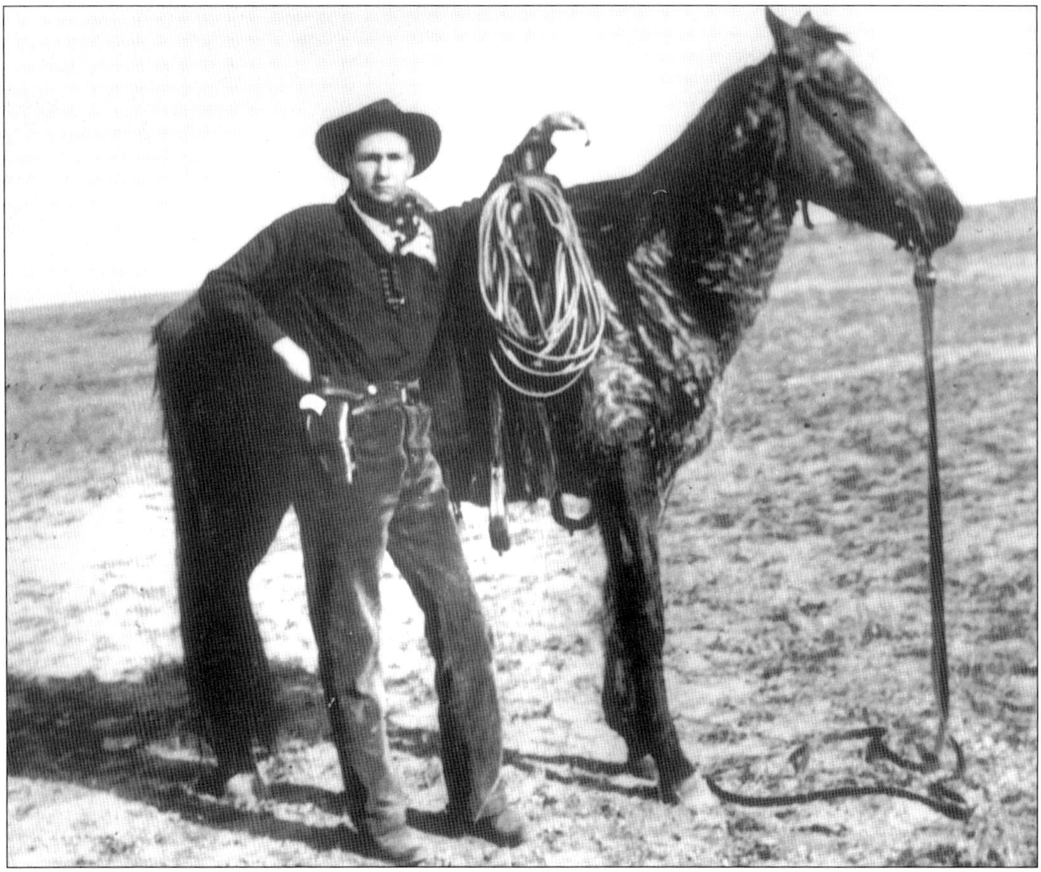

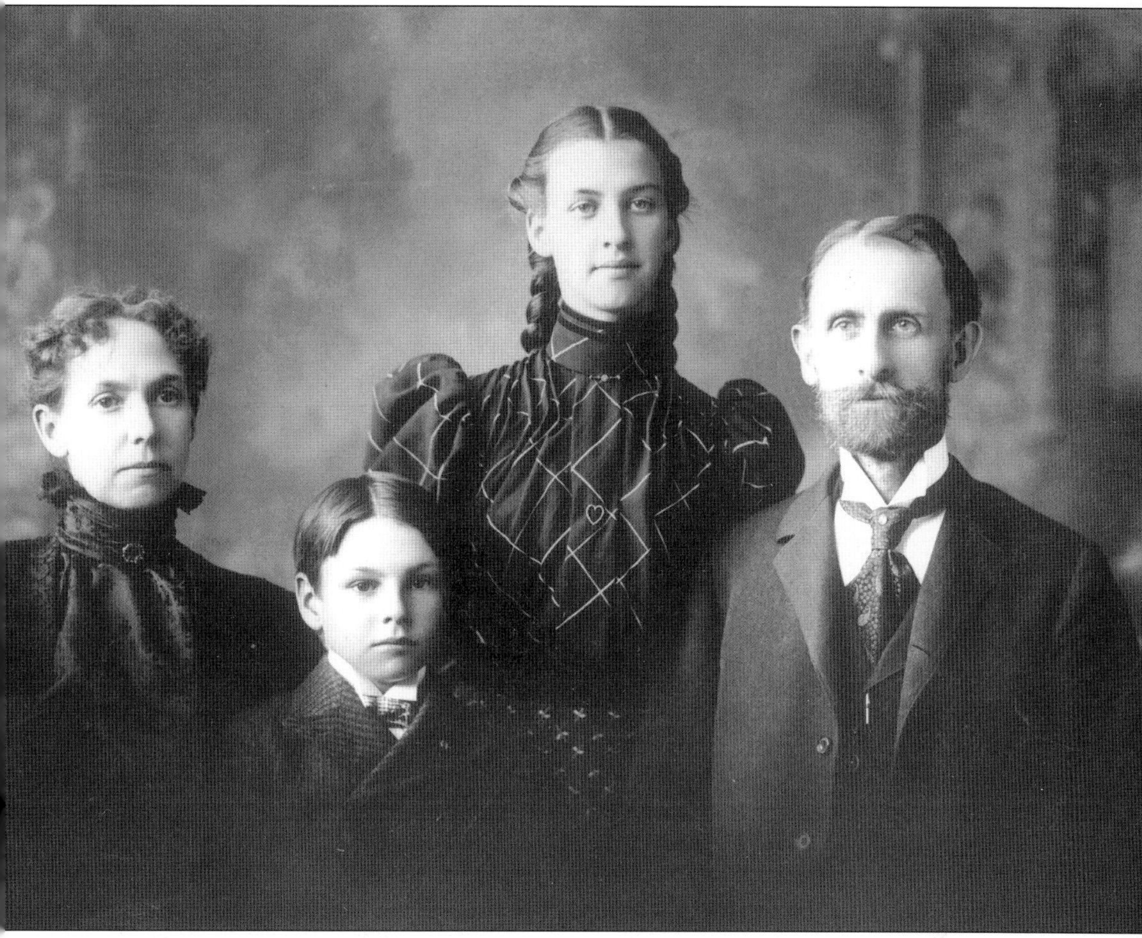

Lolly's grandmother (left) and grandfather (right) pose for a family photo with young Clifford (second from left), April 28, 1898.

(opposite) *Laura "Lolly" Lemon's father, Clifford H. Kaime, homesteaded land in Largo, New Mexico, in the early 1900s, before moving to the upper Florida River in La Plata County, Colorado in the late 1930s. Clifford was raised the son of a banker in St. Louis, but came west to go to school at the Colorado School of Mines and then go into cattle ranching in New Mexico.*

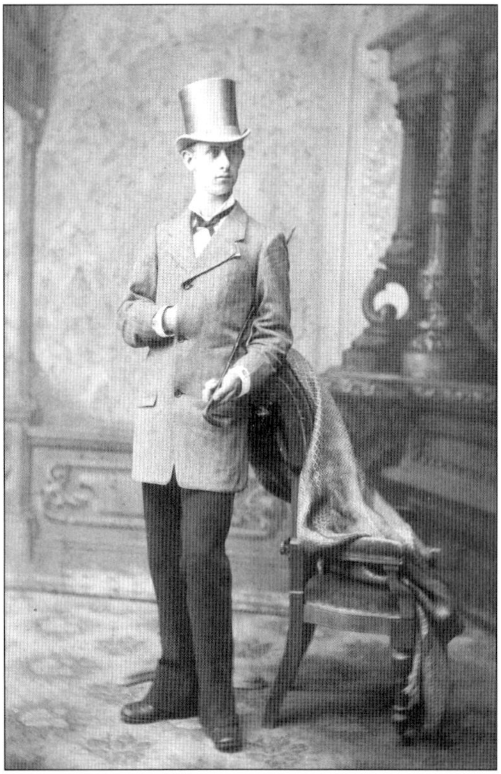

Lolly's grandfather, Edwin F. Kaime, the banker, poses for a formal picture back in St. Louis.

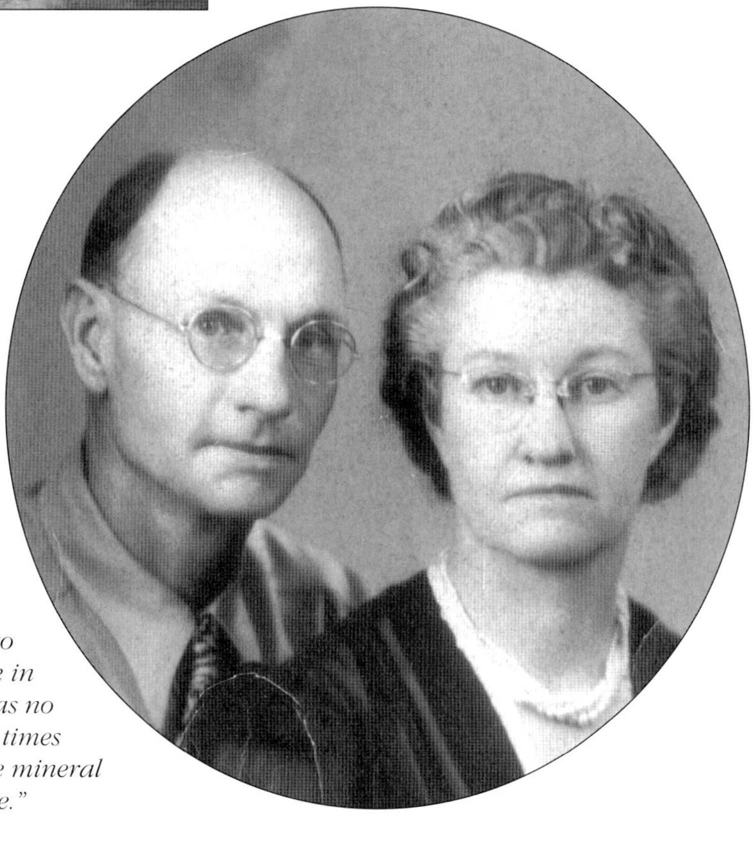

This picture is of Clifford Kaime and Lolly's mother, Gladys H. Kaime, somewhat later in life, after they had moved from New Mexico to the Florida Mesa. "My parents had the mineral rights for all that land down there in Largo, New Mexico," says Lolly, "which turned out to be the gas fields. But back in those days, when there was no money to be had and the times were hard, they sold those mineral rights for a dollar an acre."

Lolly poses with her dog on their ranch on the Florida. Before they had cattle, Lolly's parents ran sheep on their ranch. When she was young, Lolly tells us, she was a fiddle player and used to take her fiddle with her to sheep camp. "I'd take my fiddle in the evenings," says Lolly, "and I'd get to fiddling away out in the tules and the sheep would all gather around."

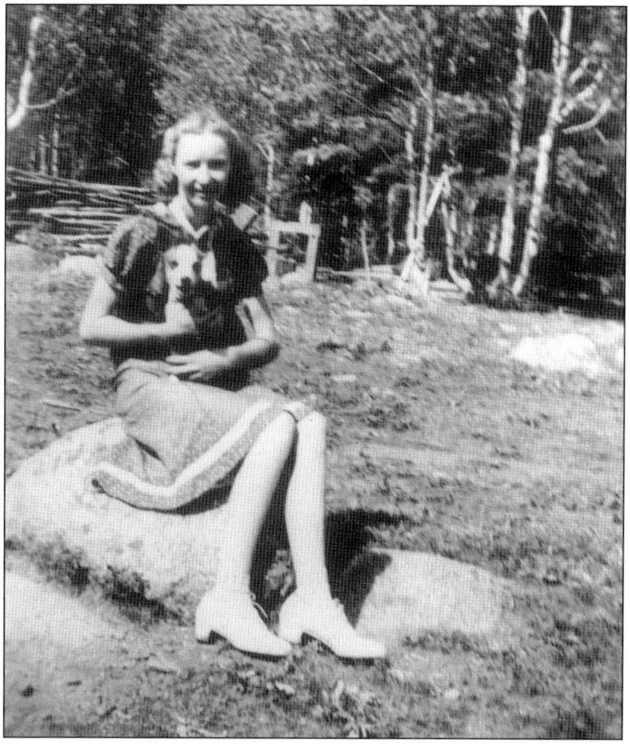

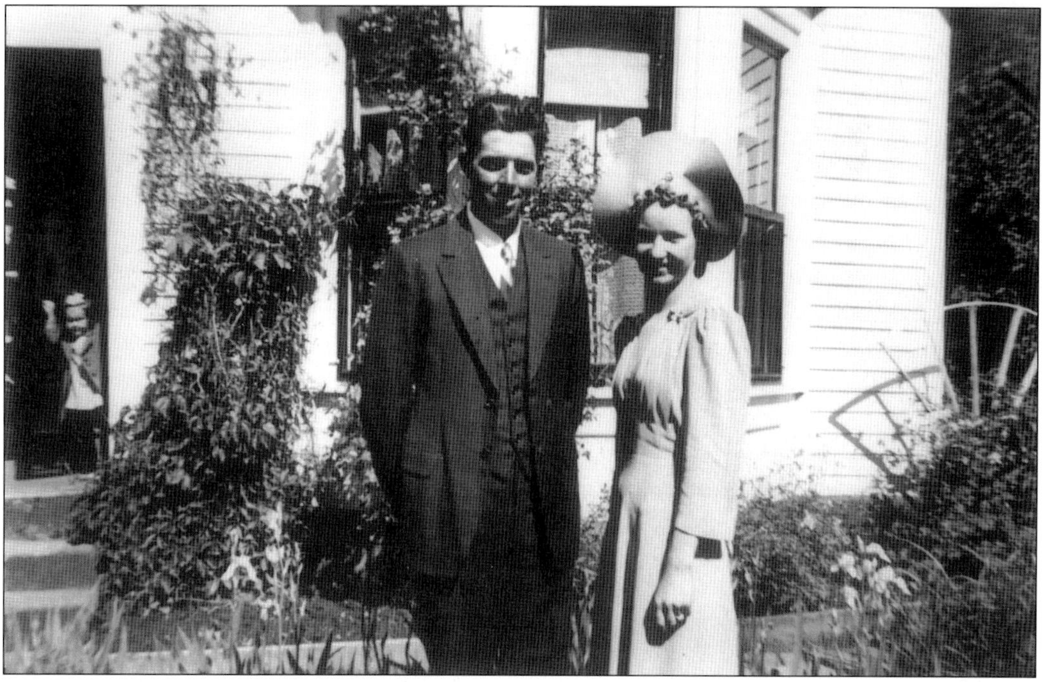

Charles and Lolly Lemon were married in 1940 in Aztec, New Mexico. As Lolly remembers it, Charles proposed to her on a horse. "He'd been dating my sister who was nine years older than I was and that fell apart," says Lolly, "so he decided he'd try the younger sister, which worked out real fine. We had 55 years of happy, married life together."

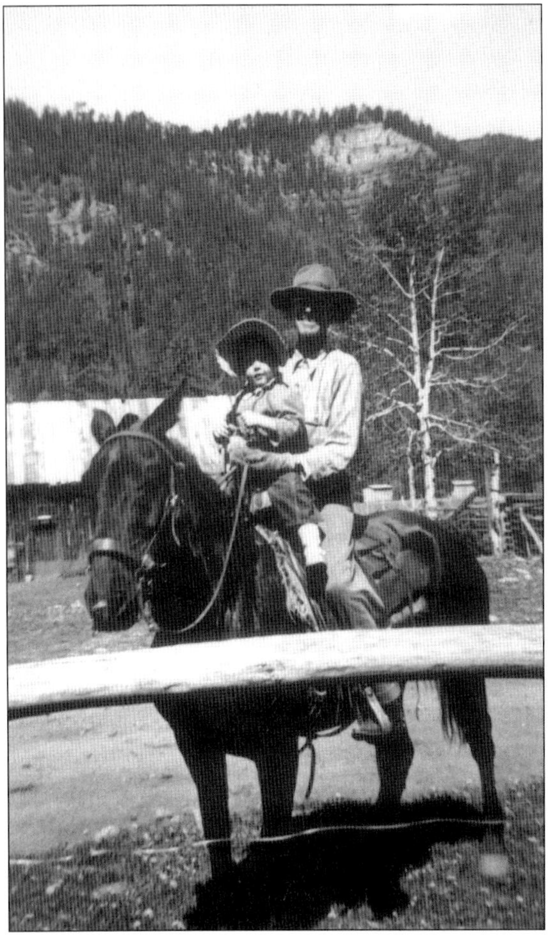

Lolly's father-in-law, Henry R. Lemon, poses here with a granddaughter on Old Cody. "Henry R.," says Lolly, "oh, mercy, him and I were the best of pals. Of course, I was married so young, I just grew up in the family, and they just taught me everything I knew."

Lolly's mother-in-law, Vivian Slack Lemon (center), sits with her sisters on the porch of the factory-built Lemon house on the old Lemon Ranch. Henry met Vivian in Durango, Colorado, went back to Missouri—where Vivian was from—to marry her, and eventually settled up on the Florida Mesa where the Lemon Reservoir is now.

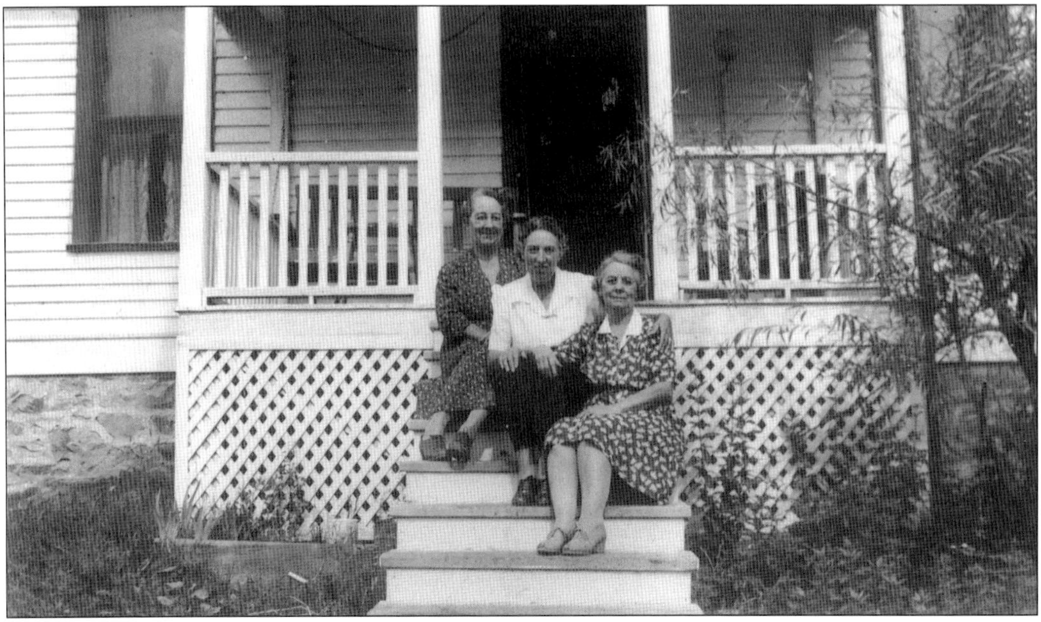

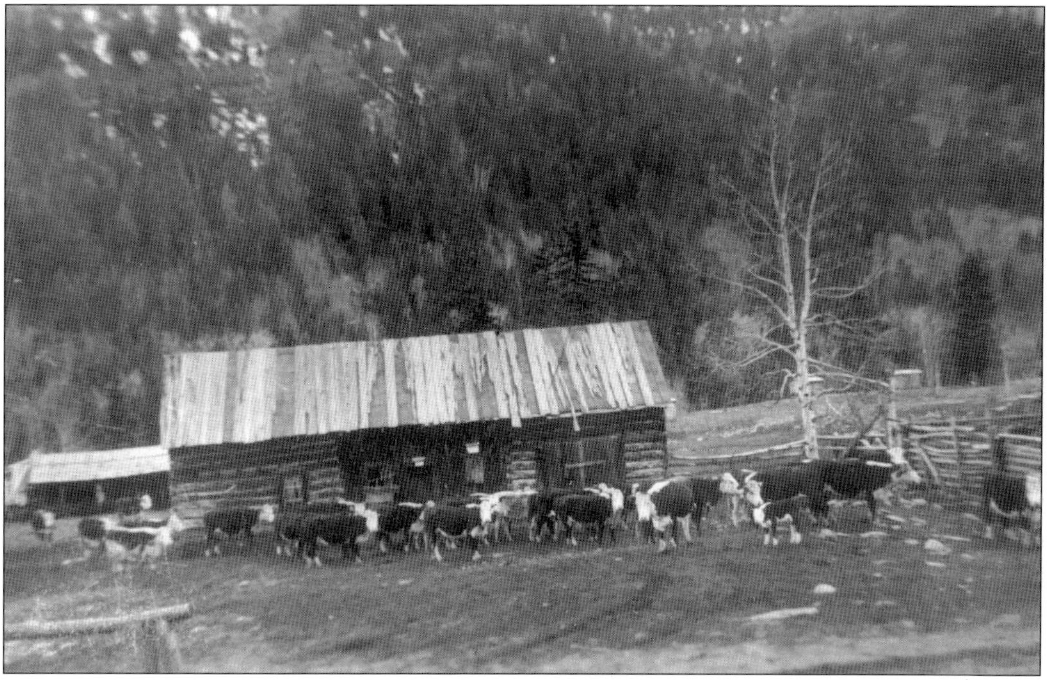

Here we see the old bunkhouse at the Lemon Reservoir site. "When we still lived up there," says Lolly, "the surveyors would come and want to make test holes and all that kind of stuff. So Henry would meet 'em at the gate with his 30–30 and tell 'em 'You're not going in.' So they'd come back saying, 'That damn Lemon!' And finally they decided to name it 'Lemon Dam.'"

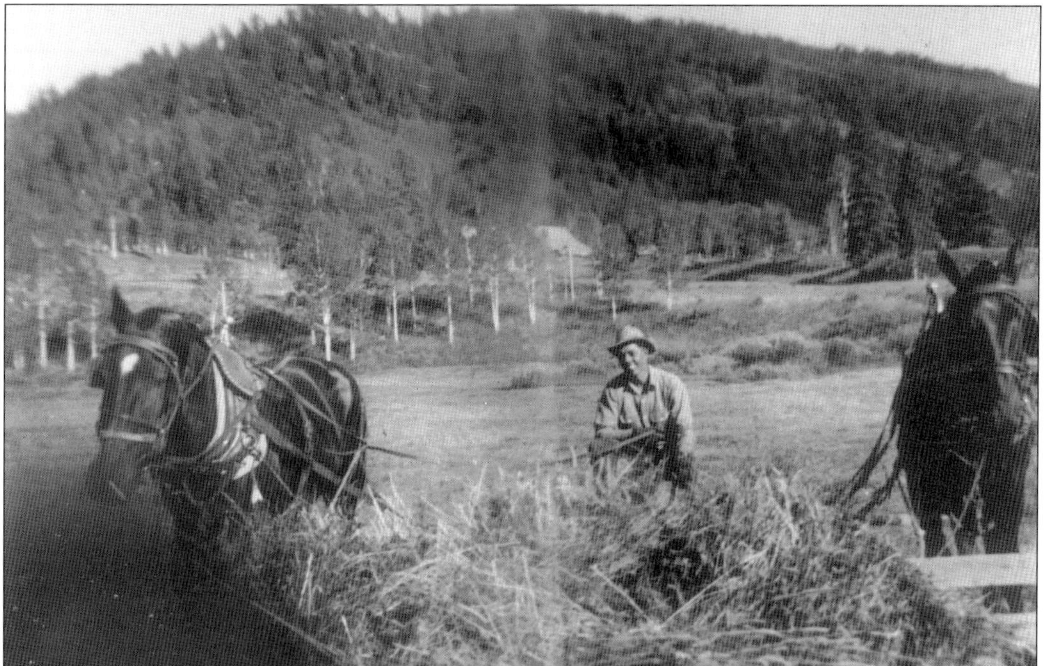

Charles is bucking hay on the old ranch.

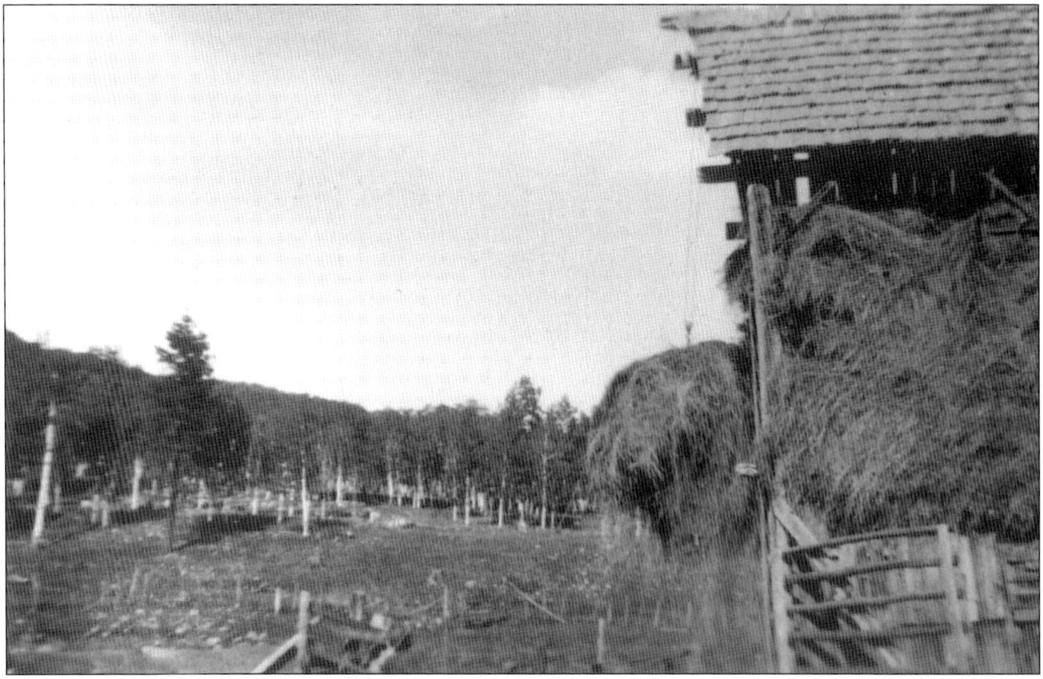

Charlie and Lolly's hay used to be put up in the barn with a harpoon fork, just as its being done here.

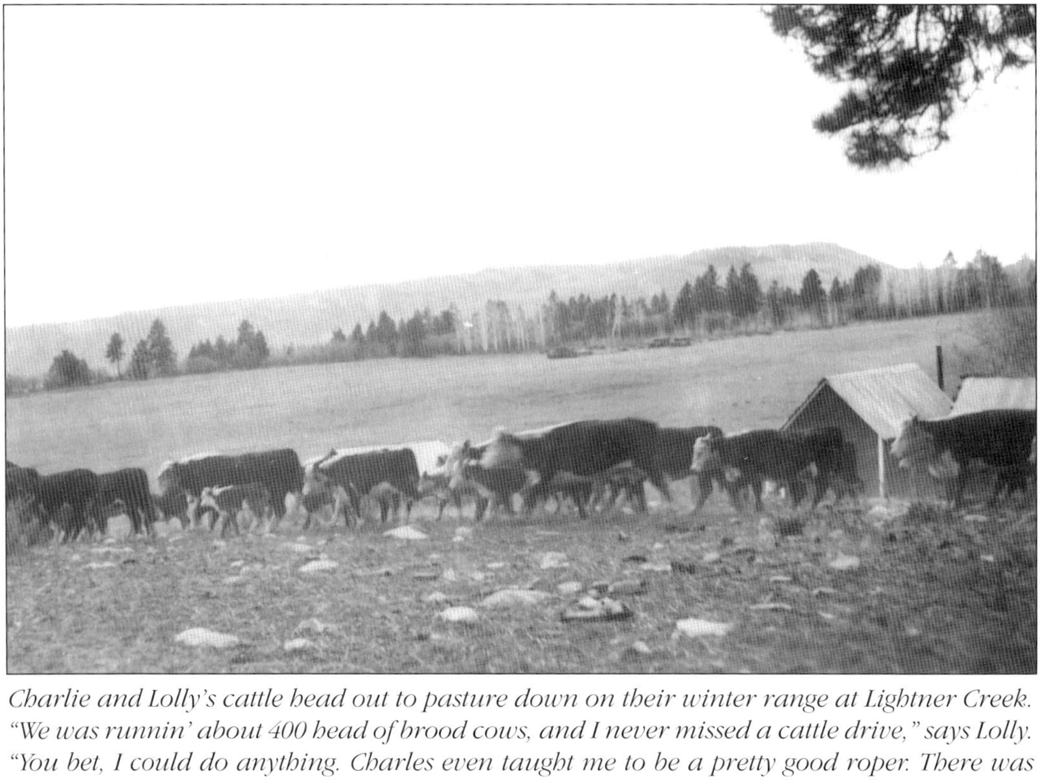

Charlie and Lolly's cattle head out to pasture down on their winter range at Lightner Creek. "We was runnin' about 400 head of brood cows, and I never missed a cattle drive," says Lolly. "You bet, I could do anything. Charles even taught me to be a pretty good roper. There was only one thing I didn't have to do and that was castrate the calves."

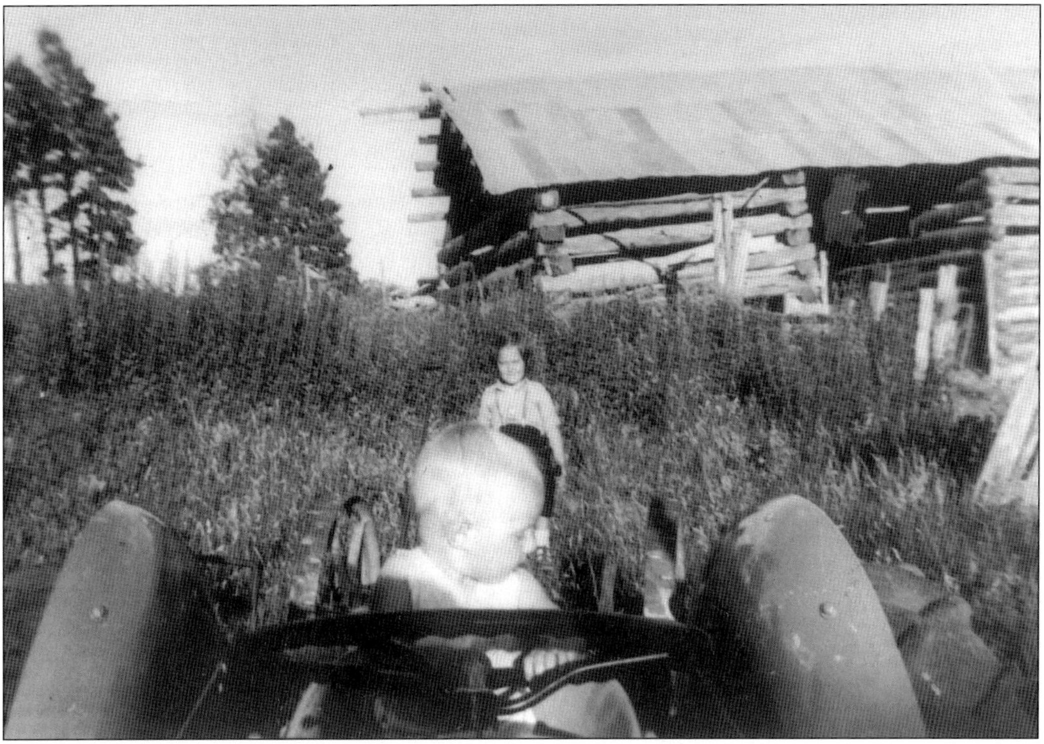

Two of the kids play on the tractor in front of the old barn on the Lightner Creek ranch.

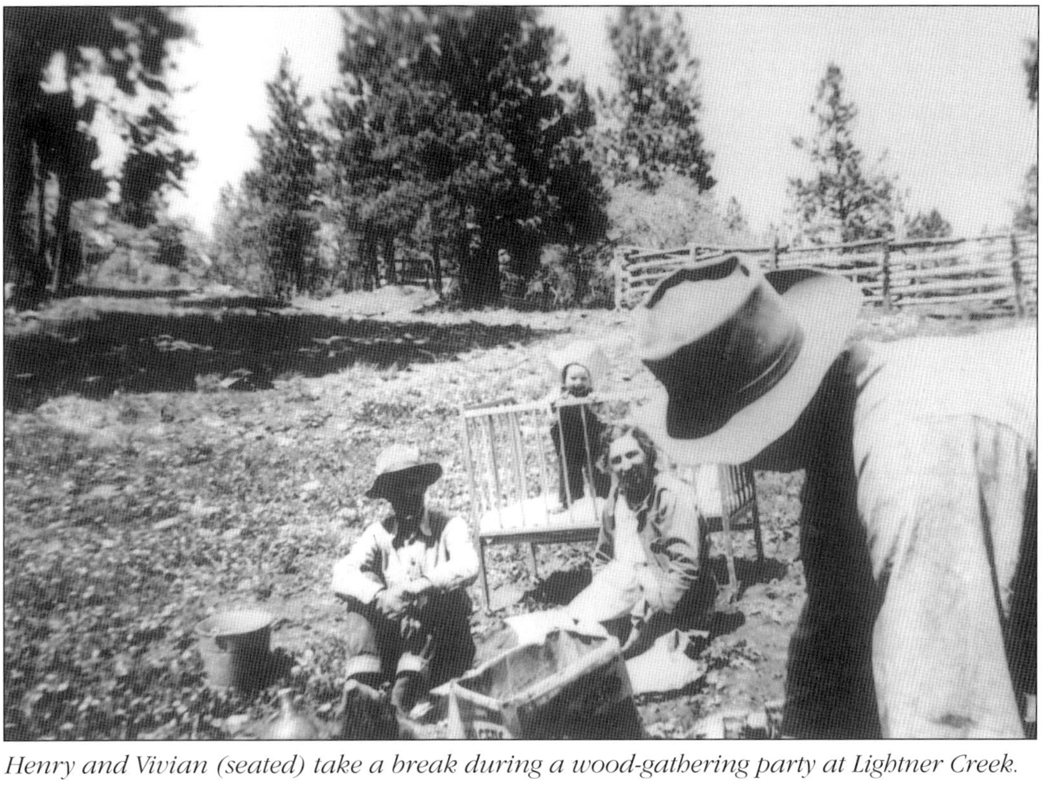

Henry and Vivian (seated) take a break during a wood-gathering party at Lightner Creek.

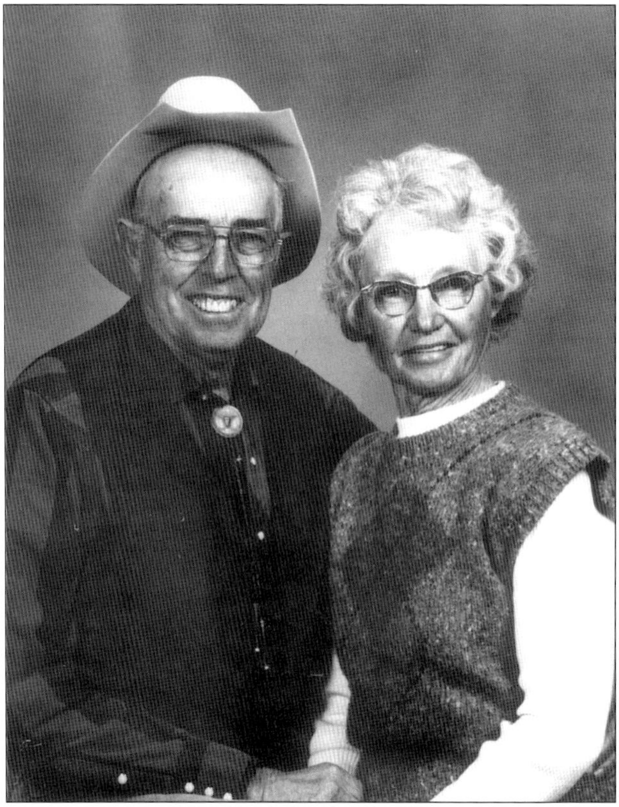

Charles and Lolly pose for their 50th anniversary. "After we got married," says Lolly, "we thought we would take a little honeymoon, you know? So we got a room in Farmington, but it clouded up that night and the next morning we got up and there was snow on the ground. So that took care of the honeymoon. We come home and started feedin' the cows."

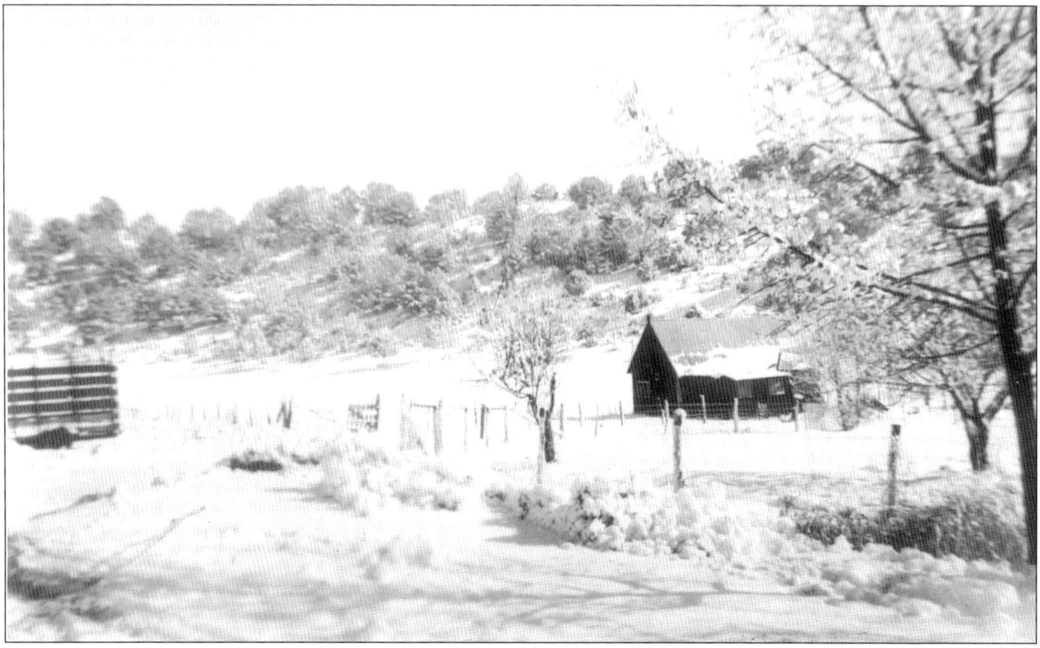

Snow falls on the ranch at Lightner Creek.

Chapter 12

The Lechner Sisters

Mary Ann and Lethia Leola Lechner

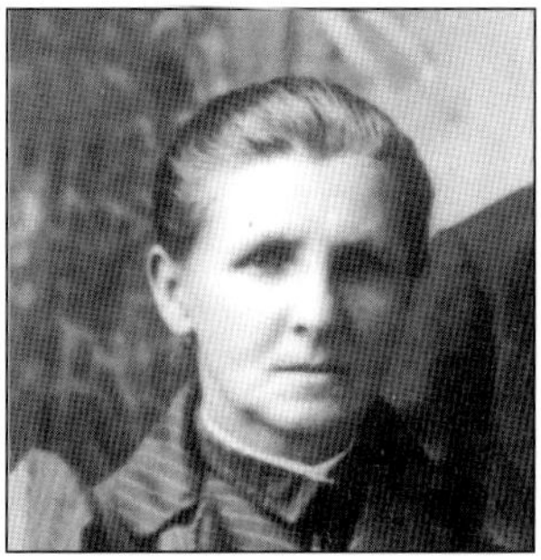

Mary Ann and Lethia Leola Lechner's grandmother, Maria Daum Lechner, left Austria for Colorado before she was married.

"Then she met our grandfather, Francis Lechner, up there around Denver," says Mary.

Francis and Maria Lechner married and came to La Plata County, Colorado, Mary and Leola tell us, in 1881. "They homesteaded up at Electra Lake. Then after they built the dam, they bought that place where Needle's store is, the old Lechner Ranch."

MARY: When we lived there at the ranch in Needles, I was about six. I can remember the Indians, all their wagons and horses, going up the road and over the hill to Ouray in the summertime.

LEOLA: I don't remember much about it, but I was born there.

MARY: You know that log house where they have a restaurant in there now? That was our uncle's house, Peter Daum's. He built that house and they lived there for years.

LEOLA: The house where I was born I guess burnt. But I remember the dances at the old schoolhouse there. We lived right west of Haviland Lake then...

MARY: Just north of Tamarron, our place joins part of Tamarron.

LEOLA: There were five brothers from up there at Needles, John, Frank, Joe, and Anthony—Anthony was our dad—and Louis...

MARY: But Joe lived in Rockwood.

LEOLA: Sometimes our Uncle Joe from Rockwood would pick us up in his Model A. Or we rode horses or walked or took a sleigh in the wintertime.

MARY: Sometimes we took the car. I started driving about, I guess I was 16, I drove twice or so. And then I started driving from here to school in Durango with a carload of kids. We went to school at St. Columba's in Durango.

LEOLA: When we started, we went to school up there at Rockwood, in the one-room schoolhouse, across Elbert Creek, way back there in the corner. We took the old school buggy. Mother used to drive it.

***

Mary and Leola's grandmother on their mother's side, Mary Washington Williams Boyce, came from Kansas. She and their grandfather, Artemis Worchester Boyce, first came over to La Plata County from Lake City—over Stony Pass and down to Silverton—by covered wagon.

"They had to hire a man to hang onto the upper side of the wagon," says Mary, "to keep them from rolling down the hill."

Mary and Leola's mother, Annie Laurie Boyce, was born on the way, in Salida, Colorado, and then moved with the family to New Mexico. "Mama and Grandma Boyce took care of cattle for different people that lived in New Mexico," says Leola. "They'd bring those cattle up and they'd take care of them up there at Cascade, clear up to Engineer Mountain, in the summertime."

MARY: That was free range then.

LEOLA: They were cowgirls.

MARY: One time my grandmother Boyce was driving the wagon and some goats scared the horses and they ran away toward this big arroyo. And Annie, our mother, took after them—she was a' horseback—and she caught the horses and stopped them right before they got to the arroyo.

LEOLA: Yup, Mama was a real cowgirl.

***

Mary and Leola's parents, Anthony and Annie, met up in north La Plata County, married, and eventually settled on the ranch at Haviland Lake.

LEOLA: We raised hay.

MARY: And potatoes, lots of potatoes.

LEOLA: And we had a milk cow.

MARY: And a pig. And dad was trapping. Us kids trapped. We made quite a bit of money. We used to catch lots of weasels and muskrats.

LEOLA: In those days, that was the thing. But our dad worked out quite a bit, too. He worked for the Forest Service, he worked for the power company up at Cascade, and he built houses. He and his brothers were contractors for Haviland Dam.

***

Mary and Leola left the ranch at Haviland Lake when they both got married. Leola moved with her husband to a ranch near Ticolote, New Mexico.

"We moved out there in '45," says Leola, "and I moved to Durango in '84."

Mary moved with her husband to a ranch near Ignacio, Colorado. "We bought a ranch down there in '49," says Mary. "Then after he passed away, I had to sell the ranch and I moved here to Durango."

"I'm not crazy about being down here," says Mary. "I always would rather been out in the country. It ain't bad here, but you don't run your life like you do out in the country."

(opposite, top) *Mary and Leola's grandmother, Maria Daum Lechner (left), and grandfather, Francis "Frank" Lechner (right), pose for a portrait with their family, including Mary and Leola's father, Anthony (second from left). Anthony was born on the old homestead where Electra Lake is now on July 6, 1889. After the dam was built at Electra, Frank and his family moved to the Lechner Ranch at Needles, Colorado.*

(opposite, bottom) *Here we see Mary and Leola's grandmother, Maria Daum Lechner, in front of her house in Durango. After their grandfather Francis died, explains Leola, "they bought this house on Third Avenue in Durango. And later, when we went to St. Columba school, we lived across the street from her."*

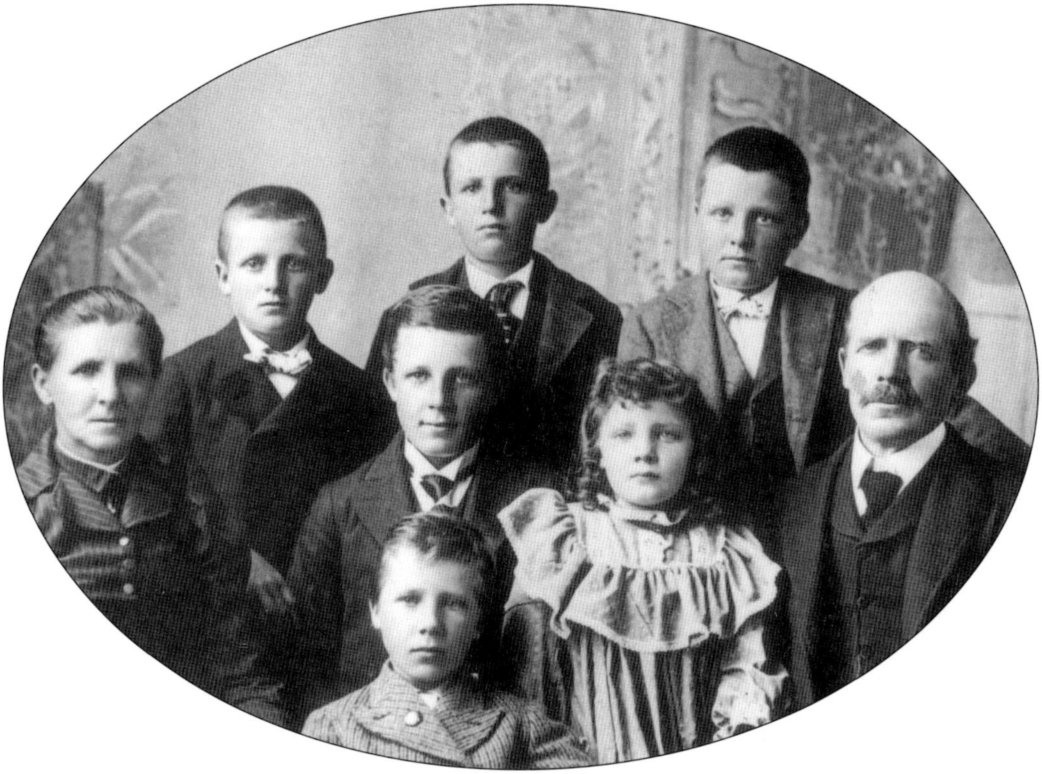

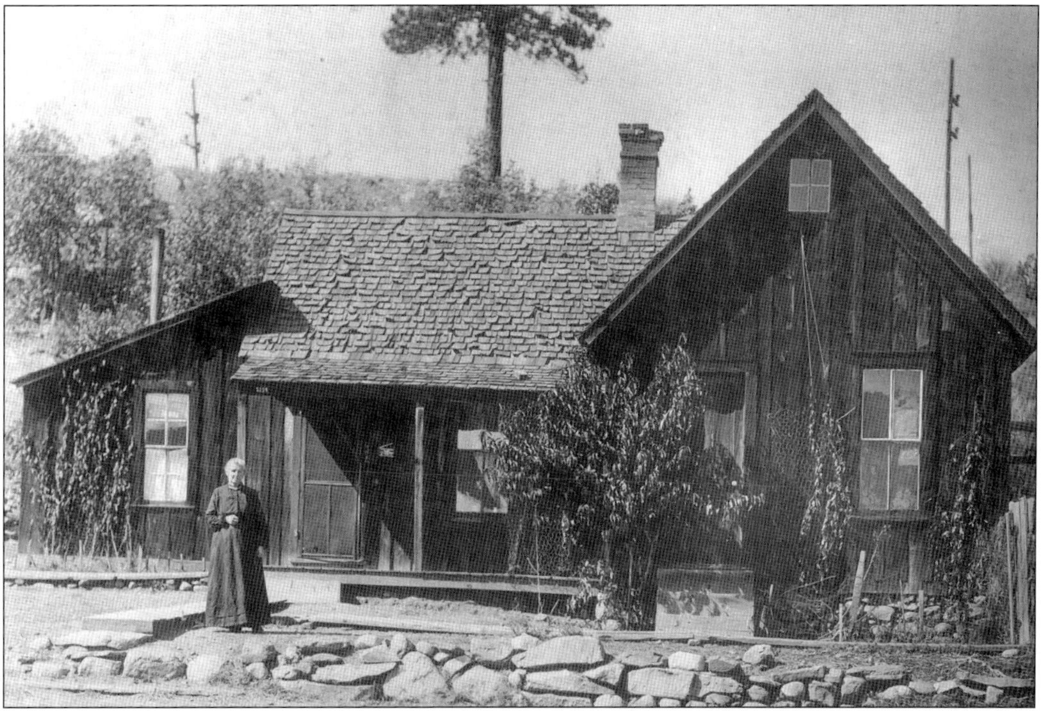

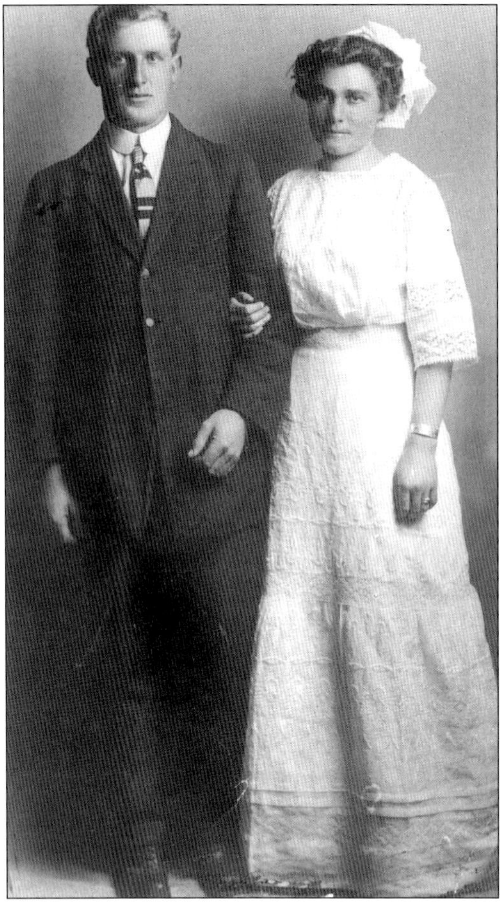

Mary and Leola's grandfather and grandmother, Francis "Frank" Lechner and Maria Daum Lechner, were married on November 4, 1882, shortly after they had emigrated from Austria to La Plata County, Colorado, via Denver in 1881. Frank, born in the Tyrolean Alps in 1857, was a soldier in the Austrian army before coming to Colorado.

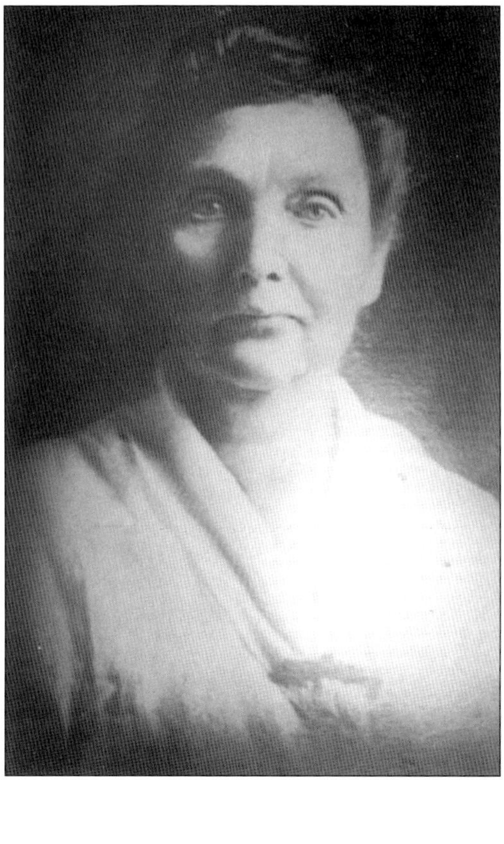

This is a photo of Maria in her later years. Francis died in 1911, so Mary and Leola never got to know their grandfather. They did get to know their grandmother, though, when they went to high school in Durango, where Maria lived after Francis died.

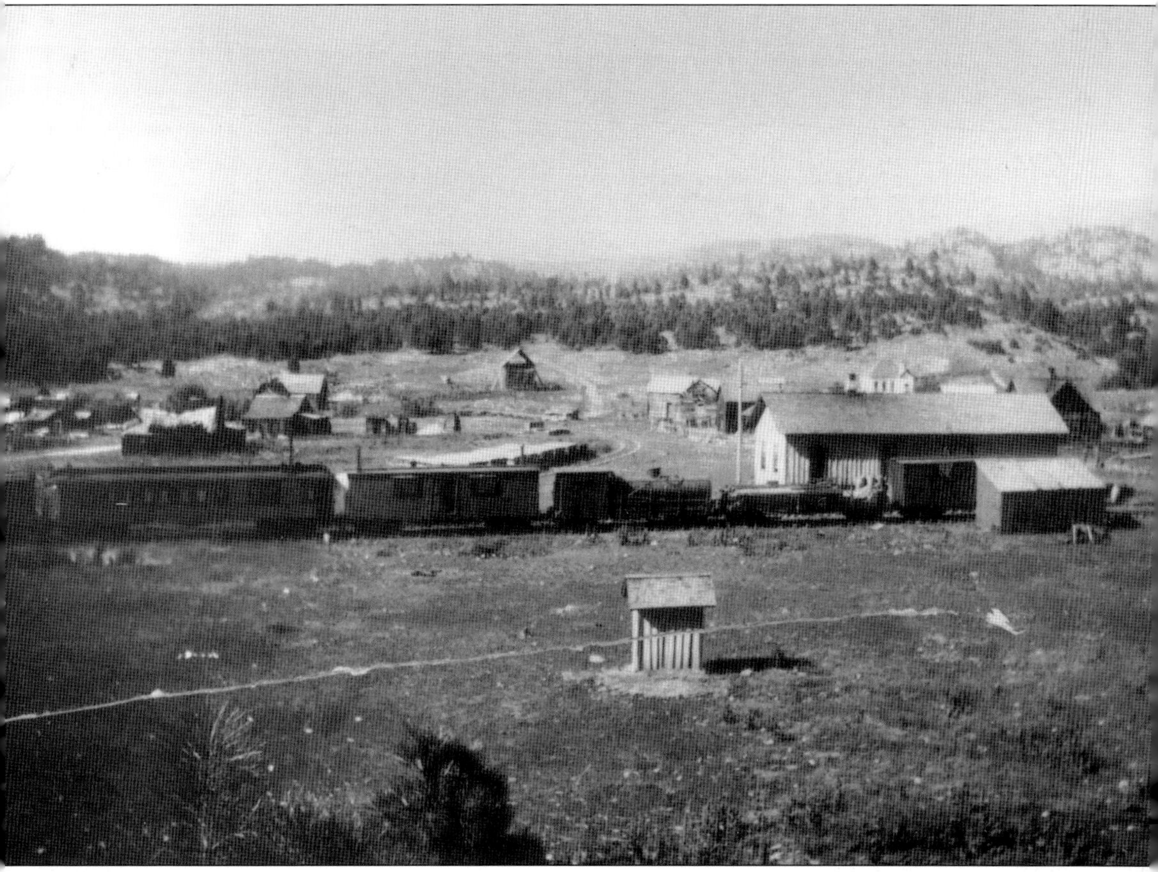

Directly behind the Denver & Rio Grande railroad depot at Rockwood, pictured here, was the ranch of Mary and Leola's uncle, Joe Lechner. Mary and Leola used to visit their cousins at the ranch. "We didn't have any other neighbors," says Leola.

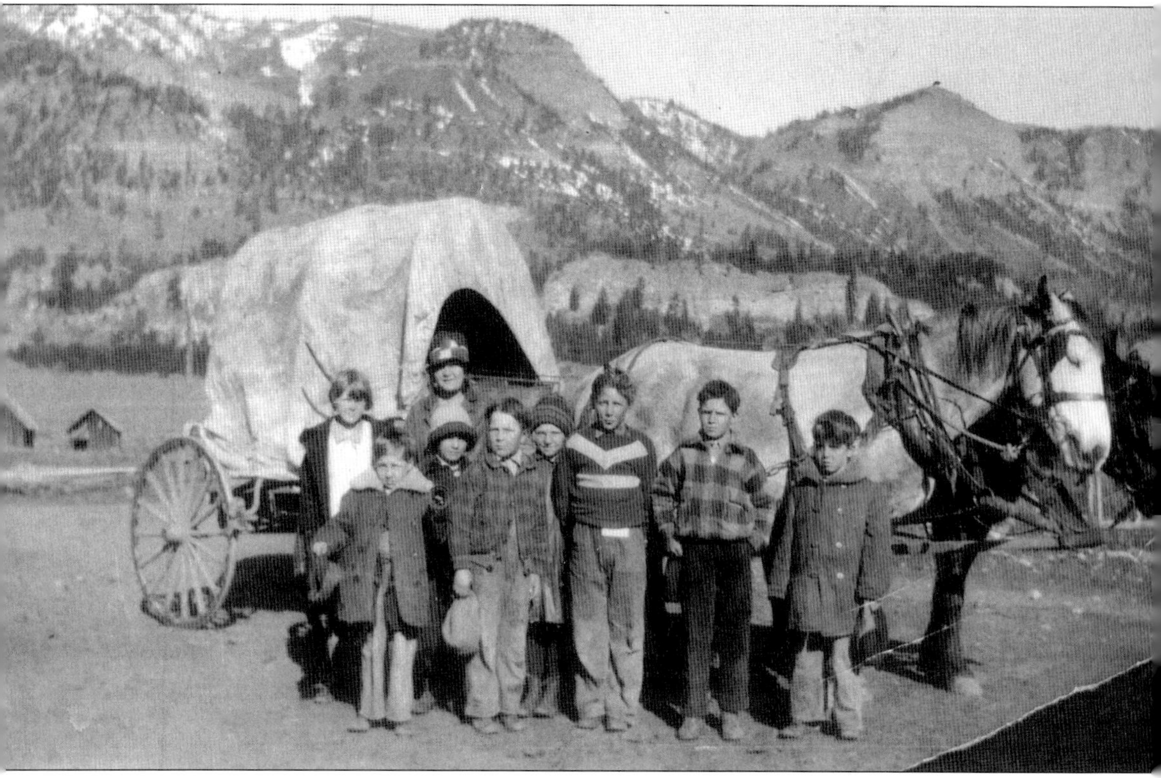

Mary and Leola Lechner grew up on a ranch just west of Haviland Lake, north of where the Tamarron resort property is now, but they went to school in Rockwood, which is south of the resort. Mary (rear, right) and Leola (front, fourth from left) used to ride to the school at Rockwood in this old wagon, the "Old School Buggy," which their mother used to drive.

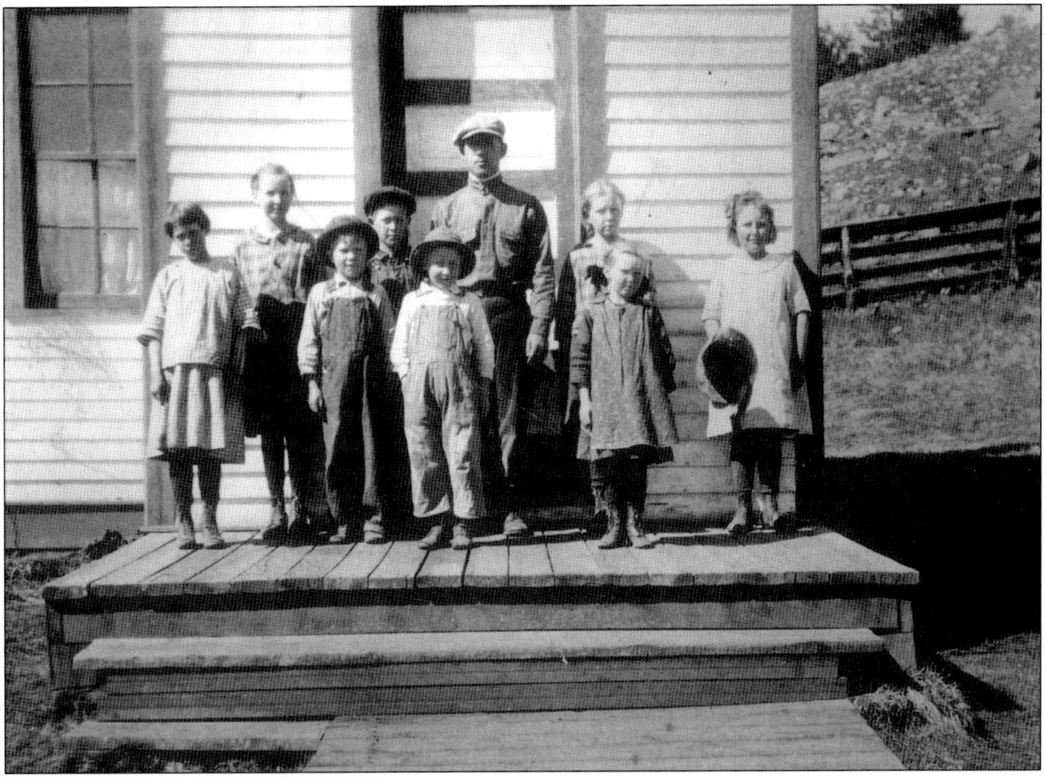

Here we see a picture of Mary (right) at the old Rockwood School.

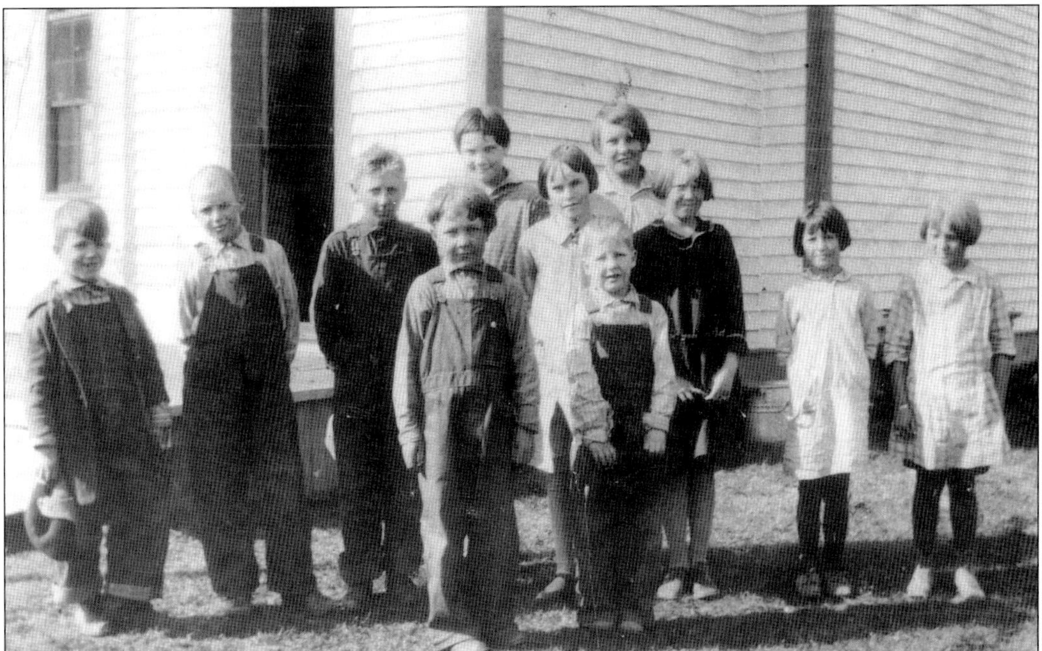

Pictured here are Mary (rear, right) and Leola (middle, extreme right) at the old Rockwood School.

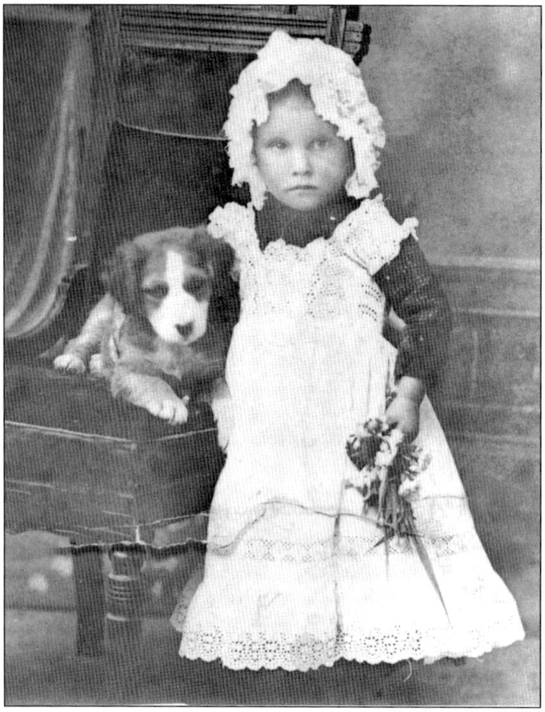

Mary and Leola's mother, Annie Laurie Boyce, shown here when she was about three years old, was born in Salida, Colorado. She came west from Kansas in a covered wagon.

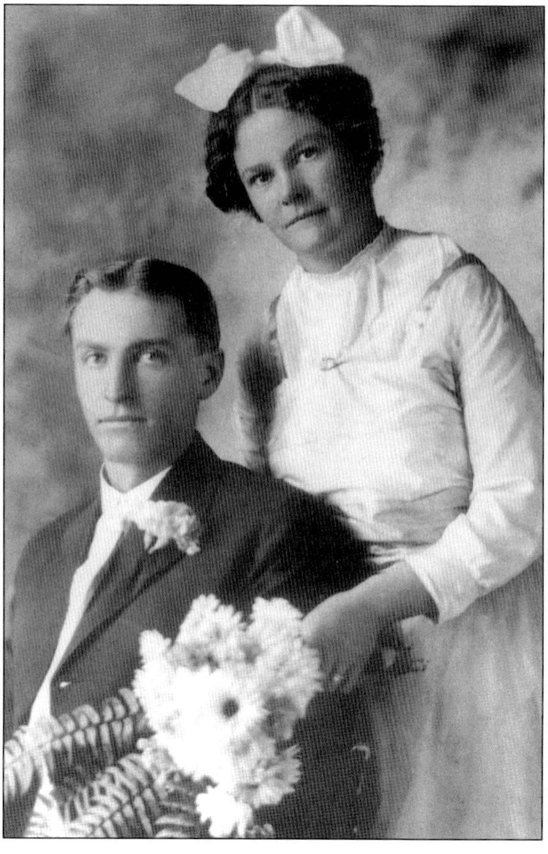

Pictured on their wedding day are Mary and Leola's parents, Anthony and Annie Lechner.

Chapter 13

But Whatever Happened To His Best Friend's Girl?

Luther L. Willbourn

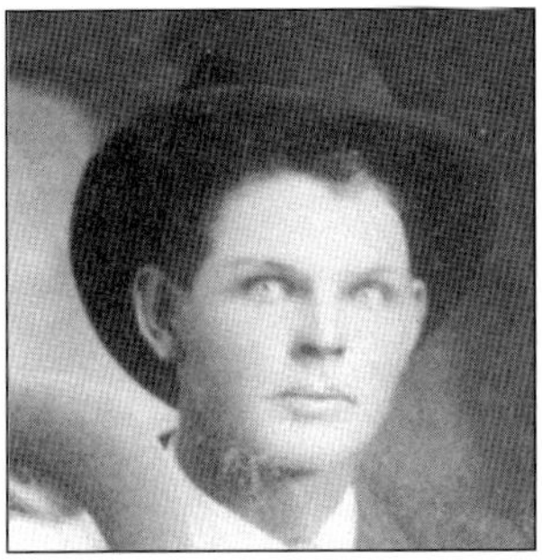

One day last spring Frances Anderson got a letter in the mail. "El Reno, Oklahoma" read the return address:

Hello,

I would like to contact any of Luther Willbourn's descendants. My dad and Luther were very good friends. I called information and they said there is one Willbourn but it is an unlisted number. Can you find someone that might know of this family?

Thank you,
Lillie (Calvert) Kappus

Frances Anderson's father, Luther L. Willbourn, came here from Oklahoma with his mother, Elizabeth Bell Willbourn, in the early 1900s, homesteading 640 acres near Bayfield, Colorado, adjoining another 640 acres his mother homesteaded right next door.

Dear Frances,

I know you are probably saying after all these years, 'why now?' My dad, Mark Calvert, was Lena Willbourn's brother. Lena was Titus Willbourn's wife. My dad and Luther went to Colorado together and worked on the Waters and Scrivner Ranch. I don't know how many years my dad worked out there, but his father became very ill so he had to come home. I think he would have gone back to Colorado, but his mother was alone and needed someone to take care of her. So he stayed, but he always talked about Luther and laughed about the things they had done. Then my dad married my mom, but I don't think he was really happy with my mom. I think my dad was always thinking about what happened in Colorado. He was always out beside the barn whittling on a stick.

The story goes that Dad wanted to marry a girl in Colorado and thought that maybe he would inherit the Waters and Scrivner Ranch. Later on, after he married my mom, Lena told him that Luther had married the girl he was sweet on and that Luther had inherited the Waters and Scrivner Ranch. I have heard since that this was not true....

Lillie Kappus

On February 12, 1909, Luther married Cora E. Lyons, daughter of Luther Martin Lyons and Kate Mahan Lyons, who had homesteaded a place just down the road in Ticolote, Colorado. Cora's father was from Texas and her mother was from County Cork, Ireland. Luther and Cora Willbourn had seven children, only two of whom, Maxine and Frances, are left.

Dear Frances,

I found the enclosed picture in some of my dad's things. Do you have any idea who it is? It had his name written on the back.

I'm anxious to see pictures, especially of your dad. I would like to see one of him in his younger days, when my dad knew him.

Lillie

Luther Willbourn ran Herefords and raised hay and grain on the land he had acquired. This included the sections he and his mom had originally homesteaded and three other ranches he had purchased, altogether totaling more than 2,000 acres.

In 1975, shortly before Luther Willbourn died, some of the kids tape-recorded some of his last recollections.

Dear Frances,

I called Cecil Calvert, my dad's brother, and talked to him. He said that about 1913 Lena and Titus Willbourn came out to Colorado to the Waters and Scrivner Ranch and worked. He said Titus and Luther roped wild horses and took them to Ft. Worth to sell.

My sister Lena says that she remembers that the boys lived in the bunk house but ate at the big house.

Do you remember anything about your Dad working at the Waters and Scrivner Ranch?

Lillie

"I was delivering cows at the agency in to Ignacio, and I got up on the end of the Florida there, and it was the last delivery in February.

"I had 43 head that time—and it was cold! But I had to get going, you know. I was helping an old buddy of mine, and he says, 'Well, you gonna take 'em?'

"I says, 'Yeah.' And I cut 'cross country. I thought it'd be faster. And it was snowin' and blowin' and colder than a nickel.

"And I'd go and break the trail, you know. There was no blazes, you know. And I'd go and break the trail and push them cows up in there and then they'd just stop.

"But I got 'em in to Ignacio and I got 'em corralled. And ol' Andy Jackson, he'd come down. And we watched 'em till past 12 that night. I'd fought them cattle all day long. And I said, 'Well, I guess I better find the livery stable.'

"He said, 'Bring your horse up there.' And we took the horse up there. And then we had to cross the river again—they had a foot bridge across the river—and so we went over. And I ate and was gettin' ready to go to sleep. So Andy says, 'Aw, I'll take you over and you can sleep in the store.'

"And I did.

"And he said, 'Don't be in any hurry about gettin' up.'

"And it was, I don't know, about nine o'clock the next mornin' before I got up."

"That's a pretty good day's work wasn't it?" asks another voice on the tape.

"Oh, yeah," says Luther, his voice trailing off, "I put in a lot of them kind of days."

And then somewhat quieter, Luther begins again. "I went to work for. . . ," the words inaudible. "They had quite a few mules. . ."

"Well, you worked for Waters and Scrivner then for how many years?" someone on the tape says, trying to get Luther started again.

Luther seems to have a hard time clearing his throat. "I think five years—two years the first time..."

"Well, you was working for them the first time, before you went back to Oklahoma, then came back and worked for them some more, right?" someone says again, a little more insistently this time.

"Yeah, well, I went to Colorado and worked for old man . . . " This name we can't make out at all. But the tape continues, "to clear out the line for the Idaho Pass, and, uh . . . "

And then the tape just goes dead.

But what about Mark Calvert, Luther Willbourn's best friend? And whatever happened to his best friend's girl?

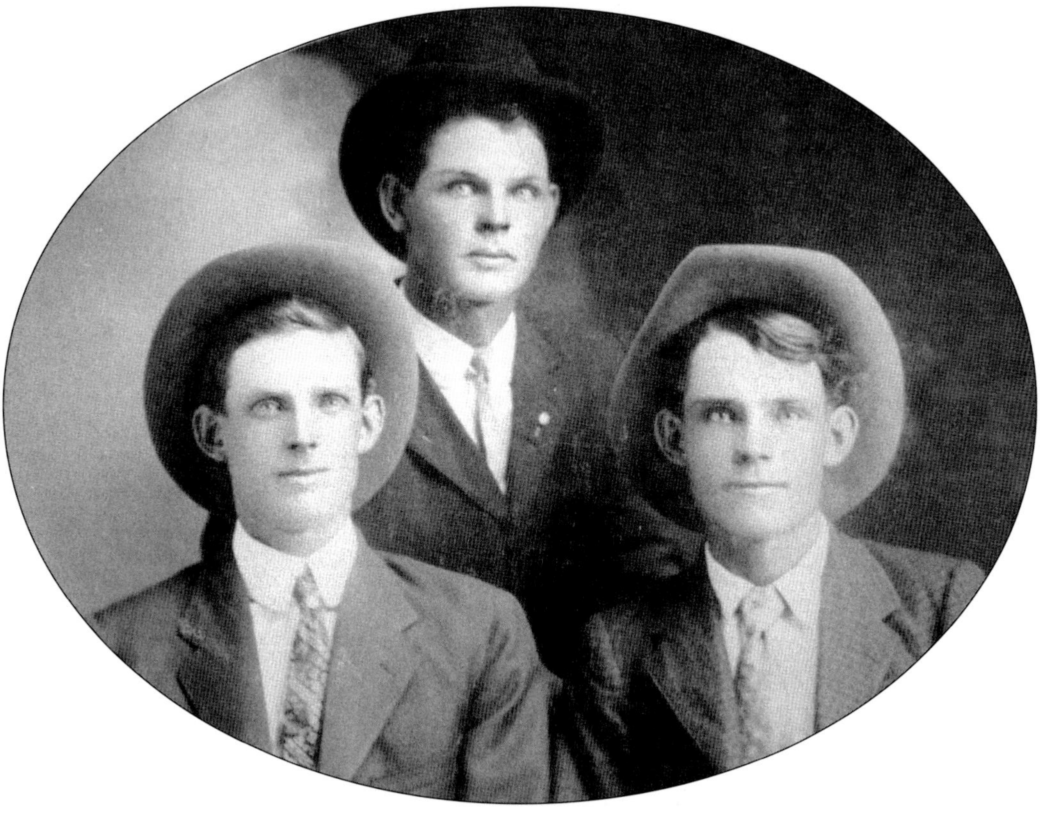

Apparently, Frances Anderson's father, Luther Willbourn (right), came from Oklahoma to La Plata County with brother Titus (possibly left) and his best friend Mark Calvert (possibly center) to work on the Waters and Scrivner Ranch in 1913. After Mark Calvert left Colorado to go back to Oklahoma and tend his ailing father, Luther supposedly married Mark Calvert's girl.

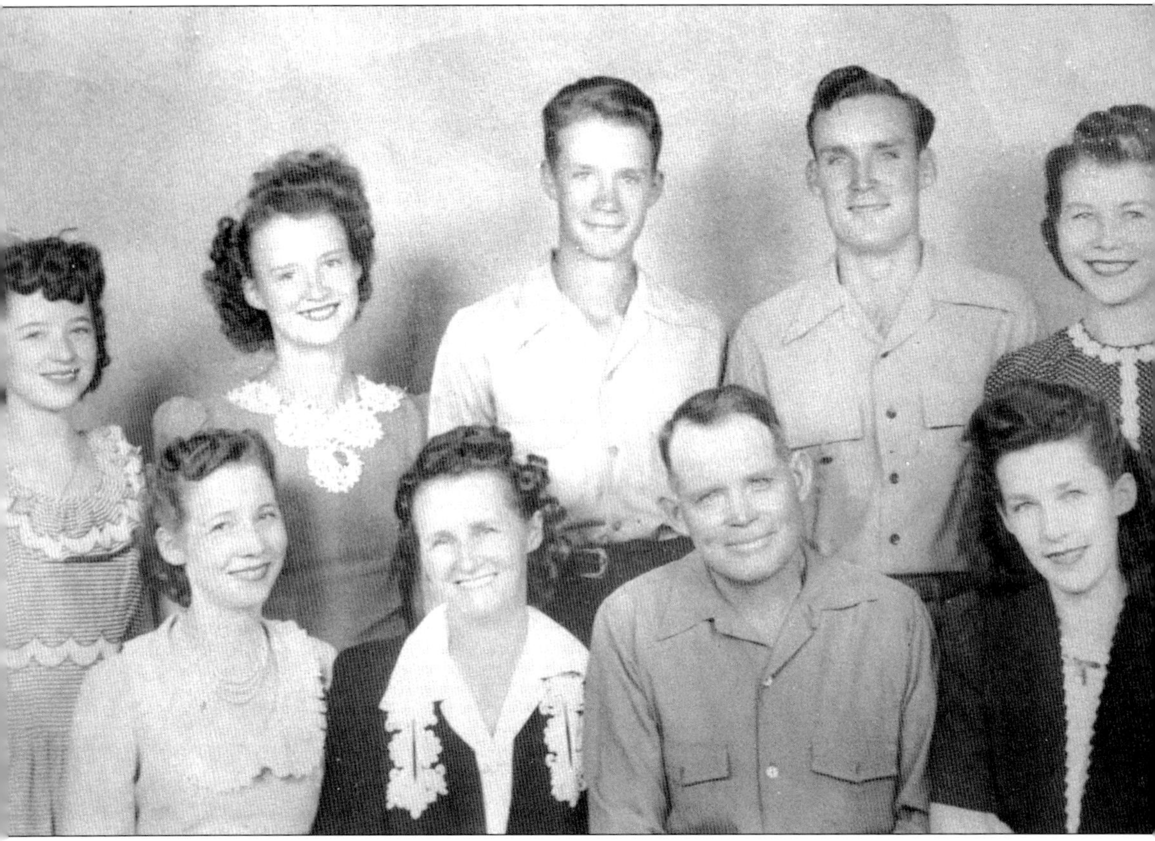

Frances Anderson's parents, Cora E. Lyons Willbourn and Luther Willbourn (front, center), pose with their family, including Frances (rear, second from left),

Francis Anderson's grandfather on her father's side, Thomas Willbourn (pictured here), was a homesteader on what was then Indian territory on the Washita River in Oklahoma. Francis Anderson's father, Luther L Willbourn, was born in Washita County, Oklahoma, on October 3, 1887.

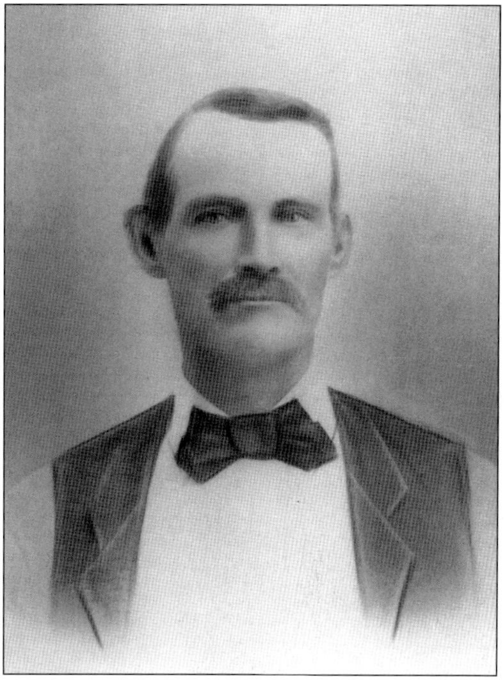

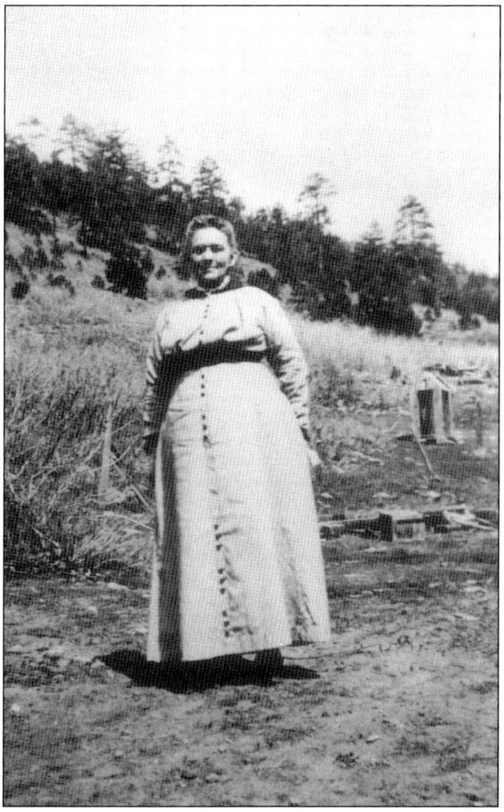

In the early 1900s, after Thomas Willbourn died, Luther came from Oklahoma to Bayfield, Colorado, with his mother, Elizabeth Bell Willbourn (pictured here). Together they homesteaded two 640-acre tracts next to each other that ultimately grew to the 2,000-acre spread known as "The Willbourn Ranch."

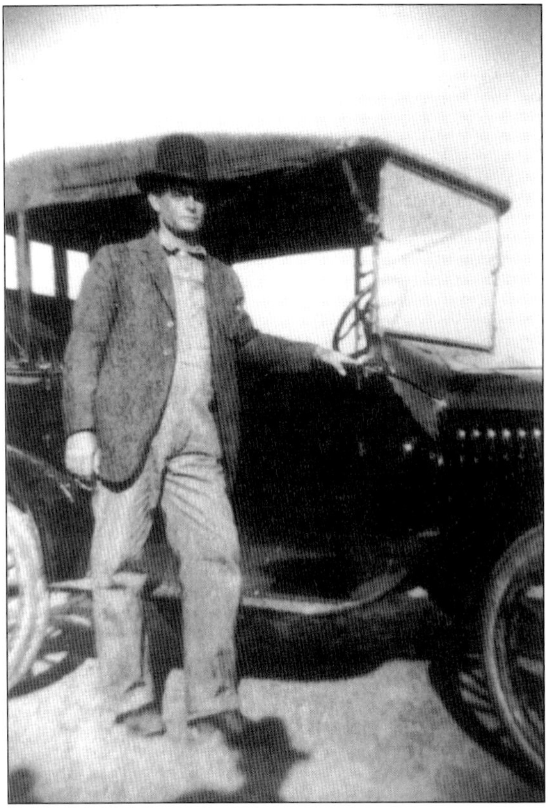

This photo is of Mark Calvert, Luther Willbourn's best friend. According to letters sent to Frances from Mark Calvert's daughter, Lillie Calvert Kappus, Luther was trail boss for several years at the Waters and Scrivner ranch and hoped to inherit the ranch when they died.

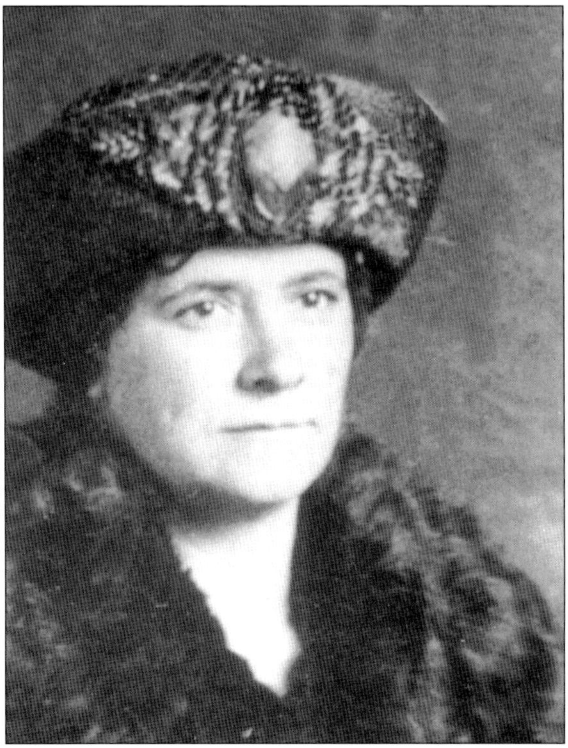

This picture is of an unidentified woman, perhaps Luther Willbourn's best friend's girl? The story goes that Mark Calvert had wanted to marry a girl in Colorado and thought that maybe he would inherit the Waters and Scrivner Ranch. Later, Mark Calvert was told that Luther had ended up with his girl and the ranch.

In fact, Luther Willbourn had already married Cora E. Lyons, daughter of Katherine Mahan Lyons (left) and Luther "Tex" Martin Lyons (right), who had homesteaded a place just down the road in Ticolote, Colorado. Cora Lyons was born in Ticolote in 1891.

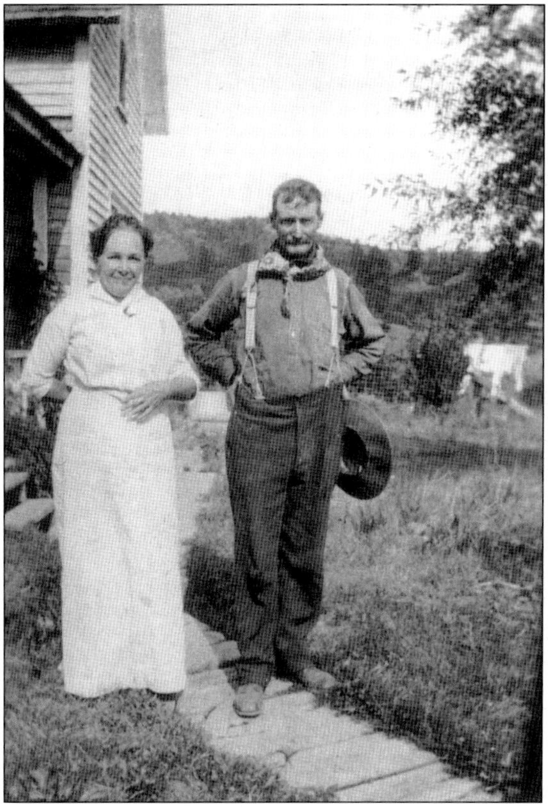

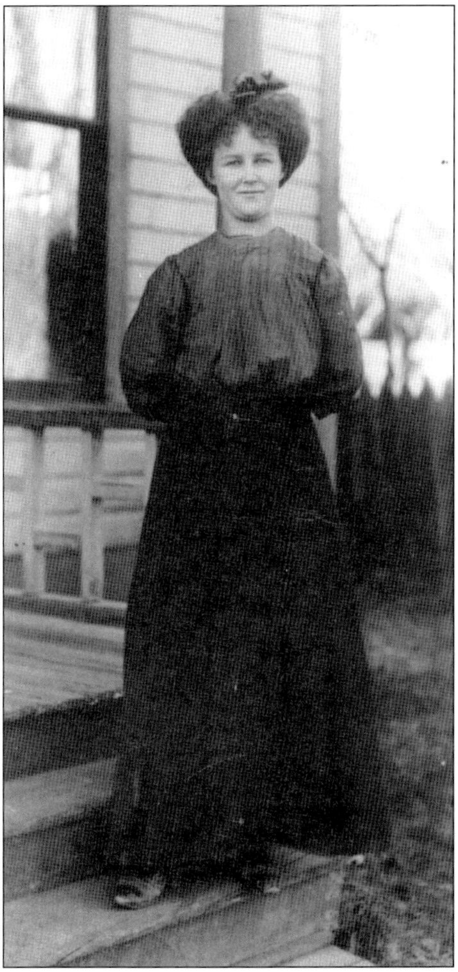

"This is going to be my wife," Luther wrote on the back of this picture of Cora, taken when she was 18 years old. "What do you think of her? I'll send you a good picture of her someday."

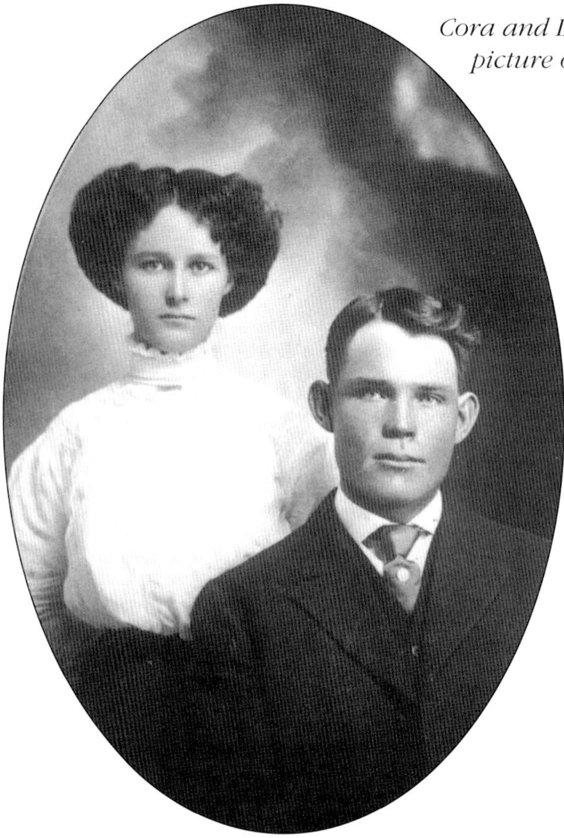

Cora and Luther Willbourn pose for their wedding picture on February 12, 1909.

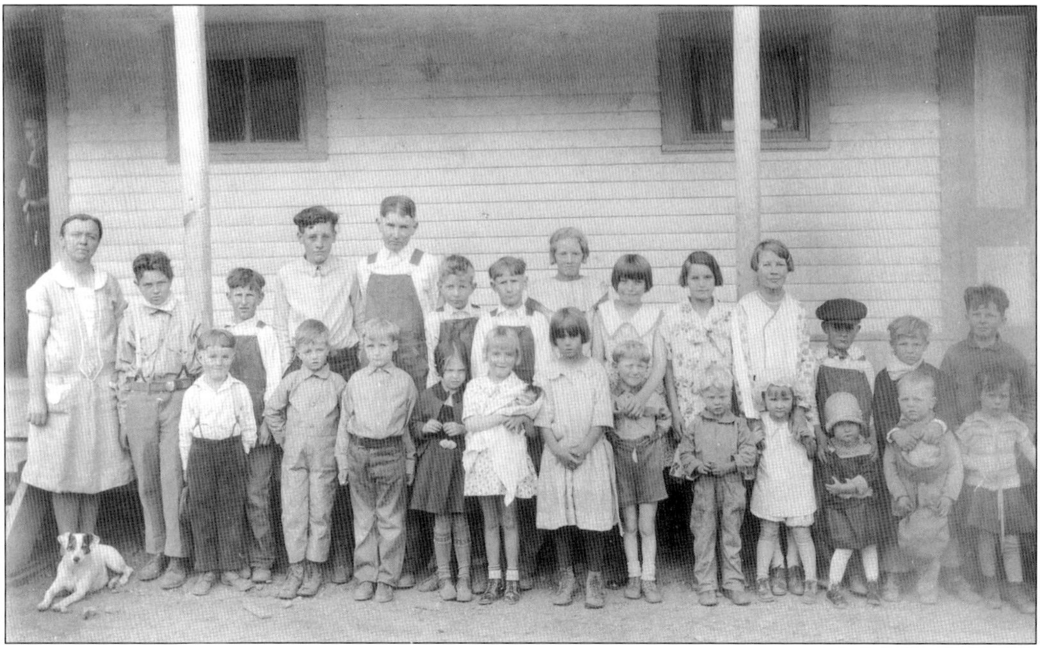

Frances (front, fourth from right) poses with her classmates at the Columbus School in Bayfield.

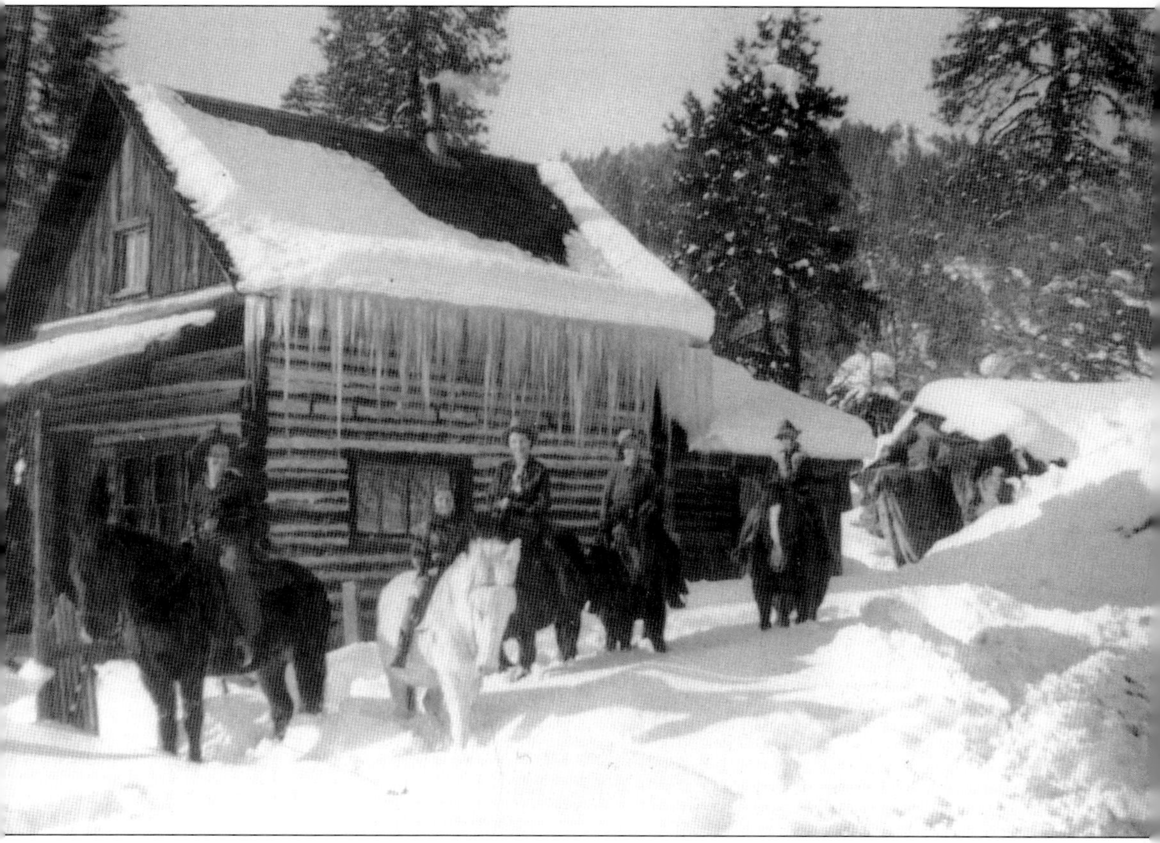

The Willbourn kids get ready to ride from the Willbourn Ranch to school in Bayfield in wintertime.

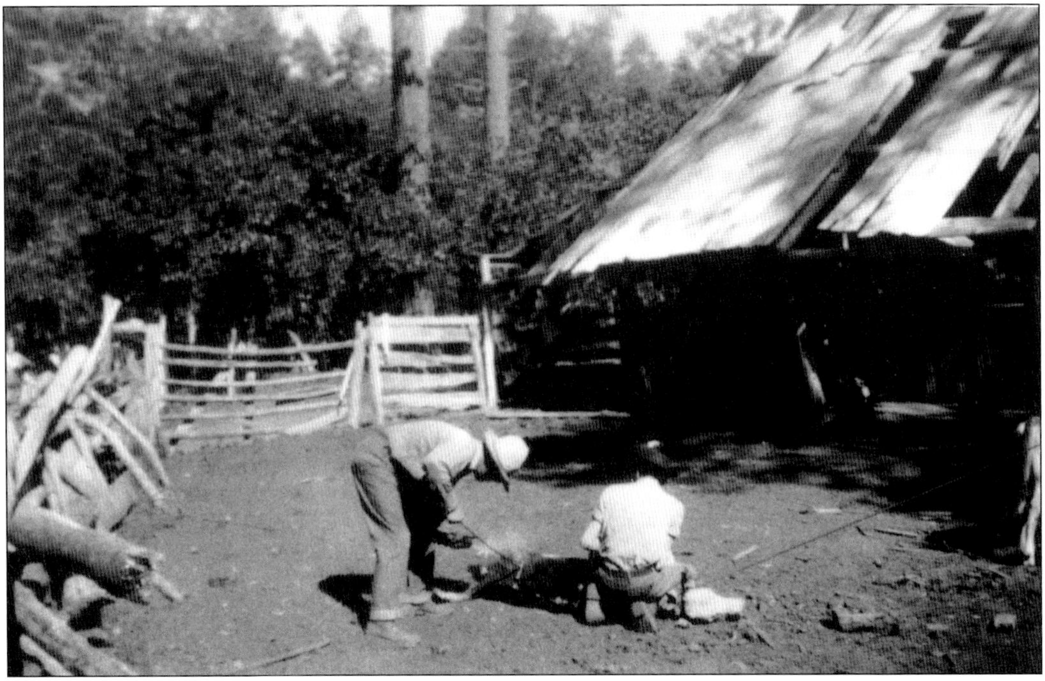

Frances' father Luther brands a calf in the corral on the old ranch.

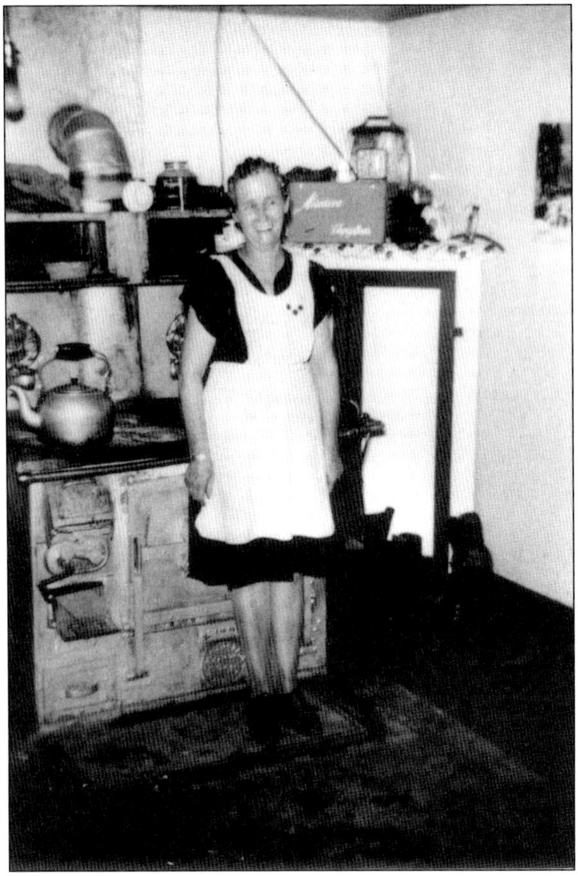

Frances' mother Cora stands in front of the cookstove at the old house.

Chapter 14

GREAT LEADERS IN THE UTE COMMUNITY

EDDIE BOX JR.

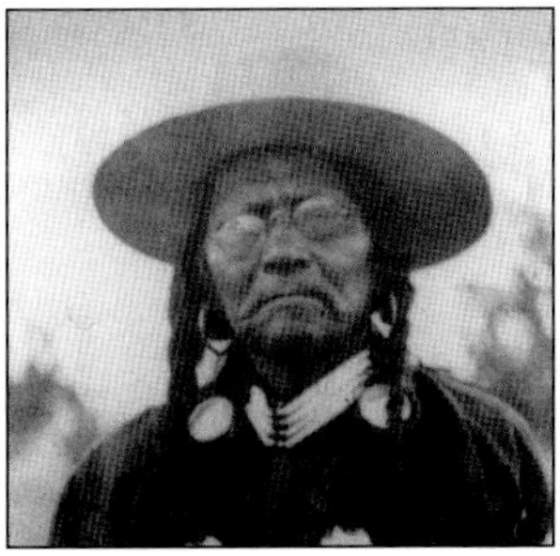

Eddie Box Jr.'s father, Eddie Box Sr., is one of the best-known and most respected seniors in the Southern Ute community. He is often called on to perform traditional ceremonies at public gatherings, part of his role as a spiritual leader. "'But I am not a medicine man,' he used to say," explains Eddie, "'I'm a traditional person.' My father always said, 'It's something else to be a medicine man. You have to give up everything you own, everything that you have, and live that type of a life. And it's very hard for anyone to do that. It takes a lot of hard work—a lot of years—before you can say you are a medicine man.'"

"He told his grandchild that the Creator offered it to him at the Sun Dance," adds Eddie's wife Betty, "but he turned it down."

"Another force that was always behind my father," continues Eddie, "was my mother. Together they accomplished a lot, just like Betty has been the same way to me, saying, 'You know, maybe this traditional way is the way it should be done, maybe this is the way we should look at something, maybe this is the way we should present ourselves,' and together that helped us accomplish a lot.

"One thing my mother told me was, 'Be aware.' But all the time when she said, 'Be aware,' it meant a lot of things. It meant be aware of what's around you, be aware of who's talking to you, be aware of your surroundings, be aware of your body, be aware. She even has that on her headstone.

"My mother passed away in 1974."

Eddie's father met his mother, Dorothy Burch Box, back in the 1940s, during the war. She was a WAC and his dad was a sailor in the Pacific.

* * *

"My dad always told me battle stories," says Eddie. "He said he made three or four invasions. He drove a landing craft—opened the door and all the troops went out—then go back out and get another load. He made four landings like that. He said it was very hard, very emotional.

"But he said that when he was on the ship his main job was loading those 20-millimeters, those big shells. He said he really was scared. Everyday he was thinking of home. He would always tell me when he was fighting the Japanese and all the planes were coming down and shooting, coming towards them, shooting, shooting, and that thing just kept coming and they'd yell like 'Get down!' Those 50-caliber shells were hitting right above him. Pieces of metal were falling down on the deck. And he said the plane came right over and he was looking at the big red star. But the pilot was dead already. He could see him leaning over."

But how did Eddie's father meet his mother?

"Back in the '40s," says Eddie, "he met Mother. He told me, back when the war was going on, my mother was going with a Pueblo. And when the war started—and that guy was also a buddy of my dad—and he told my dad, 'Take care of my girlfriend.' And he did!"

Growing up, Eddie was involved in a number of traditional ceremonies, including "sweat," and the two major dances held in the community, the Sun Dance, and the Bear Dance. "My father and my mother got involved in the Sun Dance back in the '50s," says Eddie.

"I remember they would take me to the Sun Dance in south of Towaoc, out in the sand, in the desert out there. I remember my job as a little boy then—they put on paint in the morning—and my job was to carry the paint over to my father. I remember that I used to carry those paint cans over to my father, and all of a sudden I dropped the can with the paint all over."

"The Bear Dance is the social dance of our people," says Eddie, changing the subject. "Some parts of the Bear Dance are religious, but mostly you're welcoming spring. That's the time when the bear wakes up on the mountain and starts moving around, and the dance imitates him, moving back and forth."

Eddie also remembers going to the horse races during Fiesta Days in Durango, the annual event now called Spanish Trails. "My father packed the pickup and we used to bring our tepees. They used to put us by the race track back there. And all of us kids went there. It was fun because we all got to go out and walk downtown and go to the carnival. And I remember we used to dance in the streets. They would block off the street and we would dance, traditional dances."

* * *

Probably the best-known Ute leader in recent times, other than Eddie's father, was Chief Charles Buck, or "Buckskin Charlie" as he was popularly called, a contemporary of Eddie's grandfather, Jacob Bent Box. "Buckskin Charlie," says Eddie, "got to be a law enforcement officer, which in those days was an important position in the tribe, and that goes to show he had a leadership quality." This was just as Chief Ouray before. "Ouray," says Eddie, "was kind of a diplomat. He would go in there and kind of quiet things down, even when his own people were up and at 'em."

"I'm kind of grateful for the way things turned out, though," adds Eddie. "There was a time when the tribe here had to band together. The government wanted to send all the Utes up to Utah. But Ouray didn't want to do that, and some went up there, but we stayed."

"I am a part of those who stayed," says Eddie, "and here I am, and I'm kind of grateful for that."

(opposite, top) *Eddie Box Jr.'s grandfather, Jacob Bent Box (center), was a contemporary of Chief Charles Buck or "Buckskin Charlie" (right), the last great chief of the Moache band of Utes. Eddie didn't get to meet his grandfather Jacob because he died as a result of an appendix attack before Eddie was born. (Courtesy Helen Hoskins, Southern Ute Museum)*

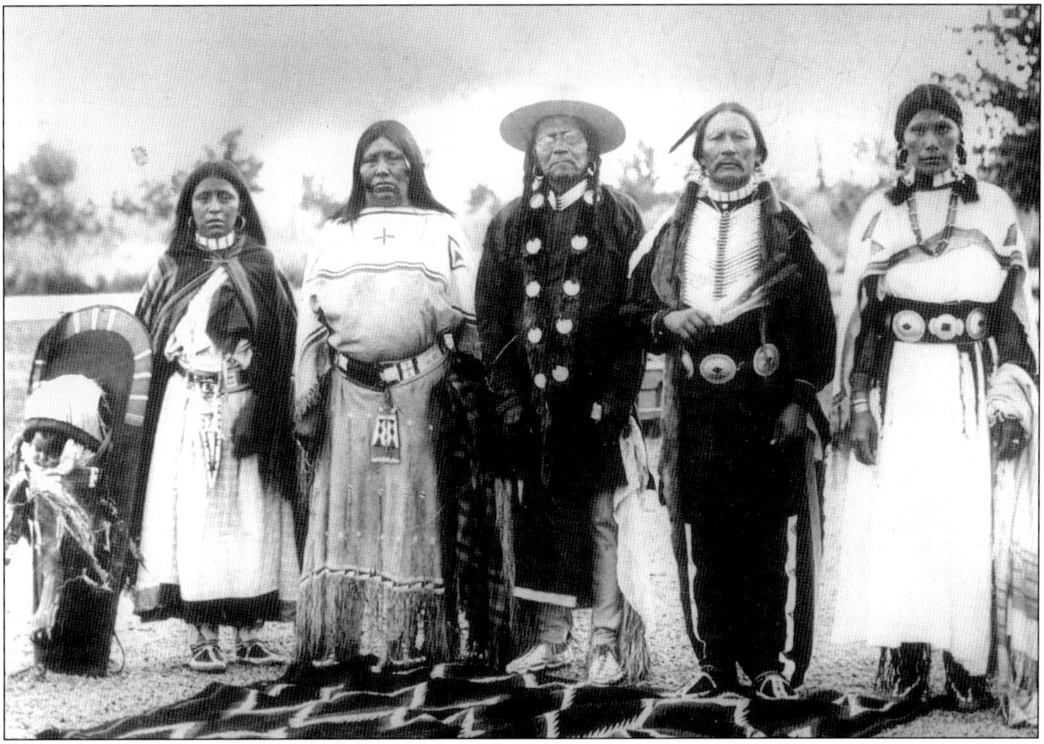

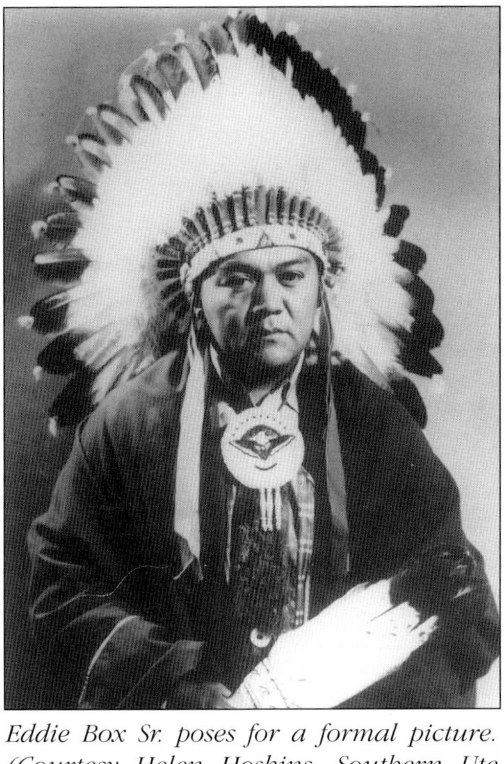

Eddie Box Sr. poses for a formal picture. (Courtesy Helen Hoskins, Southern Ute Museum)

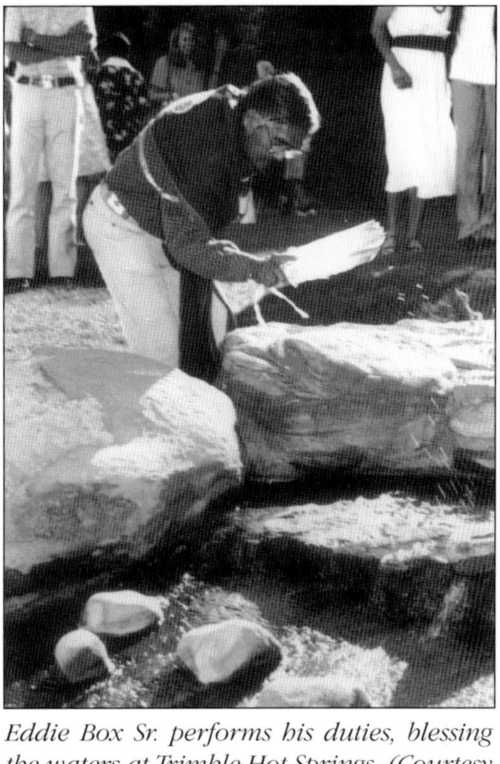

Eddie Box Sr. performs his duties, blessing the waters at Trimble Hot Springs. (Courtesy Ruedi Bear)

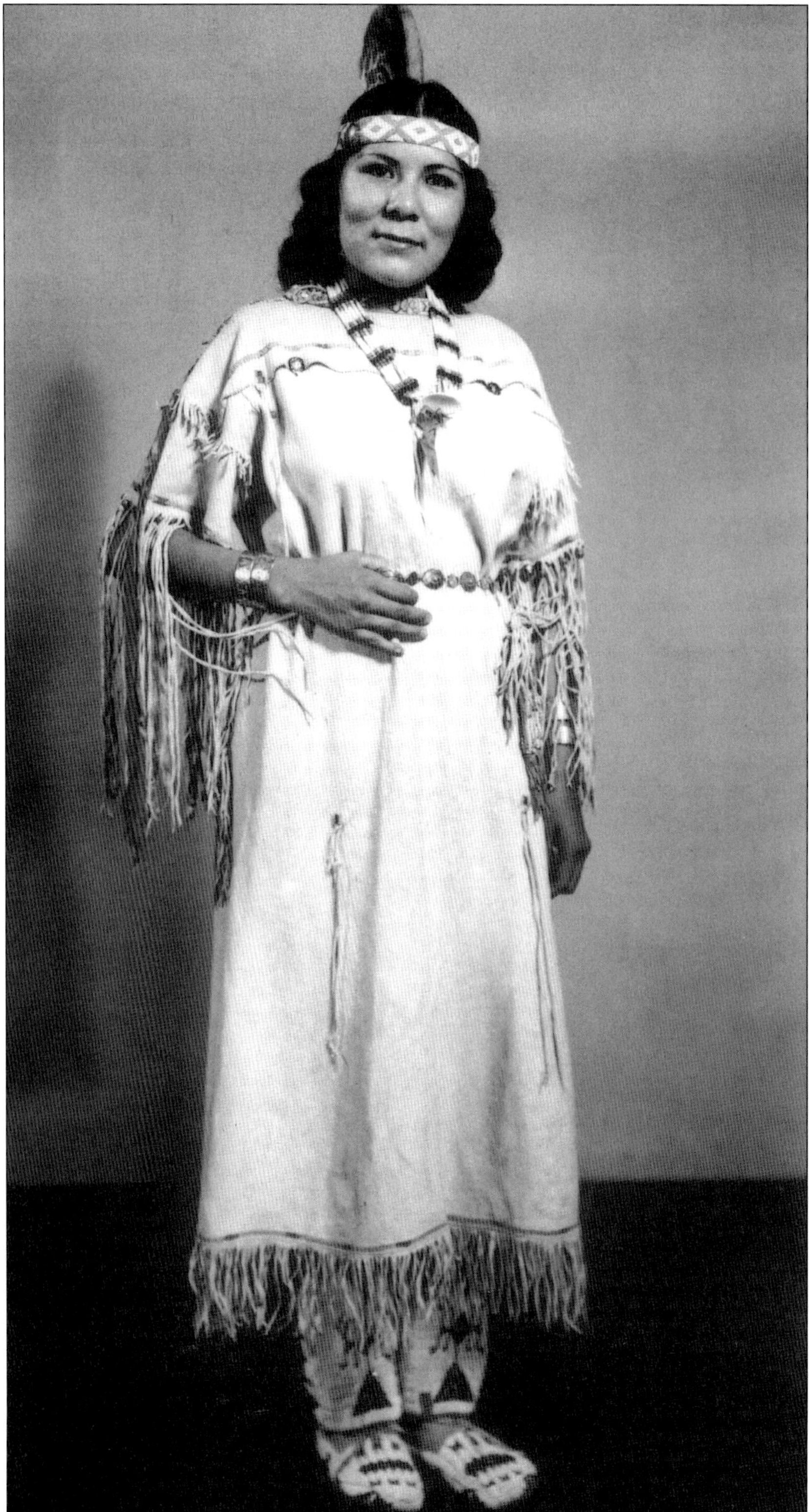

Eddie's mother, Dorothy Burch Box, poses here in traditional wear, c. 1946. (Courtesy Center of Southwest Studies, Fort Lewis College)

Buckskin Charlie, dressed in full traditional regalia, sits mounted on his horse. (Courtesy Helen Hoskins, Southern Ute Museum)

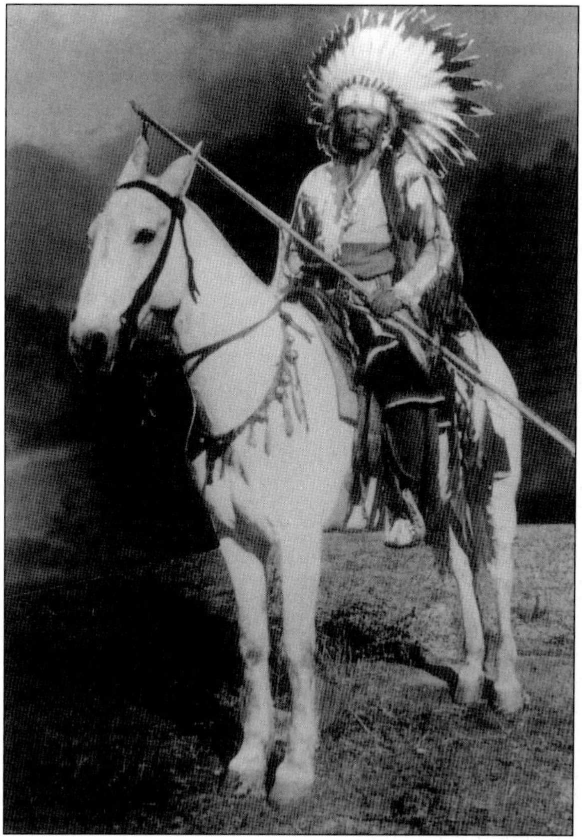

Buckskin Charlie leads the Fiesta Days parade through downtown Durango, Colorado. (Courtesy La Plata County Historical Society)

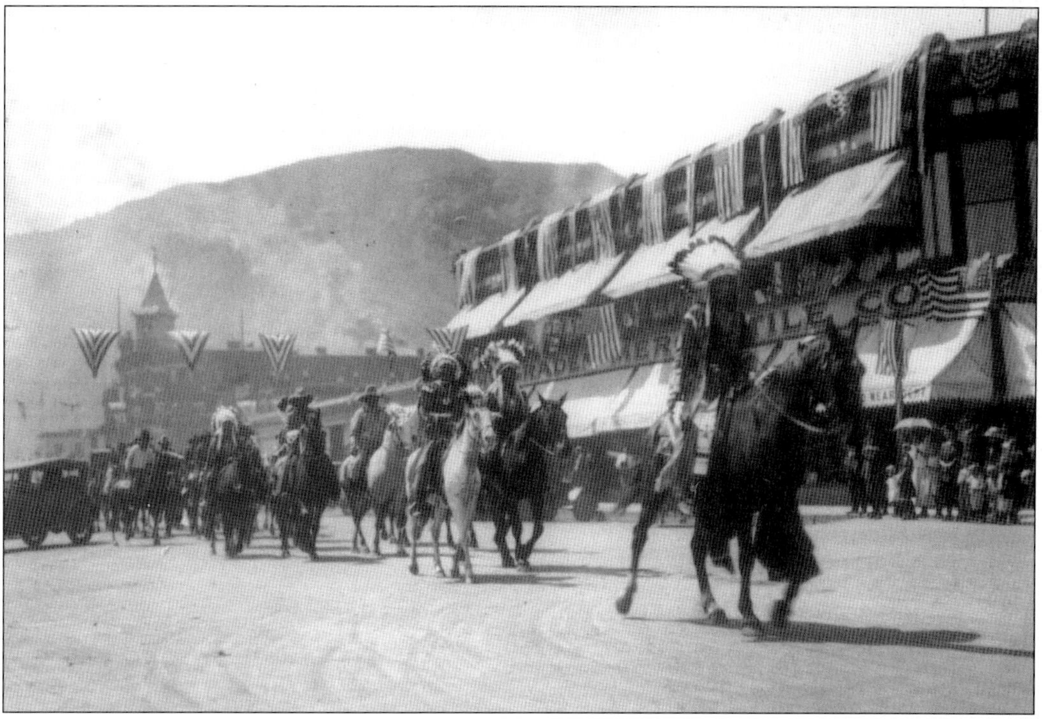

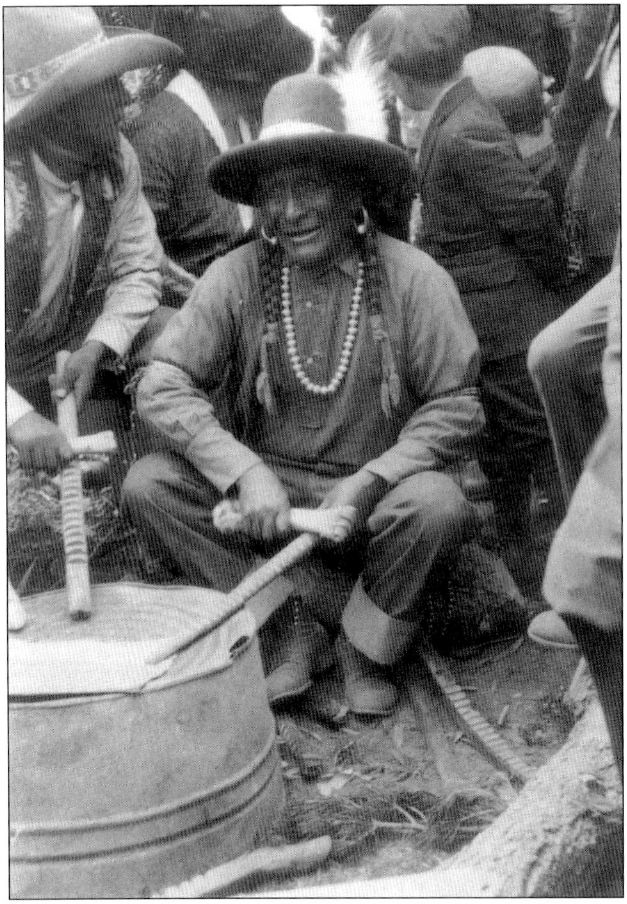

At left, bear dance musicians make music to accompany the Bear Dance by rubbing rasps against a washtub drum with deer shinbones. (Courtesy Helen Hoskins, Southern Ute Museum)

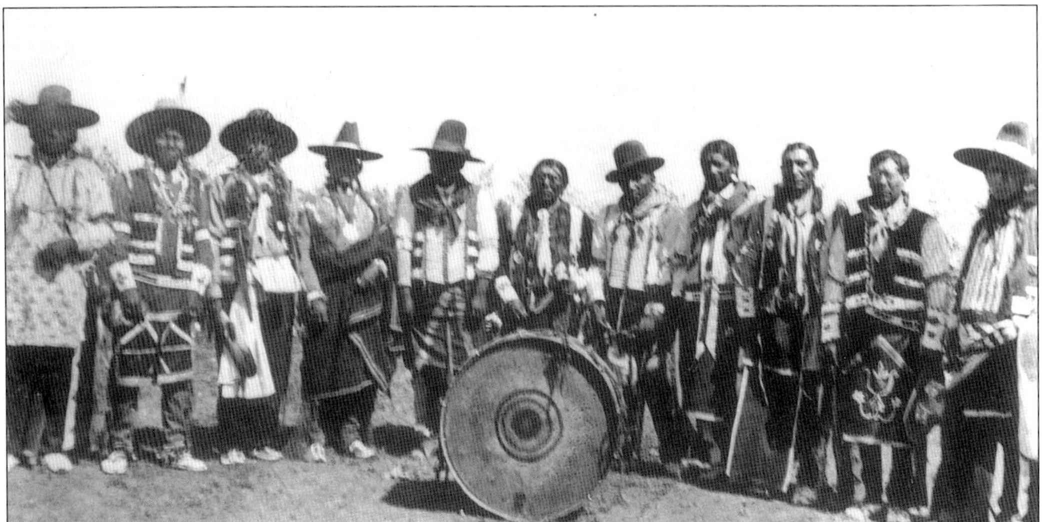

Above, bear dancers get ready to perform the Bear Dance. Standing among them is Effie Monte's father, Bird Red (second from right). (Courtesy Helen Hoskins, Southern Ute Museum)

Chapter 15

SOUTHERN UTE DOLLMAKER

EFFIE MONTE

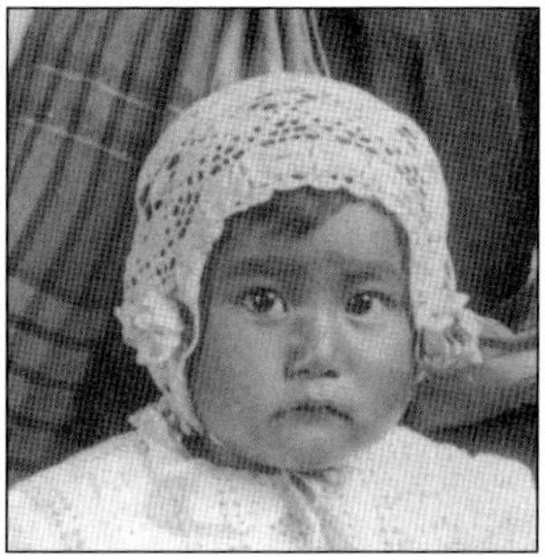

Effie Monte's mother's name was "Nana" Red. "She got her name 'Nana,'" says Effie, "because she used to be a babysitter and caretaker of young children here in town." Her mother's maiden name was Eaton. Effie used to know her grandfather, Peter Eaton, quite well. "Oh, I could write a story about him," she says. "He was the best farmer. He worked with Mr. Floyd, who used to be the superintendent here and had a lot of hay. He used to put up the hay with the old derricks with a horse tied to it and the old wagons and the hook that's hung up on top of the derrick."

"We lived right across from Grandpa," explains Effie. "They had a hacienda—a two-room house with a porch all around it."

Effie also lived just down the hill from her grandfather's sister, her great aunt. "My great aunt," says Effie, "used to have sheep, about 30 head. And she would shear them herself and she would cut the tails off the little lambs and castrate the little lambs and I used to go help her. I was about 12 years old then. And I walked up to her house on the hill and my uncle, Dick Charley, would sit right at the gate. And he'd sit there and talk to himself. He told many stories—about the old people, like Kit Carson—and he was fascinating. But my great aunt would say 'Don't listen to him because he just rambles on.'"

Effie's father, Bird Red, was a well-known traditional singer. "My father, he knew all the cultures and the traditions," says Effie, "He could sing 49 songs."

"And some of the people would dance the white man way, you know, waltz to it. He had fun with them—trying to teach them that the Indian music was the same as the white man's music—and that you could dance the steps to the rhythm of the drum and the singing."

Growing up, says Effie, "we went many places because Dad could sing and he had his own little drum." They would go to Fiesta Days, for instance. "We'd go on wagons," she remembers, "horse and wagon, and it would take us a whole day to get to Durango. I was always embarrassed as a child to go up the Main Street, sitting in the back of a wagon with my parents.

"And we used to camp there at the campgrounds in Durango. At first it was on the east side of the fairgrounds and then they moved us to the west side because many of the other Indian tribes were coming in, the Navajos and the Apaches. We had a lot to do with the Apaches, just visiting, sharing their activities."

Effie also took part in all the traditional ceremonies of the Southern Utes, including the Sun Dance and the Bear Dance.

"Yes, my father was involved in the Sun Dance," says Effie. "Three days we'd camp out. There was a way that old Indians used to enter the Sun Dance grounds and they prepared it the way they were supposed to do it—set up their shade house, set up all the cooking utensils the same way. And moving in was a traditional part of it and moving out was also a traditional part of it—where you put all your things aside, put them in different places—in a ritual way.

"The Sun Dance was held about five miles up the road, at the Sun Dance grounds, and we had our favorite shade house in the same place year after year.

"And I still go there."

And because her father was a singer and a leader of the Bear Dance for a long time, Effie also "grew up in the 'Bear Dance Chorale,' as you might say."

Effie met her late husband, John Monte, at the Bear Dance. "My husband was a dancer," she explains. "That's the way we used to do it. It was about the renewal of green plants and the birds coming back, and families too, coming out of the winter. You would have a community where everybody got together and the families introduced their sons and daughters to each other."

"Now we don't do that anymore," she laments."That's lost."

Effie's mother, Nana Red, was a very good traditional bead worker and seamstress. "She made many things," says Effie, "she could make complete outfits for adults and children and everybody. She just whipped them up in no time.

"And she loved to make cradle boards. She would make the base of it with the rawhide she'd shaped into a cradleboard. She would go out and get the willows in the springtime and make the little top, a shade, for the cradleboard.

"I used to sit and watch her do her bead work when I was small. I always did part of the Indian traditional work."

In fact, Effie has become a well-known beader herself. Most of her beadwork these days, though, is found on the little toy dolls she makes, on the little purses the dolls are carrying in their hands, on their little beaded belts. She also does quill work that can be found on the dolls' necklaces and other ornaments. "And these are traditional clothes on the dolls," Effie points out, "this is her buckskin outfit and the other doll is wearing her pow-wow traditional dress."

The designs, Effie explains, are traditional designs, "flower designs and geometric designs," for instance, "that came from the Ute people here.

"The Indian people usually work from their dreams and whatever they see or hear or the feeling they get from nature. I think it's carried from the old age—old people, the older generation, grandparents—and it just carries down.

"That's where my designs come from. It's just something I want to share with everybody, so they can see what we really come from."

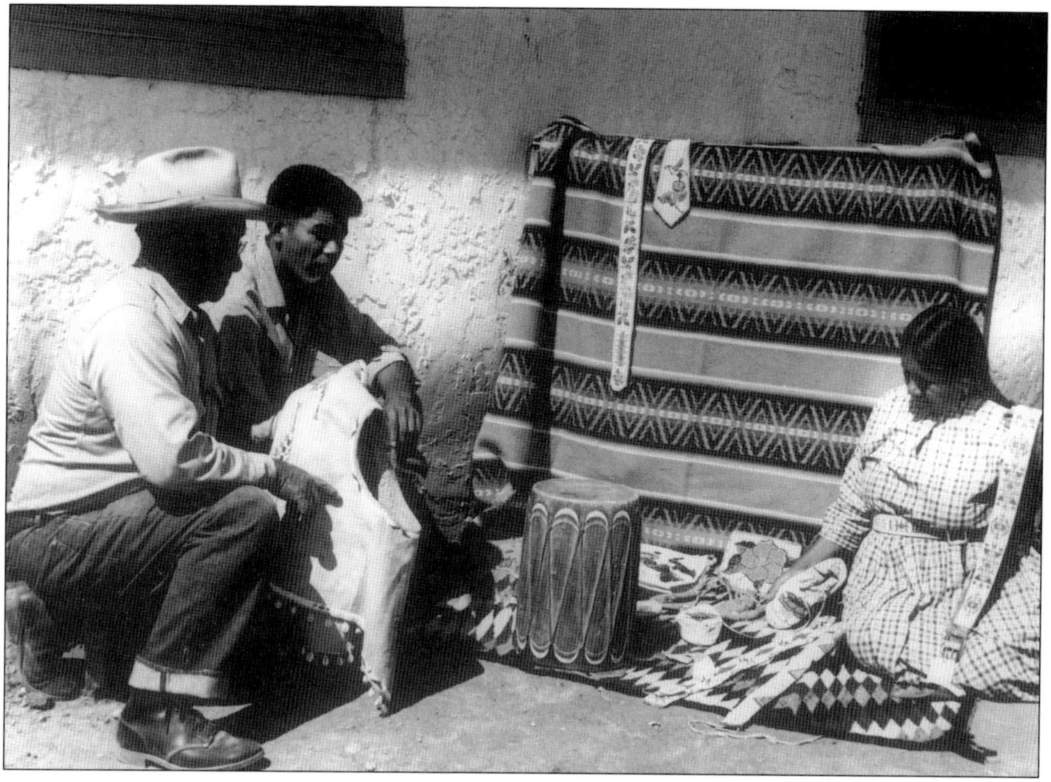

Effie Monte's father, Bird Red (left), and mother, Nana Red (right), exhibit some of Nana Red's handiwork. (Courtesy Helen Hoskins, Southern Ute Museum)

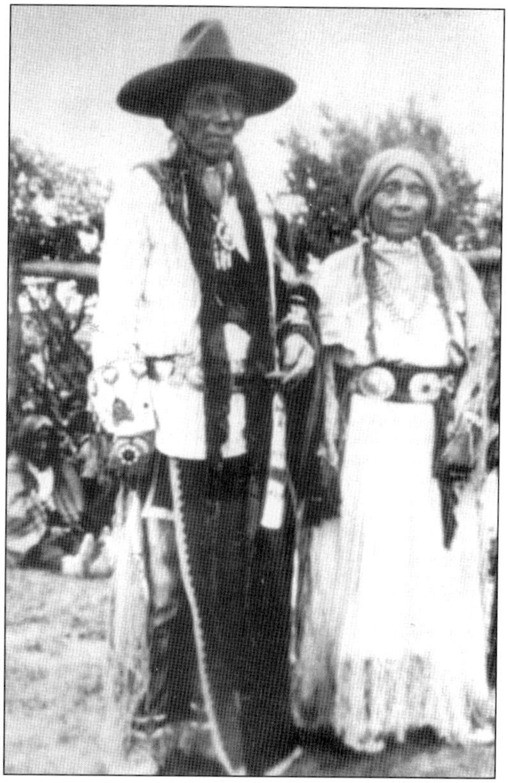

Dick Charley, standing here with Susan Bearwolf, was Effie's favorite uncle. (Courtesy Helen Hoskins, Southern Ute Museum)

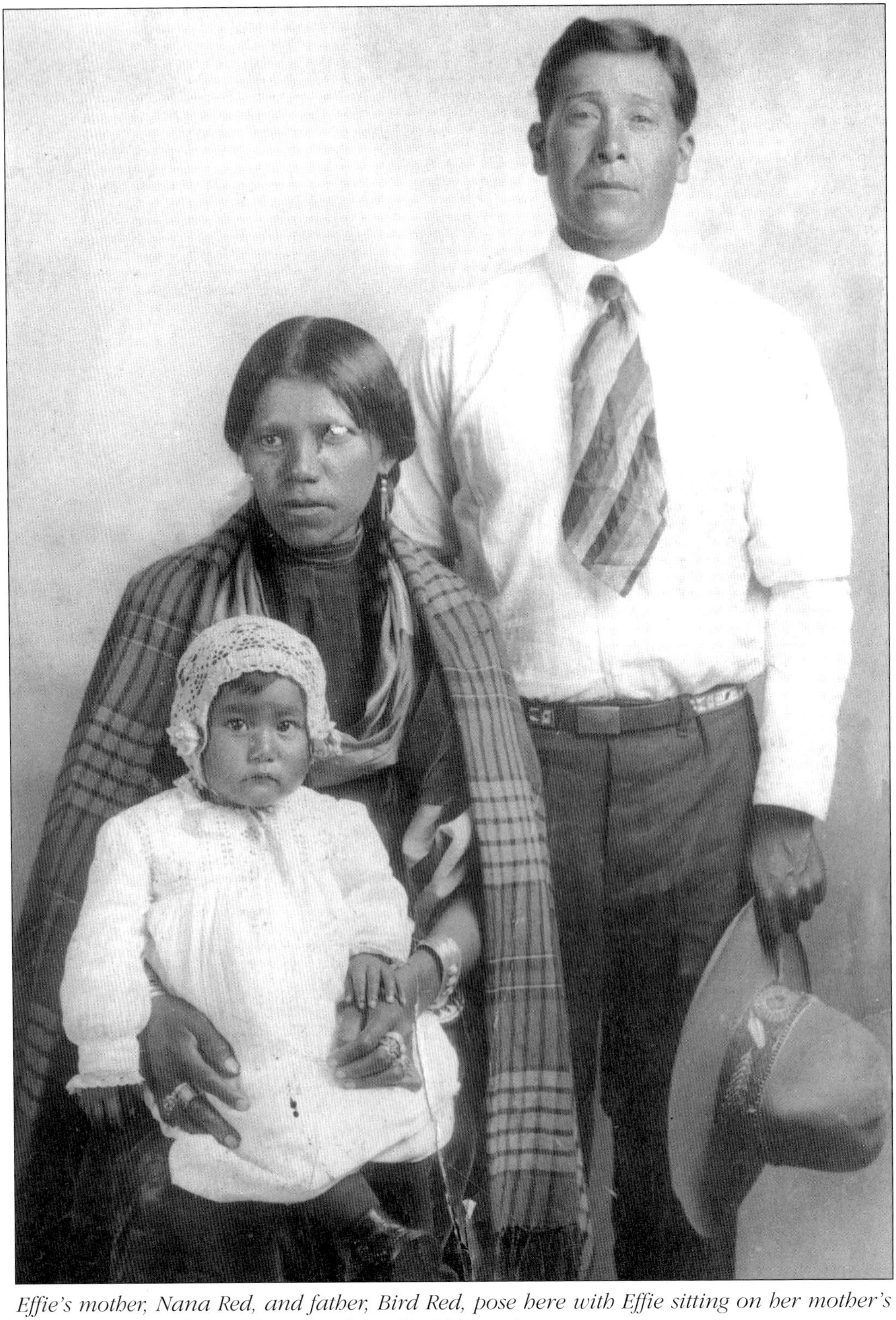

Effie's mother, Nana Red, and father, Bird Red, pose here with Effie sitting on her mother's lap. (Courtesy Helen Hoskins, Southern Ute Museum)

Chapter 16

NANÁ-MA, TOGETHER

PEARL CASIAS

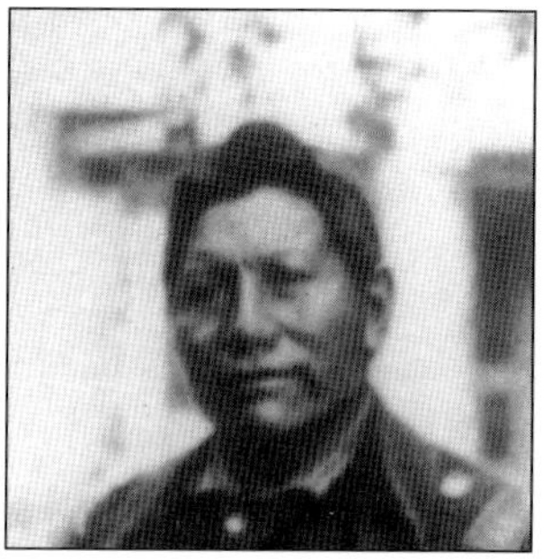

"My parents were Manuel Casias and Obdulai Tree," Pearl begins. "My father's mother was Beatrice Head, who was a descendant of Severo, and my paternal grandfather was Ben Casias. His ancestors came over from the San Luis Valley. His grandfather was a Navajo, a slave to a Spanish patron. They called him 'El Gran Casias.'"

"My mother was a Tree," says Pearl. George Tree was her father and Martha Weaver Tree was her mother. Somewhere along the line, Pearl explains, when they were compiling a census book, her mother's father's name had changed to "Weaver." But, originally, it was "Shoshone," Francisco Shoshone.

"George Tree's father was Henry Tree," continues Pearl, "and Henry Tree's father was Ankatosh."

Pearl has an interesting story about Ankatosh. During the time that Ouray was negotiating with the federal government in Washington D.C., some soldiers gave Ouray's subchiefs, including Ankatosh, some old saddles and bridles. But when Ouray found out, he told the subchiefs they had to give everything back.

"Ankatosh wasn't very happy about that," says Pearl. "So he got into a verbal and physical confrontation with Ouray, and he was going to throw him out the window, four stories up.

"But the other subchiefs stopped him and told him, 'We can't do this, he's our chief, our leader.' And Ankatosh said, 'Well, we don't understand what's going on, we don't know what he's negotiating, what he's giving up. Every time we come back, he's always richer than when we went, and our people aren't getting the benefit. So what is he doing?'

"One of the interesting stories about Chief Ouray is that shortly before he died, he asked his wife Chipeta to bring him back to the agency. And he told his wife, 'Take a dipper and dip into these bags, and for each Indian, give him a share.'

"He always had bags of money, gold and silver coins. And so a lot of the people came by and they took that and they threw it into the river. They said, 'Here's your money.'"

* * *

Pearl Casias is a great champion of Ute women. Chipeta, for instance—as Pearl points out—was perhaps a better statesperson than Ouray. "Yes," says Pearl, "I think there were a lot of instances when she tried to persuade him not to do what he actually did."

"I just want to give you some examples of some things that Ute women were historically involved in," continues Pearl.

"Traditionally, back before the Pilgrims landed at Plymouth Rock, when the Southern Ute people went to war, the women marched in front of the warriors. And they had shields that were two or three thicknesses of animal skins. And so these women went before the warriors. And the reason why they did that was that the warriors thought that women were expendable and so if they got killed it was okay. But, of course, some of us Ute women feel that we were braver, and that's why we were in the front.

"The Ute women had what they called a war society, and these were the women that went ahead of the men during the wars. And those that returned—those that were not killed during the battle—when they returned, they did a mourning dance. And that dance was only performed by the Ute women. And that dance signified an honor dance and an honor song for those warriors that fell on the battle field.

"And then in 1934 the Southern Utes were then placed on the reservation—on what is called the Southern Ute Reservation—and as years went by, our reservation was diminished. In the 1950s, we were given [the administration] of the lands that were taken from us, and women that left their homes and joined the work force were involved in the education department, social services, they assisted in day care, they were there to care for the elderly, and several women were voted into the Council membership. There was Sunshine Smith, who is still alive, Martha Mayore, she is gone to the Happy Hunting Ground, Euterpe Taylor, Edna Hood, Francis Buck.

"One of our last traditional princesses—her name was Francis Buck—she was a tribal judge during the early '50s. And since that time, even in the late '70s, Martha Burch Mayore was an associate judge, and Annabelle Eagle also was associate judge. And I hold these women in very high esteem. They were women who had courage and were able to take on a position that was generally held by men."

Pearl draws upon stories about her own grandmother, Martha Weaver Tree, to illustrate how the roles of modern Ute women have changed over the years, in courtship and marriage ceremonies, for instance.

"Traditionally, most Indians have been matrilineal," Pearl explains, "but now that's different.

"I remember when I was growing up this young man approached my grandfather and said, 'What do you think if I married your girl?' And he said, 'Well, you better ask her. I'm not going to make that determination.' He already knew, I guess, that my decision was very important to me. But, of course, that was outside of what was the tradition—because my grandmother's husband was chosen for her. She married a total stranger and lived very happily with him all of his life."

Pearl goes on to elaborate about her grandmother's marriage.

"My grandfather, George Tree, used to be a carpenter. He worked in the agency yard and he must have seen my grandmother several times. And so one day, when my grandmother turned 18, he went and talked to her brother, because she was raised by her brother and his wife (her mother died when she was about three or four years old), and he asked her brother for his sister's hand in marriage. And her brother said, 'How do you know my sister?' And my grandfather said, 'Oh, I don't know her, I've never spoken to her, I've just seen her on campus at school.' So he told my grandmother, 'George Tree is going to come by to marry you and I've already given him my permission.' And she met her husband on the day they went to the church—for the first time—on her wedding day."

There is an odd footnote to this affair.

Pearl's grandfather, George Tree, later died from tuberculosis. "And by that time," Pearl tells us, "he had built my grandmother a home and they had 80 acres.

"And he had hired Phillip Lucero, whose family lived in Durango—but they came over from Sweden because his family were aristocrats—as a partner, so he would irrigate for him. Phillip

Lucero was his ranch guy. So when my grandfather was dying and Phillip worked for him, he said, 'Now I don't have any money and I can't pay you, but I can't die being indebted to you. So I'm gonna make you a deal. I'm gonna give you my wife and I want you to raise my children.'

"So that was her second husband. She was given away twice—and without even being asked!"

Traditionally, the courting process among the Utes was quite elaborate. "According to my grandmother," says Pearl, "if a young man was interested in a young woman, he made a flute, and he would play flute music—a love song—in the vicinity of where this young woman lived. And when he felt it was time, he would come and approach the girl's parents, but there was never any communication prior to his asking for her hand."

There is another courting tradition among the Utes: the Bear Dance. "If a young woman found someone that she wanted to spend the rest of her life with," says Pearl, "she would dance out of her circle with this young man, and he would go home with her family. And that's basically how a young woman would get her 'knight in beaded armor.'"

Pearl's grandmother also told her stories about going to government boarding school.

"My grandmother was placed in the BIA school at the old Fort Lewis post," says Pearl, "and it was just like a military school. They got up at a certain time, they marched to dining room, they marched back to the dorm, they marched to school.

"My grandmother always believed in education, but she didn't approve of the way that she had been educated. I think what the government planned to do was to take the children and place them in government boarding schools so that they would be taught to assimilate with the society, and to do away with the culture, do away with the language. I know that they were forbidden to talk their language. And if they did, they had their mouths washed out with lye.

"A lot of the Indians that were taken from the reservations and placed in government boarding schools ran away, and some of them died."

* * *

Notwithstanding this kind of treatment by the government, by and large, the Utes have a reputation for getting along peacefully with their neighbors in the Four Corners area for over 100 years.

There is a special Ute word for such harmony. "*Naná-ma*," Pearl explains. "And that means 'together.'

"We were in Tribal Council the other day and Chairman Burch brought that up. We were talking to Joe Brown, who used to work with the Soil Conservation, and he said he's reformed some. But Mr. Burch reminded him, he said, 'Do you remember the 'Red Book' that we compiled and that we worked together on?' And Joe Brown said, 'Yes, I remember the book.' And Mr. Burch asked him, 'Do you remember what the title of that book was?' And Joe Brown said, 'No, it's been a few years.' And Mr. Burch said the title of that book was *Naná-ma*—'together.'"

And this book was a plan, says Pearl, "a plan that was developed by the Southern Utes and some of the government employees and the county commissioners, a plan for cooperation, for progress."

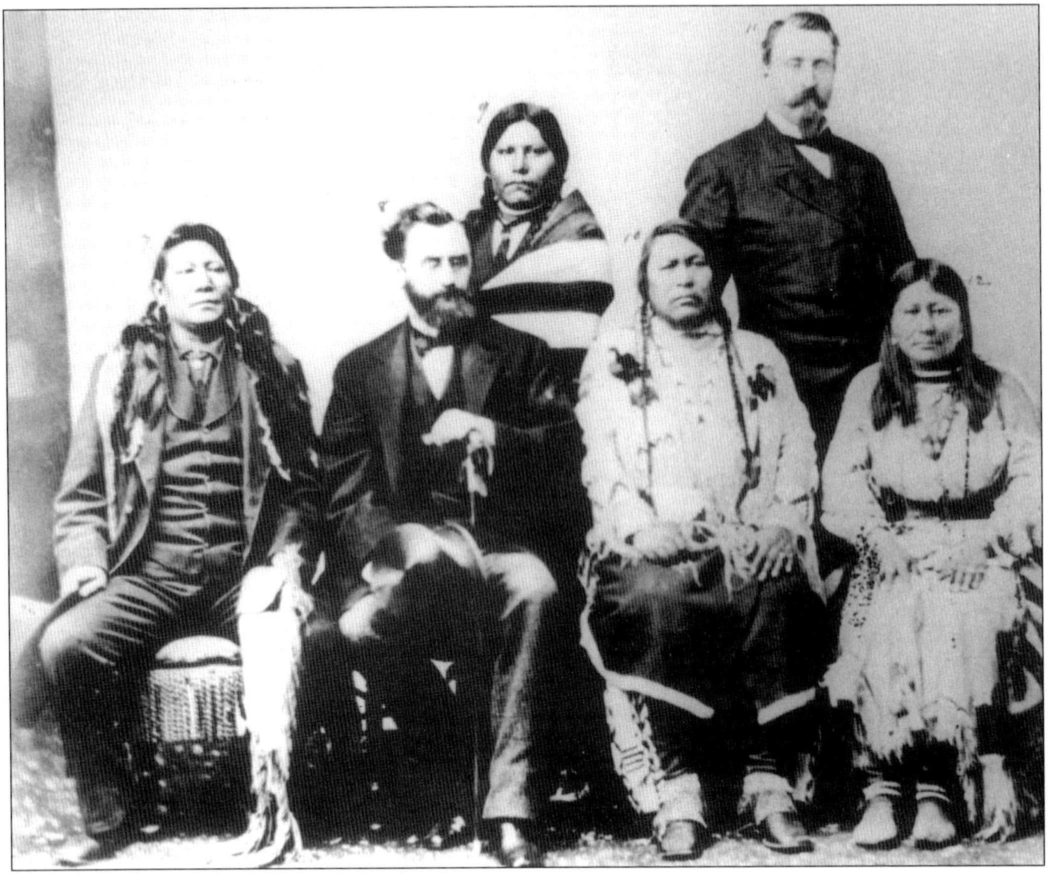

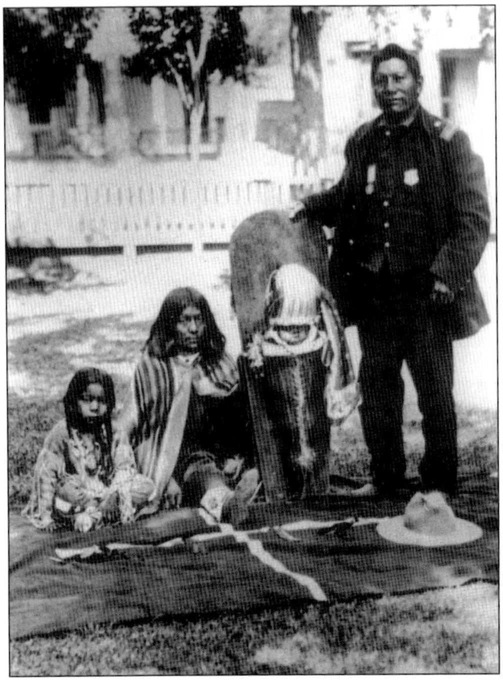

Pearl Casias' great grandfather, Ankatosh, was one of the sub-chiefs who accompanied Chief Ouray (front, second from right) and his wife Chipeta (front, right) to Washington D.C. during treaty negotiations between the Utes and the U.S. Government. (Courtesy Helen Hoskins, Southern Ute Museum)

Pearl Casias' great grandfather, Severo, poses here with his family in 1896. (Courtesy Helen Hoskins, Southern Ute Museum)

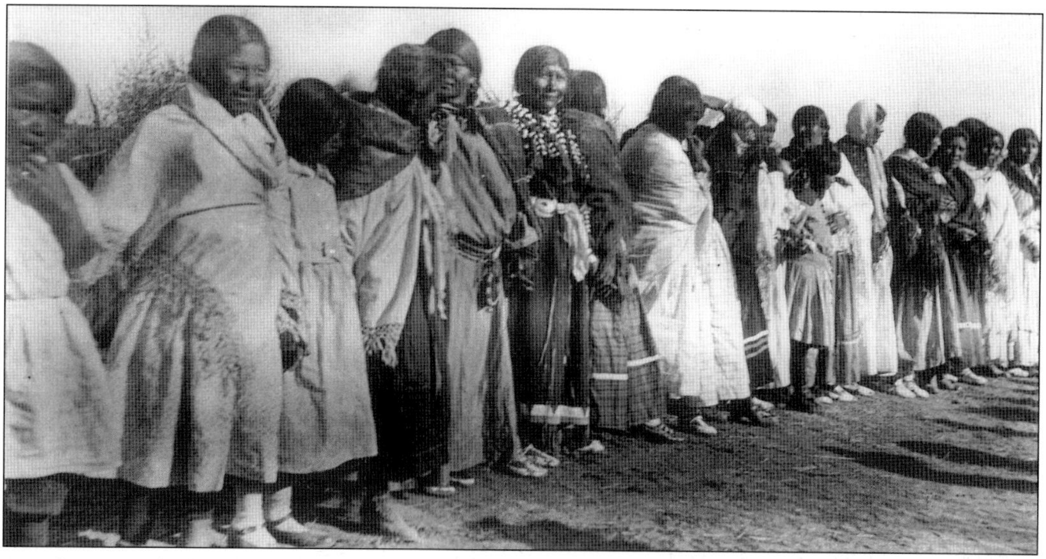

Southern Ute ladies line up for the Bear Dance, c. 1918. When the singers play a "choose-your-partner" song, the women march across the circle to the men's side, select the men they want to dance with and walk back to the center of the corral. There, the women form a line facing the singers. (Helen Hoskins, Southern Ute Museum)

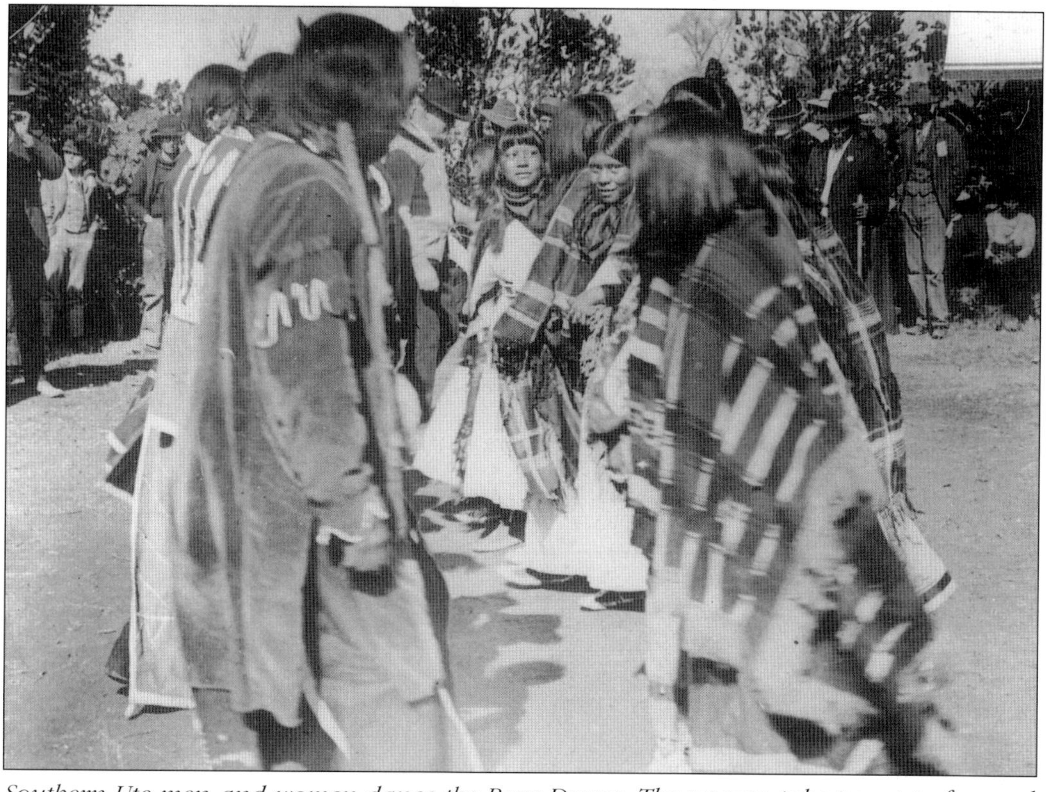

Southern Ute men and women dance the Bear Dance. The women take two steps forward and three steps back. Then the men take two steps forward and three steps back until the two lines are moving in perfect unison. (Helen Hoskins, Southern Ute Museum)

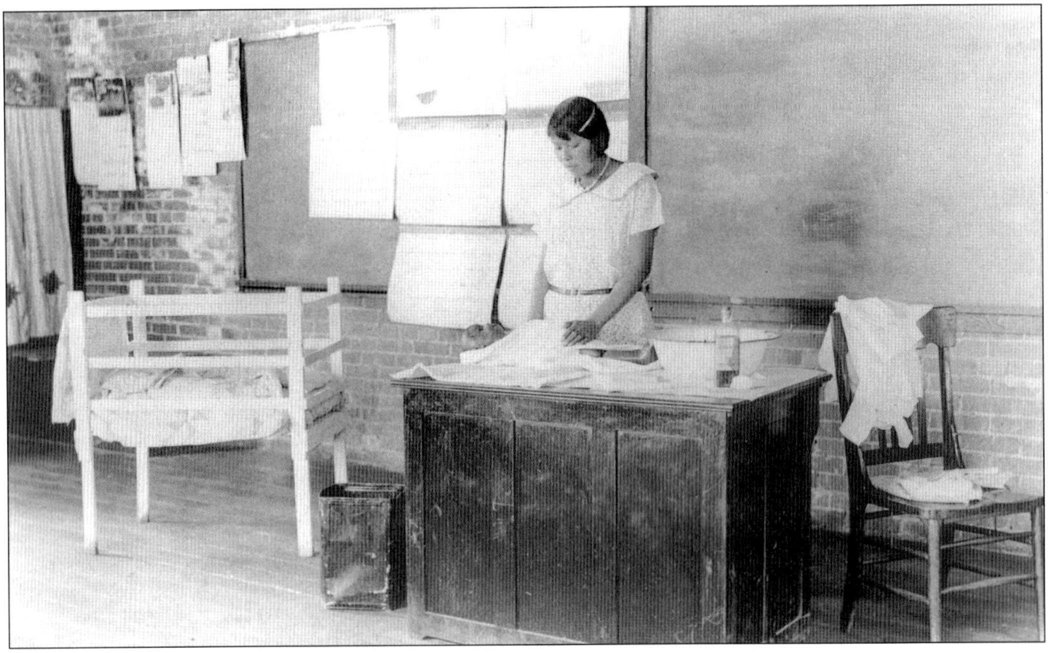

A teacher at the BIA school in Ignacio instructs students about baby care. (Helen Hoskins, Southern Ute Museum)

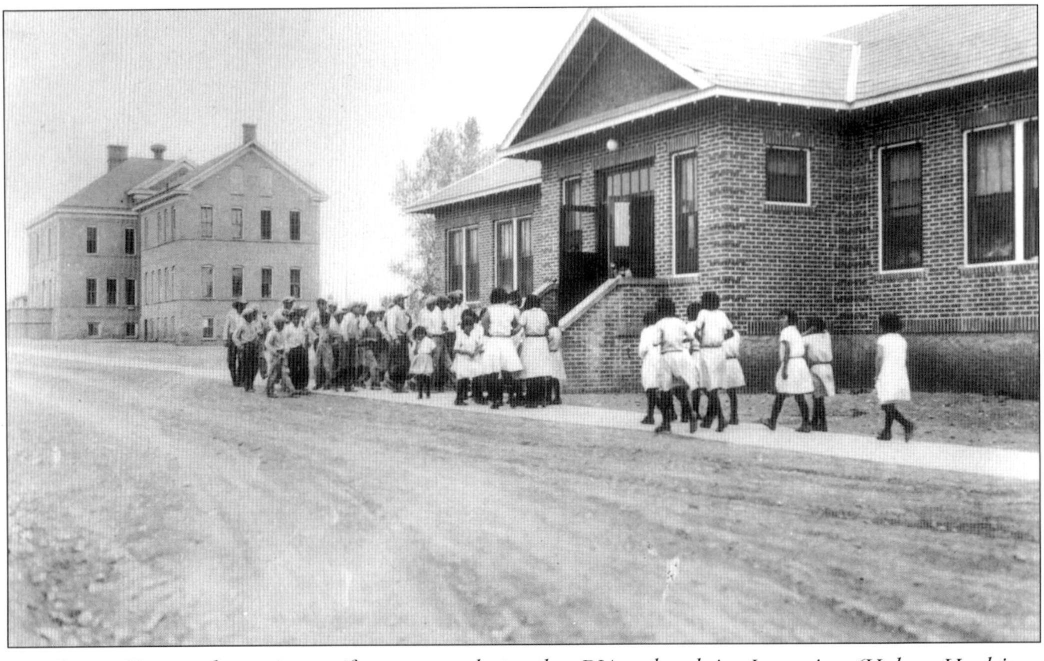

Southern Ute students in uniform march to the BIA school in Ignacio. (Helen Hoskins, Southern Ute Museum)